Disarmed

Disarmed

The Story of the Venus de Milo

GREGORY CURTIS

Sutton Publishing

First published in the United States of America by
Alfred A. Knopf

First published in the United Kingdom by
Sutton Publishing Limited
Phoenix Mill · Thrupp · Stroud
Gloucestershire · GL5 2BU

British Library Cataloguing in Publication Data
A catalogue for this book is available from the British
Library.

ISBN 0-7509-3871-4

Composed by North Market Street Graphics
Lancaster, Pennsylvania

Typeset in 11 / 13.5 Photina
Typesetting and origination by
Sutton Publishing Limited.
Printed and bound in England by
J.H. Haynes & Co. Ltd, Sparkford

For Tracy

CONTENTS

Fractured Masterpiece

M ELOS IS an Aegean island where thirty thousand people looking for a bargain vacation arrive each summer like migratory birds. When they leave, the island returns to its unlovely self. It is dull, remote, harsh—a place where the only ways to make a living are by mining, farming, fishing, and hanging on desperately until summer brings the next flock of tourists.

Unfortunately, I was not there in summer but in early spring when the weather tends toward gray skies, rain, and powerful winds. I climbed the highest hill. It is crowned by the village of Plaka, a warren of narrow streets twisting between the straight white walls of stone and stucco houses. Lost for a while, I finally began following the occasional signs that pointed toward the "ancient theater" and eventually found myself walking along a narrow dirt road. There, across from the remains of a stone wall and tower, stood a small, solitary metal sign that said in English and Greek, SITE OF THE DISCOVERY OF VENUS OF MILOS.

Behind the sign was a short but quite steep slope covered with a haphazard profusion of olive trees. Grabbing branches for balance, I made my way down the slope, about ten yards or so, to a flat area covered with grass and wildflowers.

The ruins of another wall, once the continuation of the one above, ran down the slope and there, after pulling aside a few more olive branches, I saw a white stone plaque bolted to the crumbling wall. It had inscriptions in Greek, English, German, and French. The English read HERE HAS BEEN FOUND THE VENUS OF MILOS. This area was where the statue of the goddess once stood in an arched niche in a wall. But the exact site of the discovery is impossible to locate. Landslides long ago buried the wall with its niches. It must lie somewhere beneath the olive trees whose branches I'd grabbed on the way down. Perhaps, deep in the ground, their roots entwine the missing arms.

After several minutes of trying to imagine what this place had once been like, I found myself disappointed and perplexed by exactly how lost and how untended the purported site turned out to be. I climbed back up the slope and followed the dirt road through what had once been a Greek and then a Roman city. There were the remains of a theater situated so the audience could look past the stage and out across a bay at the foot of the hill. There were the remnants of walls here and there. The long narrow field that had once been a stadium lined on one side by stone bleachers was still easy to identify. Occasionally, I ran across a part of a marble column lying on the ground.

During the next three days I talked several times with an archaeologist at the local museum, but there had been little work done at the site where the statue was discovered. But he did give me a map of the Greek city drawn after some light excavations done decades earlier. So each day I went to the ruins with that map in hand and explored. I drew my own maps and took photographs and eventually understood the layout of the ancient settlement.

Even so I found myself trying to imagine, not so much what the town had been like in ancient times, but what the ruins had been like in the spring of 1820 when the statue was uncovered. But it was impossible. The ruins have disintegrated so badly since then that I knew my mental reconstructions were mere imaginings. One fact, however, has not changed. These ruins were a lonely, isolated farmer's pasture in 1820, and they are a lonely, isolated farmer's pasture now. During my visits of several hours each day for four days the only other visitors were a herd of goats who were fenced in a distant corner.

I tromped around the ruins until I was convinced that I would never find anything more than I had already seen. I had learned only this. Melos, an island as boring in the past as it is today, may have been the first home of the Venus de Milo. But like so many other provincials who were blessed with talent, intelligence, or beauty, her life did not really begin until she arrived in Paris, the city that values both talent and intelligence but values beauty most of all.

TODAY the Venus de Milo stands, as it has for decades, in an alcove at the end of a long hallway on the ground floor of the Louvre. Entering that hallway, you can see the statue in the distance, almost eighty yards away, looming over the crowd around it. Since the crowd obscures the base and legs, the nude torso appears to be an apparition. The deep whiteness of the marble is luminescent against the browns, blacks, and grays of the hallway. Distant, pale, and shimmering, unconcerned by the hubbub around her even though she is nude, the goddess seems to float above the admiring throng. She looks fresh, forceful, and completely original, the way she must have looked to the people who saw her when she was rediscovered almost two hundred years ago.

Moving closer brings more of the statue into view, and the unexpected power of seeing her at a distance diminishes. Now she becomes familiar. Though most people in the crowd are seeing the actual statue for the first time, they all have seen her image time and again. I first saw it on the cover of a box of Classicos matches from Mexico when I was six. I remember her naked breasts and her impassive face staring into the distance. Once I saw that image, I never forgot it. How could I? The Venus de Milo permeates our culture, where her image is shorthand for lofty ideals: truth, purity, and timeless beauty. She is in advertisements and cartoons, on the covers of record albums, and part of company logos. She is reproduced as saltshakers, vases, table lamps, and rubber toys that squeak. In serious art the

Venus de Milo has inspired both homages and parodies by artists such as Rodin, Salvador Dalí, Magritte, Max Ernst, and, in more recent years, Clive Barker and Jim Dine. Her image is so powerful that it easily rises over cultural boundaries. In 1964 France sent the statue on loan to Japan. When the ship carrying her arrived in Yokohama, more than 100,000 people came just to watch it dock. By the time she left Japan, one and a half million people had come to see her, borne past her display on a moving sidewalk.

Seeing the Venus de Milo in the morning, when the tour groups are the thickest, is worth all the effort and exasperation. It can be exciting just to see the spectacle of the crowd and to hear guides speaking in any number of languages. But the best time to see the statue is late in the afternoon, in the hour or two before the museum closes. Then, with the crowds long gone and enough time to observe in solitude and without interruption, it is possible to let the familiar image from advertisements, matchboxes, and saltshakers fade away and to see the Venus de Milo for herself.

Her serenity, assurance, and great comfort with her own beauty produce a tranquillity powerful enough to be a physical pleasure. This can last for several moments, but as you begin to look closely at the statue you see something that nothing in the thousands of popular images prepares you for: The statue is fragile and lined with fractures. It was carved from two large blocks of marble, one set on top of the other. The line where the two blocks meet is visible even though somewhat hidden by the roll of drapery around her pelvis. Four large pieces, two on each side, have broken away from her hips. The lines where they fractured are easy to see from the sides and the back. Even the knot of hair on the back of her head has broken off and been reattached. The arms, of course, are missing, and so is the left foot. There are nicks and scrapes everywhere. The most damaging one aesthetically is a large gouge where the left nipple once was. Her earlobes are gone. Presumably they were broken when robbers ripped away the earrings she once wore.

The Venus de Milo

The Venus de Milo from the back

The Venus de Milo from the right

The Venus de Milo from the left

This Venus is clearly a big woman, but how big? In fact, from head to toe, she is six feet seven inches tall. Her right foot—twelve and a half inches long—is enormous. Her hips are so wide she looks as if she has had several children. Rodin described her stomach as "immense like the sea! It is the rhythmic beauty of the sea without end." Yet she seems almost weightless, as if this ton of marble could move effortlessly through the air. As you look at her, six-seven doesn't seem any more likely than either five-nine or eight feet.

And how old is she? She is not an adolescent, she is not a virgin, and she is not a crone. She could be twenty-five or thirty or fifty. Her children could be infants, or they could be old enough to have children of their own. So while most people would describe the statue as "realistic," the most obvious characteristics of a real person—height, weight, age—turn out to be elusive.

As you walk about viewing the Venus de Milo from one side and the other, she changes. Since we are accustomed to seeing her in reproductions viewed straight from the front, the changes are quite striking. From her right side she seems almost like a pillar. Her huge foot is flat on the ground, and a line goes straight up from it to her right hip and then to her right shoulder. Her leg, barely suggested beneath the folds of the drapery, is straight and bears most of her weight. Her thick hip is locked. Her stomach and her waist are also thick. She seems planted in the ground, and since she is looking away toward her left, her big hip, stomach, and waist are what defines her. They all speak of her fecundity and of her sexuality. From this perspective she is as human as a goddess can be. You can see in stone a profound truth of Greek art and religion: We share our sexuality with the gods.

Her drapery is falling down around her hip, but that doesn't concern her, because her concentration is elsewhere. Even her hair, gathered in the back, has begun to unravel. It's almost a shock to realize that, hanging free, her hair would be long enough to reach most of the way down her back. It's easy to think that she must always be exactly the way she is in the moment captured in the statue. But it's not true—that's the shock. What mood would she be in when she let her hair fall down her back? The gathered hair beginning to unravel reveals a tantalizing glimpse into her interior life, just as her partially fallen drapery does. As with many masterpieces, the statue that appears so open, even blatant, is instead filled with suggestion and withheld knowledge.

From the left side she seems not tied to the earth but ready to ascend from it. Her raised left foot makes her appear able to spring effortlessly into space. But even from this side we are excluded from her. All her concentration is on something, now invisible, that is just in front of her. What is it? Who is she, after all? How did she come to be here on a pedestal in an alcove at the end of a long corridor in the Louvre? And what is it about her that attracts and holds the attention of the world?

Disarmed

I

From Melos to Paris

OLIVIER VOUTIER was twenty-three and an ensign in the French navy when he first set foot on Greek soil. He had a high forehead, black hair, and a carefully trimmed mustache that shot straight up in a waxed point at each end. His slender, athletic build was close to being slight, but he was possessed by a romantic fervor that made him prideful and gave him a forceful appearance. He wore a well-tailored uniform that completed the picture he presented of precise military sheen. In fact, he loved wearing uniforms. Later in his life, Voutier had a weakness for the gold braids, ribbons, and medals he would win during his years of combat. He would pose for portraits wearing all his medals and with a brace of pistols tucked into his broad belt.

It was spring in the year 1820. Voutier was assigned to the *Estafette,* a two-masted warship, which for more than a month had been at anchor in the magnificent harbor on the island of Melos, a piece of rock halfway between Crete and mainland Greece. Unfortunately, to most tastes, the harbor was the only thing about Melos that was magnificent. The Greek islands in the Aegean are often idyllic, but Melos was not. Long stays in the harbor there were bleak exercises in boredom, and the *Estafette* had nothing to do but wait for orders.

Fortunately, Voutier had an escape from the boredom.

Olivier Voutier

He was interested in what was then a completely new and unformed science: archeology. On April 8 he left the *Estafette* with two sailors carrying shovels and picks. They were going to dig into the hillsides of Melos for whatever remnants of the glories of Greece and Rome they could find.

In fact, Voutier was looking for more than that. He was a young man in search of a cause, and Greece was where he found it. He saw the Greeks, heirs of classical civilization, demoralized and humiliated under the rule of the Ottoman Turks. Just a year after the long anchor at Melos he abruptly resigned his commission in the French navy and joined the Greek war for independence. He became a hero of the struggle.

That morning on Melos it wasn't difficult to find the most promising place to dig. The ruins of an ancient theater, as well as stone walls and pieces of broken columns, were still clearly visible on an escarpment on the side of the island's tallest hill. Voutier and the sailors began to dig there near the remains of a wall and circular tower that had once defended the gate of the ancient town. They found a seemingly endless number of marble fragments, as well as a bust, a carved foot, and two nicely chiseled statues missing their heads, hands, and feet.

As Voutier and the two sailors were digging, another man, a local farmer as it turned out, was also working just twenty paces away trying to remove the stones from an ancient wall to use in a structure he was building on his farm. Voutier, glancing over that way, noticed that the man had stopped digging for the moment and was staring at something in a niche he had uncovered in the wall. His posture was curious enough that Voutier went to look himself.

As Voutier drew near, he could see that the farmer was busy again, covering something with dirt. Peering into the darkness of the chamber where the farmer was working, Voutier saw a statue, or at least the upper half of one, lying on its side and still partly buried. Its odd shape made it useless as a building block, so the farmer had decided to cover it over. Voutier gave him a small bribe to dig up the statue instead. It didn't take long to push aside the accumulated dirt and stones and prop the object up. It was the nude upper body of a woman. The tip of her nose and the small bun of hair gathered at the back of her head were both broken off. There was an ugly hole in her right side that Voutier assumed was the result of some crude restoration from long ago. Stains, nicks, and scrapes, evidently from the time when it had first fallen over, covered the surface of the statue.

But despite these imperfections, Voutier sensed from the first glance that he was seeing something extraordinary. This torso was more glorious than anything he could have hoped to find when he set out that morning with the two sailors and a few picks and shovels.

Voutier insisted that the farmer search for the lower half of the statue, but his insistence revealed his excitement. Now the farmer wanted more money to continue digging. Voutier paid. He joined the farmer inside the niche, an oval enclosure about five yards wide. The walls were cut stone and had once been painted in a pattern that was still faintly visible. Overhead was an arched roof.

After a little digging here and there amid the rubble on the floor, the farmer found the lower half of the statue and brought it up out of the dirt. But the two parts couldn't be reassembled because a large section missing from the right side made it impossible to balance the top half on the lower. Yet another bribe persuaded the farmer to continue digging, but this time, since the missing piece was considerably smaller than the other two, the search took more work and time. When the farmer wanted to quit, Voutier calmly prodded him until he finally discovered the missing middle section.

At last Voutier and the farmer, perhaps with help from the two sailors, were able to place the top half of the statue on the lower. When they slid the middle section between the two larger pieces, the statue balanced, and they were able to see it as it was intended: a woman, nude from the waist up, her legs covered in wet drapery that was falling from her hips. This was of course the statue that would become known to the world as the Venus de Milo.

The farmer's only interest in the statue was what money he could get for it. But Voutier, though he had to contain himself as best he could, knew that this was an experience granted to very few. He was in the presence of a masterpiece that no one had seen for almost two thousand years. Here, in a buried niche on a minor island, was a work of art that was a culminating expression of the Greek genius. It had been reborn before his eyes, and now it stood there in full glory for him to contemplate. Voutier later wrote a single sentence to describe these first few moments: "Those who have seen the Venus de Milo are able to understand my stupefaction."

As soon as he had recovered from his astonishment, Voutier turned his attention to practical matters. To prevent a fall, the top half was removed and placed on the ground beside the lower half. Now it was time to try to claim the statue before anyone else was able to, preferably even before anyone else knew about it. Voutier hurried to the small town at the top of the hill about fifteen minutes from the ruins. There he found the only representative of the French government on the island, a vice-consul named Louis Brest.

After about thirty minutes Voutier arrived back at the niche with Vice-consul Brest in tow. While Voutier was gone, the farmer, whose name was Yorgos, had had enough time to make a thorough search of the small enclosure. He found a marble hand holding an apple, a piece of a badly mutilated arm, and two herms. Herms are quadrangular pillars about three feet high with a carved head at the top. Their purpose is no longer clear, but apparently they were usually used as some sort of boundary marker. One herm had the head of a bearded man, and the other the head of a young man. Each one was standing in an inscribed base.

Voutier had brought a sketch pad and a pencil with him on his digging expedition, and now he set to work on what would turn out to be four drawings: one of the upper half of the statue, one of the lower half, and one of each herm in its inscribed base. He copied the two inscriptions clearly enough to be read. His plan was to use the drawings to convince the captain of the *Estafette* to take the statue on board.

While he was drawing Voutier prodded Brest to buy the statue. Yorgos had decided he wanted four hundred piasters for it, about the price of a good donkey. Brest was a rotund, methodical person, thirty-one years old, who tried to maintain

Voutier's drawings of the Venus de Milo done on Melos

the dignity of his office by wearing a blue uniform with gold braid. The sudden exertion of getting to the site, the close atmosphere inside the small niche, the ancient dust that had just been disturbed and was still floating in the air, the play of light and shadows on the statue and the oddly painted brick walls—all that was too much for Vice-consul Brest. Besides, he had no official budget. If he were to buy the statue, he would have to do so with his own money and then hope to be reimbursed by the French government. While that might happen, it also might not. "Are you *sure*," he whispered to Voutier, "that it's worth that much? Please don't make me risk losing my money."

With that Voutier left the vice-consul behind and returned with his drawings to the *Estafette*. (Voutier ordered the two sailors to bury the artifacts they had found before he approached Yorgos. He was never able to return for them. It's possible they remain buried on Melos to this day.) On board he showed the drawings to his captain, a certain Robert, an intense, demanding officer known to his crew, more out of respect than fear, as Robert the Devil. Voutier tried to persuade him to sail immediately for Constantinople to get authorization from the French ambassador there to buy the statue. The drawings impressed Robert, but he had orders to wait at Melos. He couldn't ignore them because of the sudden enthusiasm of an ensign for a statue.

Voutier now gave up in frustration. That was how the navy was these days; perhaps under the emperor it would have been different. (Voutier was a passionate Bonapartist.) Now, his initial enthusiasm thwarted, he seems to have lost all interest in the statue and remained silently in the background during the events that followed. He put his drawings away with his personal effects, and though he guarded them through his long and adventurous life, it would be fifty years before he revealed them publicly.

Sulfur and vampires

MELOS appeared during some distant epoch when a volcano erupted underneath the sea and left a thin strip of land about twelve miles long with a wide opening in its northwest corner. The sea flows from there into a round bay that was once the crater of the volcano. The water is deep, and the bay, almost four miles across, is protected on all sides, making Melos the best natural harbor in the eastern Mediterranean.

As inviting as the harbor is, the land itself is unwelcoming. Melos is a large, hollow rock riddled with caverns, crevices, and catacombs. The seawater flows in and out, leaving behind salts and other minerals that combine with iron ore left from the volcanic explosion to produce smoldering fires. In former times these fires in turn ignited the sulfur, which was once abundant and had a beautiful greenish tint. The hot sulfur formed noxious clouds that fouled the water in the few springs and gave the air in the low areas a horrible stench.

For generations the principal town was in the lowlands, but by the late eighteenth century the air and water there had become so pernicious that the inhabitants were prone to contract painful or even fatal diseases. At Castro, on the side of the tallest hill on the island, the air was better and the water didn't taste of sulfur. Most of the population moved there, but it was a long climb up from the harbor that could take more than an hour. The road, such as it was, had been covered with volcanic soil that was principally tiny pieces of black glass. The footing was unsure, and each step caused a long, annoying crunch.

Melos has been continuously occupied for about six thousand years. Even before the classical age of Greece it was home to certain cult religions that seem to have been imported from Crete. There was silver there once, and high-quality alum, which had myriad medicinal uses in the ancient world. The weak and infirm made pilgrimages to the hot sulfur springs, and even healthy Greeks would come and drink deeply of the water to purge themselves.

During all those six thousand years only two events have turned the attention of the world to Melos. The first occurred in the winter of 416–415 B.C., during the Peloponnesian War, when an Athenian invasion force landed on the island. Melos had allied itself with Sparta against Athens. After a brief siege, the invaders conquered the island, put all the men to death, and sold the women and children into slavery. The Athenians then sent a colony of their own citizens to settle on the island.

Even this bloody episode would be forgotten if Thucydides in his *History* had not dramatized a council between the Athenian leaders and the leading citizens of Melos. The Athenians demanded complete surrender and a yearly tribute; in return, they pledged not to murder the men or enslave the women and children. The islanders refused in the vain hope that they could hold out long enough to be rescued by the Spartans and thus preserve their independence. The dramatization, known as the Melian Dialogue, is a staple in college introductory political science classes. It subtly shows that even those who are doomed militarily still have political power, since the Athenians really had no interest in murdering and enslaving the entire population. All they wanted was allegiance in the form of a tribute.

That left room for negotiation about the terms and amount of the tribute and any other aspects of the surrender. The Melians' failure to understand what power they had despite their military weakness led to disaster.

The second notable event in the history of Melos was the discovery of the Venus de Milo in the spring of 1820.

About four thousand people lived on Melos then. They were constantly in the grip of fears both real and imagined. The real fear was of the brutal whims of the despotic Turks who ruled them. The imagined fear was of ghosts, goblins, vampires, and other spooks. Every act of ordinary life was riddled with superstition. Before childbirth every door, chest, and window that could be locked with a key had to be opened in order to prevent a difficult delivery. Once labor began, no one present could leave and no one could come in. After childbirth a woman had immediately to step on something iron to make her and the infant strong. Also she couldn't let a star shine on her, or both she and the infant would die. Similar superstitions ruled courtship, marriage, the wedding night, child rearing, medical prevention and cures, and of course death and burial.

In particular, the people of the Aegean islands believed in vampires. When anyone died without apparent cause, the assumption was that a vampire was roaming the island by night and returning to the grave only by day. Recently buried bodies were disinterred to identify the vampire, because supposedly, a vampire's corpse didn't decompose. As it happens, corpses buried on the islands were often slow to decompose because of the salts in the volcanic soil. A preserved corpse became proof that the vampire really existed. After prayers by everyone as they gathered around the body, followed by incantations from the priest, the body was burned to extinguish the vampire.

Many of these superstitions, like so much else in life on Melos, had survived from classical times. In both eras, the inhabitants lived with their superstitious fears and their fears of distant powers and marauding pirates. Their droning folk music with its exotic time signatures—8/5, for example—was apparently little changed from ancient times. The same was true of wine making, cheese making, cotton spinning, and other domestic arts. And like their distant ancestors, the people of Melos still kept weasels as pets. The old theater may have been in ruins, but otherwise the sights and sounds of ancient Greece and 1820 Melos were surprisingly similar.

The hand with an apple

ON MELOS, as in every remote community, people were compulsively absorbed in the lives of their neighbors. News of the discovery of the extraordinary statue spread instantaneously throughout the island. Local opportunists offered Yorgos money for the sculpture in the hope of selling it again for profit. Even more bothersome, the local government, which was a group of three men known as primates, shouldered its way into the affair. In small towns the most powerful citizens are the ones with the most money or land, and the minister of the leading church. It was no different in the Greek islands. The rich, the landowners, and the Greek Orthodox priest, who was often wealthy himself, became the primates. They seem to have been an extralegal institution. Apparently, they chose their members at their own discretion and then shuffled themselves in and out of the official governing council of three men that enforced the local laws.

The primates told Yorgos that they had the authority to choose the buyer he must sell to. That was a terrible development for Vice-consul Brest. What if the primates insisted that Yorgos sell to someone who wasn't French? Brest's position as the representative of France gave him a certain amount of respect on the island and, at his request, the primates promised not to sell the statue to anyone until he had received instructions from his superiors.

Despite this promise, Brest feared that if he didn't act quickly, the statue would surely slip out of French hands. The obvious solution was for him to buy it himself. But if he did and it turned out to be worthless, he would have wasted his money. On the other hand, if it *was* a masterpiece and he allowed it to fall into the clutches of another nation, he would receive all the blame. At the very least he would never become full consul, a promotion and recognition he deeply coveted and believed he deserved. Why hadn't he bought the thing from Yorgos when he'd had the chance!

Brest was a French citizen and patriot who had never seen France. His grandfather and father had been vice-consul on Melos for decades before him. In 1780 Charles-Sigisbert Sonnini, a young Frenchman traveling in Greece and Turkey at the behest of Louis XVI, encountered Brest's grandfather, whom he described as an excellent man who had the esteem of the French navy, the European merchants in the region, and the Turks. The Greeks of Melos, Sonnini said, venerated him: "The flag of France, which flies above his house, however isolated and without any protection, was nowhere more respected." And how had France repaid his service and fine character in the twilight years of his life? "He has the misfortune of seeing himself reduced to nothing more than an agent of the consul in Smyrna."

Forty years later his grandson was still under the authority of the French consul in Smyrna, a city far across the Aegean at the end of a bay on the coast of Turkey. Brest's isolation on the island and the neglect of both him and his grandfather by the nation he loved had left him, like a spurned suitor, cautious at best and bitter at worst. And his life was often one of misery. Just a few years earlier, when he was in his late twenties, he had brought a young bride from Constantinople to live with him. When a pirate named Franco Poulo and his fifty men landed on Melos to loot and kidnap young girls, the newlyweds had to run for their lives, and Brest's bride came close to being captured. The comte de Forbin, who had just become director of the Louvre, happened to visit Brest and his wife at their home in 1817 while on a voyage in search of antiquities for the museum.

Forbin was touched by their eager hospitality, but he recorded how people from the "miserable" town stared at him through the open doorway while he consumed "bad bread, fruit, and passable wine."

In his present dilemma about the statue, Brest could turn only to the few other Frenchmen in positions of authority on Melos. These were the captains and officers of the vessels in the harbor. On April 9, the day after Voutier made his discovery, Brest asked Robert the Devil from the *Estafette* and Captain Duval d'Ailly of the *Lionne,* a ship that sailed with the *Estafette,* to come see the statue.

To protect his treasure, Yorgos had carted the upper, more valuable half of the statue to his cowshed, along with the two herms and their inscribed bases, the arm fragments, and the hand with the apple. Brest and the two captains went to Yorgos's farm and tramped past the animals and through the straw and thick manure in his cowshed to see the new discovery. The captains advised Brest to buy it, although that was probably not what he was hoping to hear. A negative opinion would have helped him justify not risking his money.

The next day, April 10, two other French vessels, the *Bonite* and the *Emulation,* arrived at Melos. Brest took their commanders to the cowshed immediately. On April 11, Captain Dauriac of the *Bonite* wrote a letter to Pierre David in Smyrna, the French consul general in the Levant who was Brest's superior. This letter is the first written description of the Venus de Milo after its discovery:

> Three days ago a peasant who was digging in his field found a white marble statue representing Venus receiving the apple of Paris. She is larger than life-size. At the moment we have only the bust down to the waist. I have been to see her. The head appears well conserved to me as well as the hair. The end of one of the breasts is broken. The peasant was told that the discovery that he

made was of great value and he believes it now because there are people who have already offered him one thousand piasters. M. Brest . . . asked me for advice about the statue, but I am not able to give him any, not knowing anything about the subject.

The next day, April 12, Brest himself wrote a letter to David to alert him to the discovery. He said that the statue was "a little mutilated; the arms are broken off and she is separated in two pieces at the waist." He describes the work as "Venus holding the apple of discord in her hand."

Both men seem to be referring to the hand holding an apple that was among the bits and pieces Yorgos found in the niche with the statue and put with the rest of the fragments in the cowshed. Its marble and dimensions were consistent with the statue's. And, as both Dauriac and Brest seem to have known, Greek statues of Venus often showed her holding an apple. The apple is the central symbol in the myth of how the Trojan War began. When the mortal Peleus and the goddess Thetis were married, the only goddess who wasn't invited was Discord. For revenge she threw a golden apple with the inscription "For the fairest" among the guests. Juno, Venus, and Minerva each claimed that the apple was meant for her. Jupiter saw nothing but trouble for himself if he chose any one of the three above the others, so he sent the goddesses to Mount Ida, where Paris, the most beautiful mortal man, was tending flocks of sheep. Each goddess appeared before him and tried to bribe him to choose her. Juno promised power and wealth. Minerva promised triumph in war. But Venus promised the most beautiful woman on earth for his wife. That decided Paris. He chose Venus and gave her the apple. The most beautiful woman on earth turned out to be Helen, the wife of Menelaus, king of Sparta. Venus helped Paris persuade Helen to leave with him for Troy. The Greeks united to bring Helen back, and the Trojan War began.

The ambitious ensign

ALONG with Voutier's sketches, Dauriac's letter, and Brest's letter, there is a fourth description of the statue from the days that followed its discovery. Its author, an ensign in the French navy who was just a month shy of his thirtieth birthday, had arrived on April 16 aboard a ship named the *Chevrette*. During the next ten years he would emerge from obscurity to become one of the most famous men in Europe. His rise began in Melos when he appropriated for himself the credit for discovering the Venus de Milo.

This ensign was the driven, indomitable, and peculiar Jules Sébastien-César Dumont d'Urville. Although he languished through his twenties as a junior officer without connections, he eventually became a rear admiral. He led three voyages around the world, during which he explored the coasts of Australia, New Zealand, and New Guinea as well as many islands in Polynesia. He established the first French presence in Antarctica. His accounts of these voyages became publishing sensations and were translated into a number of languages (although not English), thus spreading his fame throughout Europe. His work in botany earned him membership in learned societies, as did his philological studies on the languages of Oceania.

Tall and muscular, he flaunted his robustness and endured the most demanding physical hardships almost with relish. Although his crews were loyal to him because he was scrupulously fair, he was too awkward socially to be friendly with them. He usually spent evenings at sea in his cabin poring over botanical specimens and writing in his journal. By the time he became an admiral, he would wear his uniform only when in port; otherwise he was unconcerned with his physical appearance. An officer who sailed with him wrote later that he was "a tall untidy man, without stockings or cravat, wearing torn duck trousers, and unbuttoned twill coat, the whole outfit crowned

Jules Sébastien-César Dumont d'Urville, by Jerome Cartellier

by an old straw hat full of holes." When he spoke, he made a whistling sound through his teeth.

D'Urville's unconcern for appearances concealed the driving motivation of his life: a desire for fame. Born in Normandy in 1790, he lost his father seven years later. His formidable mother made the fragile boy spend hours outside in the coastal chill without a coat. She thought that would toughen him up, and evidently it did. She was repelled by affection and insisted that her son address her only in the most formal and polite language. When he was ten, d'Urville asked an uncle if any famous men came from the little town in Normandy where he was born. The answer was no. "I promised myself," d'Urville wrote, "to work twice as hard to place my name on the wings of fame. Habitually plunged in such thoughts, I had acquired an aloof and serious manner, unusual at my age."

He had joined the crew of the *Chevrette* in 1819. Although d'Urville was married with a son who was going on three, he chafed at the shore duty that had been his lot since the Bourbons' restoration to the French throne. The *Chevrette* had a mission to study the islands of the Mediterranean and the Black Sea. D'Urville was to be one of the scientists on board, his subjects being botany, entomology, and archeology. As always he performed these duties with immense energy and enthusiasm. His immediate superior officer, Lieutenant Amable Matterer, later wrote that "whenever the ship was at anchor, M. Dumont d'Urville left very early almost every day and did not return till after sunset, laden with all sorts of plants that he carefully classified and pressed. He would come aboard tired out but elated to have found some rare plants that had escaped the notice [of previous explorers]."

While the *Chevrette* was anchored at Melos, d'Urville and Matterer made excursions across the island. On April 19, after the ship had been in harbor for three days, they made the hour's climb of the large, steep hill overlooking the harbor to Castro, the main village on the island.

When they arrived at the village itself, it hardly seemed worth the effort of the climb. The houses, two stories tall with whitewashed sides and flat roofs, all looked alike. A set of bare stairs without any rail led up one wall from the street to the second story, where there was a flat terrace. During the day women sat on the terrace spinning cotton thread and often, if eighteenth- and nineteenth-century travelers are to be believed, looking provocatively at passersby.

Inside the houses the first floor was a combination stable, chicken roost, and pigsty. Garbage and muck from both humans and animals were thrown into the street, making it impossible to walk through town without fouling one's boots. The smell was nauseating. And fleas were everywhere. "The quantity of the insects is truly extraordinary," one traveler wrote. "One is covered and devoured. They spread over the head and slide into the hair."

In Castro, d'Urville and Matterer called on the French vice-consul. With two French officers in front of him, Louis Brest had only one thing on his mind. He began to tell them about the new discovery.

D'Urville and Matterer, excited by this news, asked Brest to take them to see the statue. He led them down the hill from Castro to the niche where the statue had been found. Matterer simply looked, but d'Urville assumed his role as a scientist and began to measure the niche and the bottom half of the statue, which Yorgos had not bothered to carry to his cowshed. D'Urville copied as best he could the Greek inscription on the wall of the niche, before asking what had become of the upper half. Brest gestured toward Yorgos's cowshed in a far corner of the field. The farmer's mother now sat spinning as she guarded the door. In a few moments they had walked across the field, and Yorgos let them in. Like the ships' captains before them, they waded through the manure on the floor to the place where the upper half stood. They were, according to Matterer, who used the same word as Voutier, "stupefied." The two sailors stared at the statue in silence. They also examined the herms, the arm fragments, and the hand with the apple. D'Urville was familiar with the myth of the three goddesses and the golden apple. He thought that meant the statue must have originally been part of a group with Juno, Minerva, and Paris. At last he began measuring again and taking notes.

Eventually, d'Urville asked his friend for his opinion. Matterer said he thought it was beautiful, but he mistrusted his own judgment in art. Yorgos, who from the first was eager to get the thing off his hands in exchange for some cash, offered to sell the statue to the two officers. They refused. They didn't have enough money with them. More important, though, their ship had a long and difficult mission in the Black Sea and was already crowded with crew, supplies, and scientific equipment of every description. There was no room for a heavy and unwieldy statue.

Daylight was waning now. After profuse thanks to Brest, the two men returned to the *Chevrette*. That was the end of it for Matterer but not for d'Urville. He spent the evening in his cabin and wrote, as he did each night, in his journal. He could not have known how famous the Venus de Milo would become. But along with Olivier Voutier, Captain Dauriac, Louis Brest, and even Yorgos, he sensed that the statue was not just one of thousands of antique statues but something special and powerful, something less like a thing than an event.

So, on this night of April 19, 1820, he began to create the legend that would first make him famous. From that moment everything he did or wrote was a mixture of truth, errors, and lies of omission designed to make d'Urville himself, and only him, the discoverer of the Venus de Milo. He tried and almost succeeded in sweeping everyone else, including the faithful Matterer, off the stage and out of history.

The kaptan pasha's dragoman

ON APRIL 22, three days after d'Urville and Matterer had seen the statue, their ship, the *Chevrette,* weighed anchor at Melos and sailed for Constantinople. By then the four other French ships that had been at Melos during the time of the discovery had departed as well. The *Emulation* and the *Bonite* were returning to France. The *Lionne* and the *Estafette,* with Olivier Voutier aboard, were bound for Smyrna. Now Louis Brest was left alone on the island to handle the primates as best he could.

The primates were the legal authority on the island, but exactly what the law was in 1820 is no longer clear and may not have been clear even then. Melos was part of the Ottoman Empire, but no Turk or Turkish official lived there. The Turks imposed heavy taxes that an official came around regularly to collect. And a magistrate appeared from time to time to sit as a judge in criminal cases, which he would decide according to the bribes he received. Other than this corrupt magistrate, the islanders received no governmental services of any kind in return for the burdensome taxes they paid to the Ottomans. There were no police or civil courts. There was no protection from pirates and no public works. There was not even a postal service. The whole Ottoman Empire, which at this time stretched from Persia to the Balkans, was administered by communications sent via personal messengers.

The possessions of the empire were divided into provinces, each ruled by its own pasha. The Greek islands in the Aegean formed one of the provinces. Their ruler was the kaptan pasha, who was also supreme admiral of the Turkish navy. The kaptan pasha, like most of the other pashas, used an intermediary known as a dragoman to administer the island province entrusted to him.

This peculiar position rose to importance as the Turks expanded far into Europe in the sixteenth century. The Turks did not know Western languages or customs, nor did the European powers know the Turkish language or Turkish ways. Since each side regarded the other as ignorant barbarians who were infidels besides, neither side was particularly inclined to learn the intricacies of living with the other. Dragomans bridged the gap. Typically, they were from European families who lived in Constantinople. Some of these families had been there for generations. They were hired by the European states to represent them to the Sublime Porte, as the sultan's government was known, but dragomans as a class were notoriously corrupt and devious. In the eighteenth century, England and France began sending young men to Turkey to train as dragomans in order to avoid this corruption. It was considered lonely and onerous duty. Its single attraction was that after ten or twelve years among the despicable but wealthy Turks, the young men could return home to England or France with a fortune.

In 1820 the dragoman for the kaptan pasha was a Greek prince named Nicolas Morousi, third son of the prince of Mol-

davia. Like most of the other dragomans for the Greek possessions, Morousi was a Christian who came from Constantinople.
Although he was technically a servant of the kaptan pasha,
Morousi was in fact the real ruler of the islands. The system
worked this way: the kaptan pasha had to pay a tribute to the
sultan in return for his dominion over the islands. He was then
permitted to make the tribute back, plus a profit, by taxing the
islands under his authority. But instead of collecting the taxes
himself, the kaptan pasha sold that right to his dragoman
Morousi, who could now profit by imposing any taxes he
wished. That's how dragomans acquired vast wealth. Morousi
might even sell the right to collect taxes on certain islands to still
other individuals, who would then recoup their expenses and
squeeze out *their* profit. Something like this system had been in
place since biblical times, which explains why publicans—tax
collectors—were so despised in the New Testament.

The three primates of Melos, in turn, were obliged to raise
taxes for the dragoman from the people of the island. If they
failed, the dragoman had the power to punish them with fines,
dispossession, imprisonment, or beatings. The primates lived in
terror of the dragoman. And now, just a few days after the
departure of the last French ship, a representative of Morousi
arrived at Melos. He had come to search for antique statues.

At least he said he represented the dragoman. This man was
a priest named Oconomos. Accused of embezzlement by his
superiors in the church, he had been summoned to Constantinople to account for himself. Now he had returned. He was to
find statues for the dragoman as a kind of penance to earn back
Morousi's favor. As soon as he learned of the recently discovered statue, he demanded that Yorgos sell it to him on Morousi's
account. He claimed the dragoman would settle the debt when
the statue was delivered to him.

The primates didn't know whether to believe Oconomos.
Perhaps all his claims were part of an elaborate swindle; even at
best, how could they be sure the dragoman would pay? Brest
reminded the primates that they had promised to do nothing

until he had further instructions from his superiors. Yorgos, meanwhile, had been listening to his neighbors, who had made him believe the statue was worth twenty to thirty thousand francs, a vast fortune on an island like Melos. Neither the French nor the dragoman was likely to offer that much money. They all found themselves stalemated.

The portrait of a girl

THE *CHEVRETTE*, with d'Urville and Matterer aboard, sailed straight from Melos to Constantinople and arrived there on April 28, 1820. After a few days in port the captain invited d'Urville to accompany him to a dinner on shore at the Russian embassy. There d'Urville met an assistant to the French ambassador, a man who at twenty-five had the air of someone quite at home in the halls of diplomacy and with the intrigues of the sultan's court. Marie-Louis-Jean-André-Charles Demartin du Tirac, comte de Marcellus, was a small, aquiline man who wore his wavy hair piled high on his head to conceal his receding hairline. His eyelids were hooded, his nose was long, and his mouth was small and straight. All this combined to give him an air of superiority that was somewhat misleading. In fact, he was good company. He was kindly, intelligent, and enjoyed a good laugh.

The young Marcellus had attracted the attention of the great Talleyrand, now returned to power after the restoration of the Bourbons to the French throne, who sent him first to Corsica and in 1815, when he was only twenty, to Constantinople. There he became secretary to the marquis de Rivière, the French ambassador.

At the dinner at the Russian embassy, Marcellus was impressed by d'Urville, who was spilling over with his enthusiasm for botany. He wanted to take a long hike in the countryside around Constantinople to search for specimens, and Marcellus volunteered to be his guide. D'Urville later recalled his particular pleasure during this expedition in finding a Daphne du Pont,

Demartin du Tirac, comte de Marcellus, by Ingres

a lys de Galcédoine, and a bourrache d'Orient. Marcellus, however, was more excited by d'Urville's account of the statue he
took credit for finding on Melos. The count pressed him with
questions, which d'Urville answered readily. He even showed
Marcellus the copies of the inscriptions he had made and drew
his own sketch of the statue.

The intensity of Marcellus's interest was just a bit disingen-
uous, for a secret reason of his own. He had met the Viennese
painter Johann Ender who had done a portrait of a beautiful girl

who lived on Melos. She was the daughter of a hideous old ship's pilot, who allowed Ender to paint his daughter's portrait on the condition that he show the painting only to Europeans. The old man feared that if the Turks saw the picture, they would take his daughter for the seraglio. Once Marcellus had seen this painting, he thought about the girl obsessively, although he had faint hope of ever meeting her. Now, Marcellus realized, there might be a way to fulfill his longings after all.

Marcellus brought d'Urville to the marquis de Rivière and had him repeat his story. Marcellus then asked the ambassador for permission to go to Melos to buy the statue. Rivière seemed unenthusiastic. Marcellus was becoming desperate as he saw his chance to visit the island drifting away. However, a royalist himself, he knew that Rivière was a fawning idolizer of the Bourbon monarchy. He suggested that he, Marcellus, could buy the statue for Rivière, who could then donate it to the king in homage. Although still doubtful, Rivière reluctantly agreed. He had already ordered Marcellus on a tour of the eastern Mediterranean, including Egypt and Palestine, which he considered more important. He gave Marcellus permission to go to Melos only if it didn't delay his diplomatic mission.

Either the next day or the day after, May 4 or 5, d'Urville sailed with the *Chevrette* through the Bosporus and into the Black Sea as it continued its scientific voyage. On May 6 the *Estafette* anchored in Constantinople, with Robert the Devil in command and Voutier on board. The *Estafette* had come to Constantinople in order to take Marcellus on his diplomatic tour. Now Melos had become the first stop on that tour, but the winds did not cooperate. The *Estafette* was unable to leave before May 15 and didn't arrive at Melos until a week later. During all that time it seems impossible that Marcellus and the two naval officers—Voutier, who had discovered the statue, and Robert the Devil, who had seen it—wouldn't have discussed it. And wouldn't Voutier have shown Marcellus his drawings? Evidently, he did not. In the extensive memoir Marcellus published about this voyage, he never mentions Voutier at all.

Marcellus negotiates a purchase

AS THE *ESTAFETTE* glided into the harbor at Melos early on the morning of May 22, 1820, Marcellus and the crew were in a joyful mood: After a week at sea they had at last arrived at their destination. But they were greeted by a sight so alarming and so coincidental that they couldn't help but laugh out loud. There out in the bay was the Venus. It was in a lifeboat that sat deep in the water because of its heavy load. A group of Russian sailors were rowing it toward another ship anchored in the harbor. In a memoir he published decades later, Voutier says he was incredulous. "Look," he shouted. "Someone's taking our statue away. This can't be real."

But it was. It had been more than a month since Brest had received the promise from the primates that the statue would not be sold until he had received further instructions. In the meantime French ships had come and gone from Melos, but none had brought any word from Constantinople. Oconomos had been there on the island all the while and had become more and more insistent. Finally he had promised Yorgos 750 francs and wrenched the statue away practically by force. He then had it taken down to the harbor and tried to book passage on a ship.

At this point Vice-consul Brest proved he could be both decisive and effective under the right circumstances. Claiming that the sale was illegitimate, and most likely hinting about the results of disregarding French power in the Aegean, he persuaded the captains of all the ships in the harbor to refuse to take the statue. After all, at this point the captains had nothing to lose: The wind was against them, so they couldn't leave the harbor anyway. Why not humor Brest? But Oconomos kept offering more and more money, until finally the captain of a Russian ship agreed to take the statue. His sailors rowed to shore to fetch it, rowed back, and loaded it on board as Marcellus and the sailors on the *Estafette* watched helplessly. Luckily for them, the winds had become even stronger and were still contrary to leaving the harbor.

The moment the *Estafette* anchored, Brest rowed out and came aboard. He told Marcellus what had happened. The count, annoyed by the way the vice-consul had been treated by the islanders and propelled, as he put it, "by the ardent desires of a young heart eager to fight against apparently impossible odds," resolved to seize the statue for himself at any price even if "later she would not justify the excesses of my zeal."

Marcellus immediately began the fight against apparently impossible odds. First he ordered Robert the Devil to stop the Russian ship if it should try to leave with the statue. Then he went ashore and made the long climb to Castro. Establishing himself in Brest's house, he sent for the primates. When the three men arrived, he asked to be taken to the Russian ship to see the statue. The primates refused. Angry, Marcellus began to lecture them. They had arbitrarily refused to sell the statue to the agent of France who was the first on the scene and the first to make an offer. A refusal to sell to him prohibited a sale to anyone else. Consequently, any sale that had been entered into under these conditions was null in his eyes and in the eyes of any reasonable judge. He concluded by reminding the primates that he could even use arms to enforce the sale to France. He had fifty trained men aboard his warship.

Then Marcellus bluffed. Before leaving Constantinople, he had obtained several letters of introduction, including one from the patriarch of the Greek church. He now displayed all the letters ostentatiously and read the one from the patriarch aloud. Unfortunately, as Marcellus was well aware, the letter contained only vague recommendations and said nothing specific at all about the case at hand. He hoped simple bombast would carry the day, but it didn't.

The primates began talking privately. Their discussions seemed to go on and on. Marcellus made a show of not listening.

At last the primates announced to Marcellus that Oconomos would never give up the statue now that he had it. Furthermore, the dragoman had ordered Oconomos to bring the statue to him in Constantinople. Those were facts the primates could not ignore.

By now it was late in the afternoon. As the primates began to leave, Marcellus insisted that they come to see him the next day. He sadly took the road to the port, but as soon as he was back aboard the *Estafette,* he was seized by an idea: He would go see the Venus. Robert the Devil prepared a lifeboat, and with seamen at the oars, Marcellus and several officers—most likely including Voutier—set off across the bay toward the Russian boat.

In the middle of their passage there was still enough light in the day for Marcellus to see a rider galloping across the beach toward the point of the bay closest to the Russian ship. It was Oconomos. He was signaling the Russian captain to keep the French from coming aboard his ship and seeing the statue. In response, the captain had armed his sailors. Marcellus and his companions on the lifeboat found themselves well within rifle range and exposed to possible fire.

The Russian captain, however, had second thoughts about firing on an unarmed French boat. The next French vessel to approach him would not be so defenseless. He sent a dingy out to make his apologies, although he still declined to take Marcellus on board. With that Marcellus gave up. He returned to the *Estafette* feeling that he had attempted to accomplish two things that day—to win over the primates and to see the statue—without the least result.

Still he refused to be discouraged. He even had a favorable presentiment about the outcome, especially after the goddess Venus appeared to him that night in a dream. He awoke the next day full of energy. Once again he climbed the hill to Castro, arriving there early in the morning, and immediately resumed his negotiations.

The situation had changed. The primates came to tell Marcellus that after long discussions they had decided the statue didn't belong to any single owner. As a group the entire community would send it directly to the dragoman rather than entrust it to Oconomos.

Marcellus regarded the primates' resolution as their first concession. He told them gently that he was pleased to deal with a fair community that respected France rather than with a single individual whose conduct did not inspire any confidence. Then he reminded them of how little use such a present would be in gaining the dragoman's favor. The Turks had an aversion to representations of the human form, especially for those that had been mutilated. He assured them that the dragoman would never be able to repair the damage done to the statue by time, the excavation, and the sea passage, whereas it *could* be repaired at the royal museum in Paris. Considering all that, Marcellus concluded, wouldn't it be better to sell the statue to him?

Marcellus continued to talk in a patient manner, overcoming the primates' objections one by one. At last he resorted to rereading his letters of introduction. This time his title as secretary to the French ambassador made an impression on the primates, who once again retired to consult among themselves in secret. Within an hour Marcellus saw them returning, followed by Yorgos. They expressed great regret for the delays and for any appearance of ill will. Their excuse was their perpetual fear of the dragoman. Now they were ready to sell the count the statue after all.

Marcellus accepted his victory calmly, even though just twenty-four hours earlier his task had seemed impossible. He told the primates he was very satisfied with their decision. To protect them from any reprisals, he gave them a letter for the dragoman, Prince Morousi, whom it happened that Marcellus knew well in Constantinople. They were the same age. During the previous few years they had spent long hours together sharing confidences while they hiked across the countryside and climbed the walls of ancient cities. In his letter Marcellus told his old friend of the complete devotion of the primates toward him and how they had treated him, Marcellus, with great decency.

He also addressed a letter to the French ambassador to ask that he protect the people of Melos if they should ever suffer harm because of the sale of the statue. He added that he had arrived on a warship and would have been within his rights to use force, but he had used reason rather than arms.

Marcellus then paid Yorgos 750 francs, the price the farmer had agreed upon with Oconomos, and gave another third, or 250 francs, to the primates. The sale was concluded on May 23, 1820.

The next day a lifeboat from the *Estafette* commanded by Voutier set out to take the statue from the Russian ship. He and his complement of young officers and sailors were determined to take the statue by force if necessary. In fact, they were spoiling for a fight. But they were disappointed, since the Russian captain received them politely and had his own sailors help them load the statue onto their boat.

Back at the *Estafette,* a hoist raised the statue from the lifeboat and lowered it gently onto the deck. At last Marcellus was able to see the thing he had worked so hard to buy. He was overcome with relief and admiration almost to the point of giddiness. He quoted Homer aloud before resorting to words of his own. "What superhuman beauty," he rhapsodized. "What sweet majesty. What shape divine."

After some moments of awestruck gazing, he supervised as the pieces of the statue and the other finds from the niche were sewed into sacks of canvas. He put the bust in one sack and the lower part in another. In a third sack he wrapped the two herms and their inscribed bases, the bun of hair, a left foot, a fragment of an arm, and the hand holding an apple. The sacks were then placed on padding and tightly moored in the ship's steerage.

The next morning, May 25, the *Estafette* sailed away, but not before Marcellus had had time to indulge in what he called his "caprice." He fulfilled his longing to see the girl in the painting who had been his real reason for coming to Melos.

The island girl Maritza

ON MELOS, where it was difficult to earn more than a subsistence living, the men often turned to doing business with pirates, and women became prostitutes. The men signed on to pirate vessels as sailors, or they worked as pilots guiding the pirates through the difficult passages between the islands. Sometimes these pirates were bold renegades, but just as often they were French corsairs or English privateers whose adventures were, in theory at least, sanctioned by their respective governments. Since the pirate ships used the harbor as a refuge, Melos developed a healthy economy in trading supplies needed for the ships and crews in return for pirate booty. Everything could be bought on the island, including a virgin bride.

The reputation of the women of Melos was that their beauty was matched only by their immorality. There were prostitutes and pimps of the usual kind. But there was another form of prostitution, one sanctioned by custom on the island and accepted there as hardly prostitution at all. A pirate—or an honest seaman, for that matter—who was at anchor at Melos for an extended time and saw a young unmarried woman he liked could go to her parents and ask to marry her. They would strike a bargain. The parents would certify that she was a virgin, and the sailor would agree to pay a certain amount immediately and a larger amount when he left. The more beautiful and accomplished the girl, the higher the price. The sailor agreed to pay more still if the girl was pregnant at his departure.

With the agreement made, the couple would go to the Greek Orthodox priest and be married. Later, when the sailor had gone, the marriage was annulled. The girl got a share of the money to use as a dowry to attract one of the island boys, often sailors themselves, who seemed not to mind at all. The girl had approximately the same status as a widow.

Brides could be bought this way on several other Aegean islands besides Melos, but not all. Lord Charlemont, a worldly British traveler who visited the Greek archipelago in 1749 and who was not above contracting with a prostitute himself, wrote, "These islands in which it is practiced are, unluckily, in every other respect the least worthy of a traveler's notice."

We do not know what, if anything, the painter Johann Ender told Marcellus about these customs or about the lovely girl in his portrait. But we know from the count himself that after successfully concluding his negotiations over the statue, he lost no time in turning toward his "caprice." He made inquiries and learned that the girl, whose name was Maritza, lived in a house at the highest point in Castro. He climbed up there immediately. The girl herself, who had been told he was coming, answered his knock at the door. She was surrounded by several of her sisters. Then, as if on cue in a well-rehearsed ritual, the girl's mother appeared and led Marcellus inside, where he sat on a bench while the mother talked.

Across the room was a bed. Maritza leaned against it and teased Marcellus by taking the exact pose as in Ender's painting. He stared at her and she stared at him. The mother said the girl was seventeen and was betrothed to a sailor from another island.

Maritza asked Marcellus about his ship, about Constantinople, about the distant places he had visited. He couldn't keep from exclaiming over her beauty, even in front of her. She stopped him, left, and returned with a cousin whom, as it happened, Ender had also painted. But Marcellus preferred Maritza. He asked her a few questions and was charmed by her simple answers. As he left, he gave her a coral necklace and a cake.

Or that is what he says took place. Certainly, he must have paid for the privilege of looking. According to the customs of the island, and judging by the eagerness of the mother to welcome him, Marcellus might have paid to do more than look. Perhaps he did; perhaps he did not. His infatuation was so public that the men on the *Estafette* teased him about it after they left Melos. The pilot performed an elaborate practical joke whose point was that Marcellus had left the statue behind and it was really the girl Maritza who was wrapped in the canvas belowdecks. Marcellus did not publish his account of the voyage until 1840, twenty years after the event, and even then the girl still burned in his memory. He had found two women on Melos. He appreciated the beauty of the statue, but his description of seeing it for the first time feels a little obligatory. His writing about Maritza vibrates with his lust. She was the woman he had come to the island to see.

Venus by moonlight

MARCELLUS then continued on the diplomatic tour that had been his original assignment from Rivière, the French ambassador. For five months ship and crew wandered the Aegean with the Venus wrapped in her canvas. They landed at many other islands, including Crete and Cyprus, and visited Palestine, Egypt, and Libya. All in all, everyone had a prodigiously good time. Voutier had a talent for singing and for improvising funny songs. Once at the mouth of the Nile they were out of rations and facing starvation, but a contrary wind kept them from landing. They sacrificed their last chicken to Neptune while Voutier chanted a mock-epic burlesque. Soon enough the wind changed.

In late September the ship anchored in Piraeus, the port of Athens, where Louis-François-Sébastien Fauvel, the venerable French consul, came aboard. Fauvel was both a connoisseur of art and a fervent antiquarian whose apartment near the Acropolis in Athens was filled with antiquities. Every French dignitary who visited the region stopped to see him and his collection.

Marcellus assembled the statue on the bridge of the *Estafette*. It was a warm, clear night with a full moon. Everything was quiet since there were no other ships around, and even the crew fell under the spell of the moment. For a long time Fauvel and Marcellus watched the moonlight glimmer on the marble as the ship lolled gently on the calm water of the harbor. Then they lit torches and Fauvel, who had celebrated his sixty-seventh birthday only the week before, studied the statue closely. The men spent practically the whole night that way. At last Fauvel proclaimed that it was the finest statue he knew of and came from either the school of Phidias or from the chisel of Praxiteles himself. And what was it worth? "Oh, my," Fauvel said calmly, "fifty thousand, one hundred thousand, two hundred thousand francs. A million. Anything you wish. She is priceless."

That morning, September 22, the *Estafette* sailed for Smyrna, where it arrived two days later. There it waited for the *Lionne,* a larger ship that would take the Venus and ambassador Rivière to France. On September 26 Brest arrived in Smyrna. He told Marcellus he had been looking all over the Aegean for him. The dragoman had been incensed by the sale of the statue. He had had the primates arrested and brought to him. Then, in front of officials from the other islands, he had forced the primates to their knees and whipped them himself. He also assessed a fine of seven thousand piasters, about five thousand francs at that time. He refused even to look at the letter Marcellus had written him. In a rage he fumed that it would have been better to cast the statue to the bottom of the sea rather than cede it to Marcellus and France. Marcellus told Brest that he would bring the news of this outrage to Rivière.

The *Lionne* arrived. Marcellus made sure the statue was safely transferred from the *Estafette* before leaving by land for Constantinople to report to Rivière. "In Smyrna," he remarked unsentimentally, "I left my servant, the Venus de Milo, and my dog."

In Constantinople, Marcellus told Rivière about the outrages the dragoman had committed. Rivière took the primates' complaints to the kaptan pasha, the dragoman's patron. The kaptan pasha claimed to sympathize completely with the primates, ordered restitution, and summoned the dragoman to him. Marcellus couldn't understand the conduct of his old friend Prince Morousi, but he had to leave Constantinople before he could see him again and solve the riddle. In the following months the Greek revolt began. Morousi was captured almost immediately and summarily beheaded.

The troublesome inscriptions

ON OCTOBER 24 the *Lionne* arrived in Constantinople with the statue on board. Marcellus formally presented it to the ambassador.

The marquis de Rivière was the kind of aristocrat who, a generation earlier, had made the Revolution inevitable. He was imperious toward those below him in rank and servile toward those above. Louis XVIII had consented to be the godfather of Rivière's son, but once on the throne he sent Rivière as far away as he could—to Constantinople. Rivière (his full name was Charles-François de Riffardeau de Rivière) had wavy black hair, oval eyes, and a long nose to look down. He was unkind, unfeeling, and resentful of any criticism or even any advice. Still, he had certain admirable qualities. He was recklessly brave, and he was loyal. During the Revolution he attached himself to the comte d'Artois, who was the brother of Louis XVI and Louis XVIII, and would later assume the throne as Charles X. Rivière followed the count across Europe during his exile but during Napoleon's rule frequently returned to France in disguise with messages to royalists still in the country. He was captured twice, imprisoned twice, and escaped twice. After being captured yet again, he was imprisoned until the fall of the empire.

As ambassador to Turkey, he was a complete failure. He began by dismissing everyone in the embassy who had served the empire no matter how devoted or experienced they were. Thus, at one stroke he deprived himself of anyone who knew anything about dealing with the Turks. That was in 1815. By 1820 he had mishandled affairs so badly that French traders in the

Ottoman Empire were taxed at a rate two and a half times that of any other nation. The Chamber of Commerce of Marseilles, which was the association that represented the French foreign traders, was apoplectic and demanded his recall.

Rivière, for his part, hated Constantinople. The life of the French court went on while he languished halfway around the globe. He wrote letters pleading to be relieved. In late March 1820, just twelve days before the discovery of the statue, he had written, "It would be better to die in France than to be living here, always anxious, unable to concentrate. . . . What a dreadful night! What a tomorrow!"

He wasn't interested in art and wasn't interested in the statue on Melos when he first heard about it. Marcellus had seemed so enthusiastic that it was easier to let him go than to prevent him. But when Rivière was finally presented with the statue in Constantinople, and when he finally listened to the rapturous opinions of its beauty, and when he looked at it himself, he saw that this statue could provide what was missing in his life: not art, not beauty, and not a woman, but a passage back to France. With the Venus as a gift to the king, he could leave immediately without seeming to have abandoned his post and could return to France in triumph rather than in disgrace for having botched the job he had been sent to do.

He sailed for France on the *Lionne* on October 29. Both the upper and lower halves of the statue arrived at the Louvre unharmed. So did the herms and the other pieces Marcellus had tied in the third sack. But something turned up in that third sack, something inconvenient and unwanted that no one had paid much attention to until now. It was a piece of marble that had apparently broken off the base of the statue. An inscription in Greek was carved on this broken piece, and in this inscription was the name of a sculptor, a name the Louvre hoped the world would never see.

I I

Winckelmann

THE VENUS DE MILO arrived in a Europe that had been hoping—more than that, expecting—that she, or some work like her, would eventually appear. That was because classical Greece did not seem distant to a European in the 1820s. Instead, it was a vital heritage that had recently been revived, a force that had to be understood because it was so much a part of the times. And the person who first thrust the remote Greek past into the consciousness of eighteenth-century Europe was born the son of an impoverished cobbler in Stendal, a remote and backward village in Bavaria.

"Good taste, which is becoming more prevalent throughout the world, had its origins under the skies of Greece." This seemingly innocuous sentence began a short pamphlet entitled *Reflections on the Imitation of Greek Painting and Sculpture* that changed European taste, art, and thinking forever. It was written and published in Dresden in 1755 by Johann Joachim Winckelmann, a scholar then thirty-eight, largely self-taught, who until that moment had lived in painful obscurity and poverty. At first he published only fifty copies of his pamphlet, but that small edition created a huge demand that even many later printings could not satisfy. As E. M. Butler wrote in *The Tyranny of Greece over Germany*, Winckelmann had "summoned a submerged continent to the surface of eighteenth-century life."

Johann Joachim Winckelmann, by Angelica Kauffmann

Winckelmann's influence eventually spanned Europe, but it was the French and the Germans who embraced him first. Partial translations of *Reflections* appeared in France within a year of its publication, and his ideas were adopted immediately by the French Enlightenment. Denis Diderot, whose great *Encyclopedia* dominated French intellectual life, compared him in importance to Rousseau; entries for topics such as Greece, Art, and Classicism were infused with Winckelmann's thinking. Among German speakers, his influence went deeper. Winckelmann wrote in an elevated, literary German that was rare in a place where

Latin remained the language of scholarly publications and lectures. He became the honored predecessor of writers such as Goethe, Schiller, and Hölderlin, who were the first to establish a classical literary tradition in the German language.

But his influence across Europe goes much further than that. In *Reflections* and in his later *A History of Ancient Art,* Winckelmann invented art history. Until then what had passed for art history consisted of catalogs with tedious and superficial descriptions. Art was static, and antiquity was considered all of a piece. Winckelmann's brilliant inspiration was to treat art organically and to try to understand how it grew, flourished, and declined across time. This achievement inspired at least three generations of readers. Today we know that his facts, both large and small, were often wrong. Even at the time, inconsistencies, omissions, and errors were apparent to careful readers. But these errors did not seem important compared to the way Winckelmann experienced art. For him art was mental, physical, and spiritual all at once. He taught his readers by his example to experience art the same way. "One learns nothing from reading him," Goethe remarked, "but one becomes something."

A Greek reincarnated

BORN IN 1717, Winckelmann seems to have come into the world so possessed by ancient Greece that he could have been the reincarnation of an Athenian who lived during the classical age. In his cobbler father's hut, which had a straw roof and only one room, the young boy relentlessly pleaded with his parents to send him to a school where he could learn Greek and Latin. He dug in the sand hills outside Stendal hoping to find buried urns.

Eventually his precociousness and his determination attracted attention. Through the generosity of neighbors and acquaintances, he was able to attend a series of schools and to live in Berlin, where he worked as a tutor. In 1742 he became tutor to a family named Lamprecht in the town of Hadmersleben and fell passionately in love with the son of the family, the first of many romantic attachments to young men throughout his life. But young Lamprecht rejected Winckelmann, who never recovered from the pain that caused. "I shall bury myself in gloomy silence," he wrote to the boy, and retreated for five years to a school in Seehausen, another small village.

He called those five years his "time of slavery," when he taught "mangy-headed little boys how to read the ABC's." At night during winter he wrapped himself in an old fur and sat by the fire in an armchair, where he read Greek authors until midnight. Then he slept in the chair until four, when he awoke to read for two more hours before leaving for school at six. During the summer he slept on a bench with a block of wood tied to his foot. If he moved, the block fell and awakened him for more reading.

Latin had all but eclipsed Greek in Europe at that time. The Greek authors were ignored if not forgotten, and copies of their works were quite rare. But Winckelmann managed to obtain Homer, Aeschylus, Sophocles, Plato, Xenophon, and Herodotus. Sometimes he would spend hours in a library copying a text for himself in longhand.

Finally, in 1748, when he was thirty-one, he escaped the school in Seehausen to become librarian for a Count Bunau at his castle near Dresden. Winckelmann remained there for six years. At last he had a vast library at hand, but even more important, Dresden was filled with art. There were impressive baroque buildings filled with paintings by Holbein, Correggio, Veronese, Titian, and Raphael, as well as scores of baroque statues from across Europe, all owing an obvious debt to Bernini.

Winckelmann came to hate it all. The baroque to him contained everything that was wrong in the art of his time and nothing of what made Greek art great. In particular Winckelmann hated Bernini or any work that suggested his influence. Bernini inspired art that was filled with curves and twists and false emotion. It was decadent, deceitful. It was feminine. The only thing he hated worse was rococo. It was curvy, false, decadent, deceitful, feminine, and French. Winckelmann hated the

French all his life. All his contemporaries in Europe fell short of the Greek ideal, but the French were the furthest from it of all.

Surrounded in Dresden by such horrors, he consoled himself by studying engravings of carved gems from classical times, the few antique statues that were there to see, and some plaster casts of other antiquities. On this thin foundation—formidable reading but little experience with Greek art and no travel outside Germany—Winckelmann built the theories he expressed in *Reflections on the Imitation of Greek Painting and Sculpture,* which he published in the final months of his employment with the count. No one could have guessed the gaps—the abysses—in his knowledge from reading that pamphlet. It was so confident, erudite, and original.

The "good taste" he mentioned in his first sentence came from *"le bon goût,"* which the hated French, who were the dominant arbiters of art in those days, considered the highest ideal of art. This ideal was to be found in nature. No one before Winckelmann thought to look for its origins in ancient Greece.

For him the Greeks were more natural than nature herself. He wrote, "The only way for us to become great or, if this be possible, inimitable, is to imitate the ancients." Nature itself is too complicated to imitate, but "the imitation of the Greeks can teach us to become knowledgeable more quickly, for it shows us on the one hand the essence of what is otherwise dispersed through all of nature, and, on the other, the extent to which the most perfect nature can boldly, yet wisely, rise above itself." This was precisely where the vile Bernini went wrong: "Bernini, by directing young artists primarily toward the most beautiful in nature, was not showing them the shortest way."

And what was it about Greek art that gave it such perfection?

The general and most distinctive characteristics of the Greek masterpieces are, finally, a noble simplicity and quiet grandeur, both in posture and expression. Just as the depths of the sea always remain calm however much

the surface may rage, so does the expression of the figures of the Greeks reveal a great and composed soul
even in the midst of passion.

For the next half-century the phrases "noble simplicity" and
"quiet grandeur" replaced "good taste" as the highest ideal of
art. It's a testament to the power of Winckelmann's ideas that
these phrases survived and triumphed even though he used the
Laocoön as his example of a work that shows the perfection
Greek art could achieve. This sculpture is a complicated composition of a father, two sons, and writhing snakes that Winckelmann had never seen, that he dated incorrectly, and that has
many fine qualities but is neither simple nor quiet at all.

In September 1755, just three months after publishing *Reflections,* Winckelmann left Dresden for Rome. Dresden was then
the capital of Saxony. Its king, queen, and entire court were
Catholic and regularly received visitors from the Vatican, some
of whom were collectors of ancient art. Winckelmann's talents
as a scholar had become evident by then, and he had begun to
receive offers to come to Rome. At that time Rome, not Greece,
was considered to be the place where the legacy of classical civilization was preserved. But to be allowed to study the ancient
artifacts in the Vatican and in the private palaces of notables in
the church, Winckelmann would have to convert to Catholicism. He knew he belonged in Rome, but the mere thought of
conversion troubled him. He disliked religion in any form, and
his deceased parents, whose memory he cherished, had been
devout Lutherans. He had withstood the temptation for several
years, but finally he succumbed and left for Rome in the company of a young priest.

Signor Giovanni

NOW ALMOST forty, Winckelmann was a rather handsome
man with short, dark hair and a broad chest and shoulders that

make him appear more athletic than one would expect. He had a straight mouth, a strong nose, and deep oval eyes. In Rome he became a visible but rather enigmatic figure. The nineteenth-century British historian Vernon Lee described him this way:

> A German priest, a hanger-on . . . a sort of pedant after the German fashion, a kind of humble companion, eating what the charity of his employer gave him . . . a cynical, pleasure-loving, information-seeking man, hanging on to the rich and intelligent painter Raphael Mengs, and who yet gave himself strange airs towards Roman artists and antiquaries. There he was, continually poring over books, though no lover of literature; continually examining works of art, though no artist, clambering on the pedestal of statues and into holes of excavations. What was he about? What was he trying to do?

Casanova, the great lover and diarist, also knew him slightly in Rome. He came to visit Winckelmann one day in his study, "where normally he was always alone engrossed in deciphering antique characters." But this time Casanova saw him "withdrawing quickly from a young boy." Casanova hesitated so that Winckelmann could recover and pretend that nothing had happened. But the scholar was determined to give an account of himself. "Not only am I not a pederast," he said, "but all my life I have said that it is inconceivable that this taste had so seduced the human species. If I said that after what you have just seen, you would judge me to be a hypocrite. But . . ." Winckelmann claimed that since his Greeks were all unapologetic "buggers," he felt it was his scholarly duty to try to understand the practice. "It is now four years that I am working on the matter, choosing the prettiest [boys]; but it is useless. When I set myself to the task, I do not come. I see always to my confusion that a woman is preferable in every respect." This preposterous lie couldn't have fooled anyone, least of all Casanova. One can't help thinking Winckelmann told it more out of habit than from fear of exposure. Rome attracted rich homosexuals from all over Europe; society there was discreet but indulgent. Nevertheless, Winckelmann, after a lifetime of sponging off friends and patrons yet doing whatever he pleased, found evasion and prevarication came naturally to him.

In 1764 he published his *History of Ancient Art* in four volumes. The scope of this work is so ambitious, its notion of Greece is so idealized, its descriptions of individual works are so passionate, and both its facts and its conclusions are so wrong that it's almost impossible for a modern reader to know what to make of it. Perhaps it's best seen as a weird, unintended precursor to fantasy novels, a work that creates an imaginary universe so convincing that it manages to attach itself to the things we know are real and changes how we see them.

But readers in 1764 didn't share this confusion. *History of Ancient Art* was considered to be one of the greatest intellectual achievements of the age, having done for art what years earlier Newton had done for science. Three of his ideas in particular continued to affect thinking and taste for the next half-century. First, although Winckelmann believed there were a variety of reasons that art flourished in ancient Greece—the climate was benign; athletes competed in the nude, allowing artists to study the human form in all its attitudes—the most important reason was that the Greeks enjoyed political liberty: "The independence of Greece is to be regarded as the most prominent of the causes, originating in its constitution and government, of its superiority in art."

Next, Winckelmann thought Greek art was not static but cyclical, just as he believed history itself was. It began, advanced, enjoyed a period of full development, then declined into decadence:

> One can distinguish four stages of style in the art of the Greeks, and particularly in their sculpture. These are the straight and the hard style, the great and angular style,

the beautiful and flowing style, and the style of the imitators. The first style for the most part lasted until Phidias, the second until Praxiteles, Lysippus and Apelles; the third will have waned with the latter and their school, and the fourth lasted until the decay of art. At full bloom it did not last long: for from the age of Pericles until the death of Alexander, at which the glory of art began to decline, was a space of about one hundred and twenty years.

Last, Winckelmann's ecstatic descriptions of individual works created a completely new way of seeing art and responding to it. Here, at enough length to convey its originality and power, is his description of the Apollo Belvedere, the most famous statue in the world before the discovery of the Venus de Milo:

His height is above that of man and his attitude declares his divine grandeur. An eternal springtime, like that which reigns in the happy fields of Elysium, clothes his body with the charms of youth and softly shines on the proud structure of his limbs. To understand this masterpiece you must fathom intellectual beauties and become, if possible, a divine creator; for here there is nothing mortal, nothing subject to human needs. This body, marked by no vein, moved by no nerve, is animated by a celestial spirit which courses like a sweet vapor through every part. . . . Like the soft tendrils of the vine, his beautiful hair flows round to be perfumed by the essence of the gods, and tied with charming care by the hands of the Graces. In the presence of this miracle of art I forget the whole universe and my soul acquires a loftiness appropriate to its dignity. From admiration I pass to ecstasy, I feel my breast dilate and rise as if I were filled with the spirit of prophecy; I am transported to Delos and the sacred groves of Lycia—places Apollo honored with his presence—and the statue seems to come alive like the beautiful creation of Pygmalion.

No one had ever written about art this way before. Who else had ever smelled perfume wafting from the hair of a statue? "The only precedent for this passage," wrote the British critic Hugh Honour, "is to be found in the Christian mystics." The belief that art could lead to revelation, that it could replace religion as a path to the divine, began with Winckelmann.

All the while he was in Rome, wealthy friends and noble patrons offered to pay for Winckelmann to visit and study in Greece. He always found some excuse not to accept. One can't help but think he was afraid to confront whatever he might find there. After a lifetime of laborious study, all of it in poverty except for the last few years in Rome, he might not have survived his despair if the stones on the top of the Acropolis in Athens failed to fulfill his expectations. And it would be even worse if somehow those mute stones disproved his theories. When the pressure to go to Greece became too great, he made the bizarre choice—in 1768, when he was fifty-one years old—to return to Germany instead.

Munich, Vienna, the Tyrol—he found them all so appalling that he took to bed with a fever that left him almost delusional. Determined to return to Rome, early that June he made his way alone to Trieste, where, as evasive as he had been with Casanova, he registered in a dockside hotel using an assumed name and began looking for a ship to take him to Venice.

A man named Francesco Arcangeli had the neighboring room. He and Signor Giovanni, as Winckelmann was calling himself, took to having coffee and meals together. Signor Giovanni showed his new friend two gold and two silver medals he had received from important patrons. Arcangeli then conceived of a plot.

He entered his new friend's room around ten o'clock on the morning of June 8, 1768, with a long dagger and a rope knotted into a noose. In a sudden movement he tried to strangle Winckelmann, but the scholar proved to be unexpectedly strong. Arcangeli stabbed him several times with the dagger and even then had difficulty escaping Winckelmann's grip. When he freed himself at last, Arcangeli fled but was soon captured. Winckelmann, covered with blood, somehow got to his feet and staggered downstairs. "Look what he did to me," he said to a waiter who had heard the commotion. Then he lost the power to speak. These hyperventilated events, which seem as if they must have come from the final act of an opera, concluded eight hours later when Winckelmann, who had been in agonizing pain all the while, died from his wounds.

Over the years the story grew that Winckelmann had been murdered by a street tough he had picked up on the docks of Trieste. When the director Pier Paolo Pasolini was murdered in Rome in 1975 during a still mysterious incident involving a young ruffian, the newspapers in Italy compared it to Winckelmann's murder. But Arcangeli's motive seems to have been pure greed and only greed. He was a petty thief by trade. While testifying at his trial he never accused Winckelmann of making any advances, a charge that might have helped his case. Instead he simply confessed and was condemned to death. On a piazza in front of a large crowd, his body was pulled apart on a wheel.

Perfection by imitation

EVEN BEFORE his death, Winckelmann had destroyed the taste for the baroque and rococo. In their place, classical Greek style became the inspiration for painting, sculpture, architecture, and even fashion. These changes occurred during a time when interest in art began to expand to include a rising bourgeois class as well as the traditional small elite of intellectuals, wealthy nobility, and church officials. By the end of the eighteenth century, salons in Paris might attract more than seven hundred visitors a day, most of them representatives of the new classes, who were serious and high-minded to a fault. In 1720 there were only nineteen art academies in all of Europe; by 1790, when the French Revolution had just begun, there were more than a hundred. A new idea—that art could encourage commerce—pushed this steady growth. In time the academies all would teach, in the letter and spirit of Winckelmann, that perfection in art was achieved by imitating the ancients.

Herculaneum and Pompeii, the Roman cities that had been covered in A.D. 79 by a sudden eruption of Mount Vesuvius, had been rediscovered in 1738 and 1748, respectively. Now, in the final third of the eighteenth century, voyagers to Greece began to write travelogues and publish prints of drawings for an eager audience. They braved the fleas and other insects that rained from the ceilings of local lodgings at night and infested the ruins where shepherds still let their flocks graze. These travelers ignored as well the repulsive stench from the latrines near the monuments and the way the thuggish Turkish guards extracted exorbitant bribes to view the sites. Instead, books such as *Ruines des plus beaux monuments de la Grèce* (1758) and *Antiquities of Athens* (1762) contained drawings of wistful, lovely scenes of broken pillars and ferns bursting through the cracks of abandoned temples. Printing after printing sold out. In particular, *Voyage du jeune anacharsis en Grèce* by Jean-Jacques Barthélemy (1788) went through many editions in the original French and in every other European language, including Greek. This novel purports to be the journey of a young prince through classical Greece, but its account of ancient people and times was regarded as authentic by its many readers.

In Paris in the 1760s, as a worldly observer noted, "Everything is *à la grecque*. The interior and exterior decoration of buildings, furniture, fabrics, jewelry of all kinds, everything in Paris is *à la grecque*." Travelers to Rome rushed to see the Laocoön and the Apollo Belvedere with all the expectation and excitement that is reserved today for the Sistine Chapel. Josiah Wedgwood began to mass-produce fine china. John Flaxman, his principal designer, copied his vases and plaques from Greek originals he found in the British Museum. Flaxman also produced a popular series of prints of scenes from Homer.

For fine artists, Winckelmann's basic ideas seemed to reveal hidden but powerful natural laws: Good taste began in Greece; the only way to achieve great art was by imitating the ancients; the greatness in Greek art lay in its "noble simplicity" and "quiet grandeur." These ideas inspired neoclassicism, a movement of artists such as the French painter Jacques-Louis David, the Italian sculptor Antonio Canova, and the English architect Sir John Soane, whose work began to appear in the years after Winckelmann's death. Their principal aesthetic was imitation of the noble simplicity of classical Greek art.

Winckelmann's belief that Greek art flourished because of the political freedom in classical times became almost a mantra for orators during the French Revolution. His conception of art as moving through a cycle of four distinct periods lasted well into the nineteenth century, when it became a dividing point between the neoclassicists and the romantics. And his belief that art can reveal the divine as well as or better than religion is still with us today.

Winckelmann was the intellectual, emotional, and spiritual father of every aspect of the classical obsession that would last in Europe well past the 1820s. Without the profound change in taste and thinking that he inspired, there would have been no passion for *la grecque* in Paris. But more important, there would have been no paintings by David, no sculptures by Canova, no buildings by Sir John Soane, no Wedgwood china, no prints by John Flaxman. And the Venus de Milo would never have excited the interest of the French ships' captains and ambitious ensigns who anchored at Melos in 1820. She would have remained in the niche, covered over by the farmer Yorgos, and never arrived in Paris to become the reigning goddess of the Louvre.

III

In the Hallways of the Louvre

THE VENUS DE MILO arrived in Paris in February 1821. The city, after ten years of revolution beginning in 1789, followed by sixteen years of submission to Napoleon's will, followed by five years of exhaustion and stagnation, had recently awakened to find itself once again the place where life seemed fullest, gayest, and prettiest. The foreign soldiers who had occupied the city after Waterloo had all left. The reparations demanded of the French government for the Napoleonic Wars had been paid. The Bourbons were back on the throne in the person of Louis XVIII, the brother of the guillotined Louis XVI, but he reigned as a constitutional monarch and was by nature neither oppressive nor vindictive. The economy, stalled by the reparations and several years of drought and poor harvests, took off in 1820. At last France was free of war, free of fear, and free of the absolute power of the emperor.

Suddenly, French taste and French style dominated Europe. Elegant shops in Paris were filled with luxurious baubles like a pair of pistols set with gold and pearls that shot perfume instead of bullets. Even the emperor of Austria bought lace, gloves, and stockings for his wife in Paris. French cuisine returned to its pre-eminence. Paris had more than three thousand restaurants and three to four thousand cafés. Even at the best of them the bill for dinner was still reasonable, especially when compared with prices in London or other European capitals. But the food was only part of the experience at a Parisian restaurant. One traveler wrote,

> No other capital of Europe can boast of such luxurious establishments open day and night with varied menus, in which one can have a meal at any time, and where one can enjoy peace and solitude among the crowd. Writers, princes, artists, judges, ministers, deputies, soldiers, foreigners from all over, Croesuses of all classes and ages, beauties from the north or south—how many races and eccentrics the viewer sees!

There were broad boulevards lined with trees and crowded with shops, cafés, and theaters. In the evening people strolled there or stopped at a café for a lemonade, a beer, or an ice. Just watching the passing crowd was rich entertainment. Peddlers, bootblacks, sword swallowers, jugglers, acrobats, pickpockets, and fortune-tellers made the boulevards a perpetual fair.

Indulgences that were forbidden in other countries were tolerated, if not encouraged, in Paris. There was gambling, drinking, and prostitution. Well-dressed women walked alone amid the luxurious shops and restaurants of the Palais Royal. They would take their customers to a room in an attic or underground to a small closet in a cellar where, according to an English guidebook of the era, the two would indulge in "frightful and unimaginable sensuality . . . such as no Englishman can conceive." Thus warned, the English swarmed across the channel and into Paris. In London there was even a famous after-dinner toast: "London and liberty! Edinburgh and education! Paris and pocket money!"

All this is recognizable in Paris still. But in many other ways the city of 1821 was not at all like the Paris of today. There was no Eiffel Tower. There was no Sacré-Coeur looking down across the city from atop Montmartre. The Place de la Concorde was mud and ditches. The banks of the Seine were mud, not stone, and lined with public baths and laundries. The Arc de Triomphe, which wouldn't be completed for fifteen more years, was nothing but four pitiful stumps.

The population was 800,000, by far the largest of any city on the Continent, and growing daily. Although the boulevards were spacious, the streets were narrow, crooked, and dark. Houses were built with the upper floors overhanging the lower ones so that slop could be poured out the windows into the street. The mess would lie there until passing horses, carriages, or pedestrians pressed it into the mud. Then the rain transformed it all into a black sludge. People who walked in the streets fouled their boots, trousers, skirts, and gloves. Arriving at a destination in spotless clothes was a sign of wealth, since it meant one could afford a carriage. The stench was overwhelming. What sewers there were ran directly into the Seine, where people bathed and drew drinking water.

Many people were sensible enough to drink only wine, but that was not enough to prevent general devastation from disease. Life expectancy was only thirty-nine. Diseases like tuberculosis and hepatitis were rampant, and every few years an epidemic of cholera would sweep through the city.

A skilled worker might earn as much as fifteen francs a day, but a general laborer earned only three francs. Women and children who worked received much less. A family of four needed about six francs a day to live, so the families of average laborers were condemned to hopeless poverty. Even among better-paid workers, illness or injuries that reduced the number of days worked could send a family from comfort to poverty in short order. About half the people in Paris were paupers.

Presiding over all this was the improbable figure of Louis XVIII. After Napoleon's defeat at Waterloo, Louis had been no one's first choice to assume control of France, but he was after all the rightful heir to the throne. He weighed more than 350 pounds. For most of his reign he could move about only in a wheelchair. As a young man he had married the ugliest noblewoman in Europe. Her eyebrows grew up her forehead, and she refused to bathe. Fat as he was and awful as she was, they had no children. She died during their exile, so Louis was now a widower without an heir. It seemed impossible that the blubbery and diffident king would marry now and produce children. He was infatuated with the comtesse du Cayla, but his sex life with her was limited to taking snuff from between her breasts. When she was on her way to see the king, the royal guards, though continuing to stand motionless while staring straight ahead, would commence a chorus of sniffing.

During his years in exile Louis had perfected a withering stare, but he was only passably intelligent and seemed hardly up to the task at hand. Nevertheless, he surprised everyone by outmaneuvering any threats to his power and by ruling on the whole sensibly and fairly. In particular he prevented the reactionary nobility, who had returned to France lusting for revenge, from instituting a new era of executions and persecution.

Although the laws stiffened and loosened from time to time, the censorship by which Napoleon had stifled free expression was relaxed during the Restoration. The arts, which had languished during the empire, returned with almost explosive force. In 1820 Lamartine published *Méditations poétique,* the first work of French romantic poetry, and it became a sensation. Even the king read it. A new generation of artists, writers, and musicians was about to appear: Hugo, Delacroix, Berlioz, Balzac, Stendhal, Dumas, among many others. One reason the Venus de Milo became so famous so quickly is that she arrived in France at the precise moment when the neoclassicism of the past gave way to the romanticism of the future. Since the neoclassicists, like Winckelmann, believed in imitating classical art, and since the romantics, also like Winckelmann, believed that great art was the result of personal and political freedom, each side could embrace the Venus de Milo in its fight against the other.

The looted masterpieces

ONCE IN Paris, the Venus de Milo would be placed in the Louvre, the former palace that had been transformed into an art museum, although in 1821 it looked radically different than it does now. It was just half the present size, consisting only of the Cour Carrée (the Sully Wing today) and the long building that runs west from the Cour Carrée for almost a quarter mile along the right bank of the Seine (the Denon Wing today). Both the Cour Carrée and the long gallery had a dilapidated, abandoned air that Napoleon's efforts at reconstruction had failed to dissipate.

The Arc de Triomphe du Carrousel was there, too, standing in front of the Tuileries Palace, which burned to the ground in 1871. The Tuileries began at the end of the long gallery and ran perpendicular from the Seine to the present Rue de Rivoli. The palace had been Napoleon's residence in Paris, just as now it was Louis XVIII's. But when the king happened to gaze out his window toward the spot where I. M. Pei's glass pyramid now stands, an area that today is an immense open plaza, he saw nothing but a maze of sagging, dispirited tenements lining dismal streets thick with mud and putrid refuse. The forlorn souls who lived there were among the most wretched inhabitants of Paris, indeed of all France. Balzac described this "intimate alliance of squalor and splendor" in *Cousin Bette*:

> These houses . . . lie wrapped in the perpetual shadow cast by the high galleries of the Louvre, blackened on this side by the north wind. The gloom, the silence, the glacial air, the hollow sunken ground level, combine to make these houses seem so many crypts, or living tombs. If, passing in a cab through this dead area, one happens to glance down the impasse du Doyenne, a chill strikes one's heart, one wonders who can possibly live here and what may happen here at night, at the hour

when the alley becomes a place of cut-throats, when the vices of Paris, shrouded in night's mantle, move as they will.

Although there had been plans under the ancien régime to transform the Louvre from an abandoned palace to a museum, they never really progressed. Then the Revolution came. The new government seized the property of both the king and the Catholic Church and found itself in possession of many price-less works of art. The Louvre was the natural place to display these treasures. After about a year of feverish renovations, it opened as a public museum on August 10, 1793, a date that was chosen because it was exactly one year after the fall of the monarchy. The paintings all hung in the Grande Galerie, which was lit by windows in the walls. On cloudy days it was too dark to see the paintings properly, while on sunny days it was too bright. And the paintings were hung neither chronologically nor by school but haphazardly high and low on the wall and pressed tightly together in every available space.

The Terror would begin just weeks later, but outside France the armies of the revolutionary government were having sur-prising success. French troops had just occupied Belgium, although it would require another six months to secure their hold. During the occupation, there was random pillage of the usual kind, but the Convention—the revolutionary government dominated by the extremists Danton and Robespierre—autho-rized systematic theft as well. In June 1794 the revolutionary gov-ernment proposed "to send secretly after the armies educated citizens who would be charged with recognizing and having carefully transported the masterpieces found in the countries where our armies have penetrated." Consequently experts in art arrived in the conquered land, bearing lists of the finest works and where to find them. They then went down the lists, looting the property of nobles and churches and sending their booty on to the Louvre. (Experts in books and manuscripts did the same for the national library. Botanists took plants for the former Garden of the King, now the Museum of Natural History.) These thefts were described as war reparations, the price the conquered land must pay to the French for liberating them from the onerous weight of their kings and nobility.

When the first shipment of art from Brussels arrived in Paris, a delegate to the ruling Convention announced why it was right to bring these treasures to France: "These immortal works are no longer in a foreign land: they are today deposited in the native land of arts and of genius, in the native land of liberty and of sainted equality, the homeland of the French Republic." Art could flourish only in France because only France was free—as free as the ancient Greeks. That made France also the rightful heir of the masterpieces of antiquity. Another speaker a few months later declared, "There is only we who are able to appreciate them [ancient statues] and we who can elevate them in temples worthy of them and their illustrious makers."

Winckelmann's work, simplified and politicized, became the bedrock of the Revolution's thinking about art. In October 1794, as the Terror faded after the execution of Robespierre three months earlier, the Convention appointed a committee to make a new translation of Winckelmann that could be used as a reference book. The committee reported that this work was "one of the best elementary and classic texts that it is possible to put in the hands of young people in order to introduce them to the knowledge of the beauty of Antiquity and to form the taste of those who hope to become artists." This new edition of Winckelmann was to be placed in each museum and each important library in the republic.

The Revolution's taste for antiquity spread across all society. The Convention had set the example when it ordered all its official furniture made from Greek or Roman models. Soon furniture everywhere copied classical Greek forms, especially in the cafés. Stores sold medallions and cameos in the antique style. After the Terror, when life became easier, women began dressing themselves coquettishly as Athenians in robes of linen. The government tried unsuccessfully to replace the usual religious and civil holidays with Greek festivals. There were classical decorations, high priests, and Greek temples made of cardboard. One official wanted to reinstate the Olympic games. Another wanted gymnastic exercises during the festivals in imitation of the Greeks. Public buildings, scientific discoveries, and the units in the new metric system of weights and measures were all given Greek names. That inspired this verse from a song in a music hall revue declaring that nowadays, in order to understand French well, one should learn Greek:

> *Myriagramme, Panthéon,*
> *Mètre, kilomètre, oxygène,*
> *Litre, centilitre, Odéon,*
> *Prytanée, hectare, hydrogène,*
> *Les Grecs ont pour nous tant d'attraits*
> *Que, de nos jours, pour bien entendre*
> *Et bien comprendre le français,*
> *C'est le grec qu'il faudrait apprendre.*

When Napoleon, only twenty-seven, assumed command of the French army in Italy in 1796, he knew that removing art from any lands he conquered was simply part of his mission, a part he zealously discharged. He sent the works back in large convoys whose arrival in Paris was celebrated with a holiday of parades and celebrations. The first such shipment, which was welcomed to Paris by a huge procession around the Champs de Mars, included the famous four horses of Venice (which Napoleon later installed atop the Arc de Triomphe du Carrousel); paintings by Raphael, Titian, and Veronese; and ancient statues including the Capitoline Venus and the Apollo Belvedere. The latter, which Winckelmann had described so passionately, was considered the single greatest work of art to have survived from the antique world.

While Napoleon was in power, he continued this wholesale pillage. But he did not depend on groups of "educated citizens" to find the masterpieces. Instead he appointed an official connoisseur, Dominique-Vivant Denon, who not only directed the Louvre and other state museums but also rushed into each newly conquered territory, sometimes while the battle was still in the balance, in order to choose which of the available master-pieces to send back to Paris.

Today the Louvre is divided into three wings, one of which is named after Denon. Born Dominique-Vivant de Non, he changed his name during the Revolution to disguise his noble lineage. He was a sensualist, known for his taste for actresses, who really did participate in the sort of group debauches in remote country châteaux that have become a cliché of pornography. He was a dilettante who painted prolifically if forgettably; staged a moderately successful comic play; wrote a sexy little novel, set in a remote château, titled *Point de Lendemain (No Tomorrow)*, which most recently resurfaced as a motif in Milan Kundera's novel *Slowness* and has a cult following in France; and published engaging memoirs and travelogues. But most of all he was a connoisseur both of art and of people.

With people his connoisseurship took the form of a charming sycophancy. Denon managed the seemingly impossible by ingratiating himself with—in succession—Louis XV, Louis XVI, Robespierre, and Napoleon. He knew Voltaire, Frederick II, Catherine the Great, Danton, and Talleyrand, the wily diplomat who was brilliant and slippery enough to become minister of foreign affairs for Napoleon and then for Louis XVIII. And he was an intimate friend of Josephine's long before she married Napoleon.

He first encountered Napoleon at a reception given by Talleyrand. Denon was used to such occasions and quite at ease; Napoleon was still a young officer, gauche and rather timid. Denon kindly offered him a glass of lemonade. They fell into conversation about Italy and the Mediterranean, which Denon knew well, and about Corsica, Napoleon's birthplace, about which Denon knew nothing, although he knew how to talk as if he did. Napoleon never forgot the agreeable impression Denon made on him.

Under the empire Denon's official title was general director of museums. In that role he commissioned paintings of the emperor and his victories from leading artists such as Jacques-Louis David. He also mounted regular exhibits that were generally successful. Primarily, however, he accompanied Napoleon on his campaigns and remained behind after the fighting to select artworks and arrange for them to be carefully packed and sent to Paris. He did not loot indiscriminately. Instead he took only the best and left behind the merely good, often agonizing over the distinction.

The Musée Napoléon, as the Louvre was called during the Empire, became Denon's masterpiece. Visitors could not believe what they saw. One recalled that the artworks "are displayed in such profusion that in the midst of so much beauty the eye no longer knows where to rest." Another kept remarking, "Is this really real?" And everywhere in the crowds were invalids, soldiers in tattered uniforms, and ordinary workers, all with skin weathered by the sun. They mutely pondered this profusion of beauty, none of which had ever before been available for people like them to see.

The masterpieces reclaimed

NAPOLEON himself had no interest in art. His taste was neither good nor bad but nonexistent. He thought that art was simply an imitation of nature and that there was no merit in mere imitation of any kind. His motivation in removing art to France seems to have been simply that he wanted to take the best from any country he dominated. That to him was what a conqueror did. Whenever Napoleon was shown around the Louvre, even during the glorious heights of the Musée Napoléon, he tried to proceed from room to room without stopping at all. If a work was specifically drawn to his attention, he might ask the name of the artist, after which he would stare straight ahead at the piece without expression.

There was one exception. Napoleon was proud of the Apollo Belvedere. It was by far the single greatest possession of the Musée Napoléon. The emperor himself occasionally conducted dignitaries in private to gaze upon the statue and, in turn, upon the emperor illuminated by its radiant glory.

After Winckelmann published his ecstatic description in his *History of Ancient Art,* and before the arrival of the Venus de Milo in Paris, it is impossible to overestimate the grip the Apollo Belvedere had on the European imagination. It was almost as if the French had inaugurated the policy of looting with it in mind. Even before Napoleon's Italian campaign, while the revolutionary armies were still busy subjugating Belgium, an influential delegate in the government announced, "Certainly, if our victorious armies penetrate into Italy, the removal of the Apollo Belvedere . . . would be the most brilliant conquest." The German poet and philosopher Friedrich Schiller, perhaps forgetting for the moment his revered Winckelmann, said that no mere mortal could describe "this celestial mixture of accessibility and severity, benevolence and gravity, majesty and mildness." Veneration for the Apollo Belvedere was a sign of sophistication and educated taste. Copies were everywhere—in royal courts, in museums, and on rich estates. In 1819 the French writer Stendhal made a single remark in dismissing the United States as a cultural desert: "Can one find anywhere in that so prosperous and rich America a single copy, in marble, of the Apollo Belvedere?" The plaque on the statue in the Musée Napoléon, which the emperor himself had attached to the base, described it as "the most sublime statue that time has preserved for us." For three centuries it had been the pride of the Vatican until "heroes, guided by Victory, came to take it away and set it forever by the banks of the Seine."

This gloating boast almost proved accurate, since Denon's Musée Napoléon very nearly survived the emperor's fall. After Napoleon's first abdication, in 1814, the treaty that placed Louis XVIII on the throne specifically ceded ownership of all stolen art in the museum to France. The European powers against

Napoleon thought Louis was so weak that his hold on the throne was tentative at best. Leaving the artworks in France was a simple, if expensive, way to avoid creating resentment in France against the new regime.

But after Napoleon escaped from Elba, returned for the Hundred Days, and was defeated at Waterloo, the allies were not in such an accommodating mood. Now they wanted their artworks back. As English, German, and Austrian troops occupied Paris, some of them were detailed to the Louvre to remove paintings and statues. Denon was distraught. He did what he could to fight the confiscations, but in the end he was powerless. Paintings by Van Dyck, Rembrandt, Raphael, Titian, Tintoretto, Veronese, Caravaggio, and many other masters were all carted away. An armed squadron seized the Apollo Belvedere and returned it to the Vatican. Today it stands in the Octagonal Court of the Pio-Clementine Museum in the Vatican. The Laocoön is nearby.

In all, the allies reclaimed more than five thousand works, including 2,065 paintings, 130 statues in stone, 150 bas-reliefs, 289 bronzes, and many vases, drawings, miniatures, enamels, wooden sculptures, and other diverse objets d'art. Afterward, as Louis XVIII toured the Louvre to observe what remained, he remarked calmly, "We are still rich." But that was not the general view. A popular woodcut from the time shows a French artist crying into his handkerchief in front of the Louvre as a troop of soldiers with muskets wheel the Apollo Belvedere away.

Artist, lover

UPON TAKING the throne, Louis XVIII left Denon in his post for the moment, but he installed the comte de Forbin immediately below him in the administration of the museum. As the king was beginning his tour of the Louvre, he said, "Monsieur Denon and you, Monsieur de Forbin, who know this temple, show me and explain to me these marvels." Denon understood as well as anyone the subtleties in the apparently casual comments of a king. That Louis would address him and Forbin as equals meant that Denon's days as director of the museum were numbered. He resigned and devoted the remaining years of his life to writing a history of art. In 1816 Louis XVIII elevated Louis-Nicolas-Philippe-Auguste, comte de Forbin, to the office of director.

We have encountered Forbin before, dining with Vice-consul Brest at his home on Melos in 1817. Now, as head of the Louvre, he would be the one to receive the Venus de Milo at the museum, oversee any restoration, and direct its placement and display. Forbin had a reputation as a playboy and a dilettante, but he turned out to be an effective executive. He inherited the Louvre at a critical moment, when its newly acquired collections had been stripped and its finances were limited, its future direction unclear. By the time he began to retire from his duties—in 1828, after the first in a long, painful series of strokes—he had so revived the Louvre that it was once again the leading museum in the Western world.

Forbin became director when he was thirty-nine years old. Tall, perhaps ever so slightly too thin, he was still young and robust enough to maintain his reputation as the handsomest man in France. He had an oval face, a high forehead, and a great mass of curly black hair. He dressed elegantly, almost to the point of dandyism, and his spectacular appearance was set off by his pleasant manners. He appeared easy, natural, at home with himself. His conversation sparkled. He could improvise comic verses effortlessly. His voice was musical, softened by a lilting, southern accent that came from his childhood in Provence.

His famous looks went hand in hand with his reputation as a lover. Napoleon's beautiful but completely daffy sister, Princess Pauline Borghese, was one of Forbin's mistresses. Her exquisite form is still on display in the Villa Borghese in Rome, where Canova sculpted her as Venus reclining nude upon a couch.

Louis-Nicolas-Philippe-Auguste, comte de Forbin,
by Ingres

Forbin had a succession of other mistresses and was a prized, highly visible guest in the best salons of Restoration Paris. He had a long flirtation with Madame Récamier, the greatest beauty of the era, whose portrait by David hangs in the Louvre. Purportedly a virgin—at any rate, her marriage to a much older banker, who may have been her own father, was never consummated—she used Forbin's infatuation to tantalize another of her admirers, the writer Benjamin Constant. Madame Récamier goaded Constant so effectively that he challenged Forbin to a duel during which, after some tempestuous posturing, neither man was hurt.

Forbin had had an obsession with painting since he was just a boy. He was born in 1777 in a château on the banks of the

Durance to one of the oldest aristocratic families in the south of France. After his family moved to Aix-en-Provence, they enrolled him in an art school. There he met François-Marius Granet, the son of a bricklayer, who became his closest friend and the most important and enduring emotional attachment of his life. (Today there is a museum devoted to Granet's work in Aix.)

During the Revolution, Forbin's family lost their property. At sixteen he witnessed the executions of both his father and his uncle on the guillotine. For the rest of his life Forbin suffered from bouts of brooding loneliness. Although he had a brother, sisters, many cousins, and eventually a wife and two daughters of his own, he was reserved and unemotional about family ties. He was unable to trust them or let them sustain him. "I am a little surprised by the silence of your sisters," he once wrote to Granet, "but I know from experience what family relations are."

In 1798, after some time spent dodging revolutionary armies in the south, Forbin was living in Paris, where he studied at the school of David, then the leading artist in France. Forbin persuaded David to admit Granet and even paid his tuition of twelve francs a month. Forbin wrote several years later that this time together "cemented the affection between the two sons of Provence and came to unite them more forcefully each day."

At David's school some sixty students and their easels were crowded into one room at the Louvre. The only light came from long, narrow windows high in the walls. The more advanced students surrounded a live model—always nude and always male—on a platform. The other students worked from plaster casts or, if they were new to the school, copied engravings. Every day or so, usually around noon, David would arrive, immaculately dressed, and stride magisterially from student to student, commenting on their work and intoning about art. He was then working on his great masterpiece *The Rape of the Sabine Women,* now in the Louvre. "I want to return art to the principles that Greek artists followed," he lectured to his students one day. "I want to create pure Greek. I nourish my eyes with antique statues and I intend even to imitate some of them. The Greeks didn't have any scruples about reproducing a composition, a movement, a style that already existed. They put all their care, all their art toward perfecting an idea that they already had before them." He said that all art since Phidias was mannered, false, theatrical, ugly, ignoble. He told his students that they should not look at any of the paintings in the long galleries of the Louvre. They should let their eyes fall only on antique Greek statues. They should ignore all statues, whether Greek or Roman, created since Alexander the Great. All of this was, of course, pure Winckelmann.

Forbin was twenty when he heard these declamations by David. They would not determine his taste forever, and David himself deviated from them often enough. But the lessons, as well as Forbin's loyalty to his imperious and blustering teacher, would influence his reaction to the statue found on Melos twenty years later.

According to a fellow student, Forbin was the "soul" of the school: "Forbin carried, under his extremely simple clothes, all the ease and the slightly mocking familiarity of a gentleman in the midst of young people with whom he had nothing in common except their age." In this time of revolutionary fervor he did not use either his title or the aristocratic "de" before his name. Instead he won the students over with his elegance, his wit, and even his extraordinary height and bearing. He could speak fluent Italian. In French his pleasant Provençal patois gave a wry nuance to his jokes and puns. Sometimes he would grab whatever came to hand, a cane or a broken leg from an easel, and go dancing around the room singing comic verses he improvised and beating time with the stick in his hand like the leading man in a musical farce. In fact, during those years he wrote a successful comic play called *Sterne à Paris*.

In June 1799 he married a woman he later glumly described as the only daughter of a rich man of Burgundy. Their first child, a daughter named Lydia, was born eleven months later. Shortly after that Forbin left to live and travel in Italy with Granet.

Forbin returned to France long enough to have a second daughter, Valentine, who was born in December 1804. But only a few months later, back in Italy, Forbin met Pauline, Napoleon's sister. They lived together openly for two years, a situation that produced no end of jealousies and intrigues. Pauline finally tired of him in 1807. To get rid of him before he could cause more trouble, Napoleon sent him to the army in Portugal, where Forbin, confounding the assumptions about him, fought so bravely that he was awarded the Legion of Honor.

He continued to paint and exhibited successfully in several salons. He published *Charles Barimore,* a steamy novel that became a sensation among titled women of the Empire. His liaison with Pauline had helped make his painting fashionable, although when he encountered her again by chance in 1812, she pretended to have forgotten him entirely.

The greatest frustration of his life was that Granet preferred to live in Italy rather than Paris. Forbin wrote Granet pleading letters and hurt, accusing love poems. But Granet had established a household in Rome with the wife of an Italian gentleman, a woman Granet called Nena, whom he adored. In time they both became great favorites of Forbin's younger daughter, Valentine. Granet returned to Paris only when Forbin secured a position and a good salary for him at the Louvre in 1827. Finally, in 1831, Granet moved in with Forbin, who had become increasingly feeble after continued strokes. Granet took care of him until Forbin's death in 1841. By then Nena's husband had died, and at last Granet was able to marry her. He was sixty-eight, and she was seventy-six. They had been lovers since their youth.

The unhappy husband

BY CONTRAST with the Musée Napoléon, it was a bare and forlorn Louvre that Forbin inherited from Denon in 1816. In particular, it was empty of impressive antiquities. The Apollo Belvedere was back in the Vatican. Worse, that very year, the British parliament voted to purchase from Lord Elgin the marble reliefs he had ripped from the pediments of the Parthenon and transported to London. Now called the Elgin marbles, they were undeniably from the age of classical Greece. Their provenance and their beauty provoked spasms of jealousy in German and French connoisseurs. The Elgin marbles were placed in the British Museum, which in a single stroke became the leading institution in Europe.

Forbin didn't waste time moping. He immediately set out on a voyage to the Aegean and to Egypt in search of antiquities to buy for the Louvre. It was during this trip that he dined with Brest. While on Melos, he sketched the ruins of the Roman theater. As he worked, he stood not too far from the place where the Venus de Milo would be discovered three years later. In Cairo he disguised himself as an Arab and silently explored the mosques and other mysterious corners of the Arab quarter. He even visited the slave market, where he bid unsuccessfully on a young Circassian girl. Along the way, he did buy some antiquities for the museum, but nothing that would seize the imagination of Europe.

Upon his return, he became obsessed with the idea of sending French artists to England to make casts of the Elgin marbles for the Louvre. Then he expanded the notion to other massive casts, including one of Michelangelo's *Moses*. He wanted to commission Ingres and three other French artists to copy the ceiling of the Sistine Chapel, exhibit it at one of the yearly salons at the Louvre, and then place it permanently in Notre Dame. These schemes, which seem preposterous today, were to Forbin "proof of [France's] love of the arts and our eagerness to bring together such precious means of study for our artists." He was again merely repeating the ideas of Winckelmann, which had by now become accepted wisdom: Arts flourished where there was an accumulation of masterpieces or copies of masterpieces for artists to study and imitate.

Of course, an original masterpiece was considered infinitely more valuable than a copy. With the Apollo Belvedere returned to the Vatican and the Elgin marbles the property of the British Museum, France had no equivalent example of antique art. This lamentable situation was not just a blow to national pride; it was a lack in what France could offer her artists for study and inspiration. In the future, French arts would suffer because of it and consequently lag behind artists in England and Italy, perhaps for generations. France, instead of advancing as the third great civilization in Europe after classical Greece and Renaissance Italy, would slip slowly into the second-rate. It was a problem for which there appeared to be no solution.

In addition to his worries about the museum, Forbin was on the brink of despair over his health, his family, and his legacy as an artist. He was now in his early forties and time had begun to erode both his looks and his constitution. He had frequent colds that he could not cure. Often he suffered from the sensation that all the blood was rushing out of his head. He stopped drinking and ate only simple foods, but any physical effort exhausted him. Still, he pushed himself to work harder, uncertain how much longer he would be able to work at all.

As he worried about his health he also brooded about his family. He hadn't been the best of husbands, but at a time when most marriages were arranged, especially among Forbin's social class, a wife and husband having separate lives and separate lovers was common and accepted. His wife despised Paris and insisted on living in her family's château in Burgundy with her mother and her two daughters. Forbin visited them there, sometimes staying a month or longer, but these visits were always painful. His wife was a lazy, ineffective woman who spent most of her days bickering endlessly with her mother. Forbin hated his mother-in-law passionately. Now widowed, she controlled the family fortune with tight fists.

Forbin's daughters, Lydia and Valentine, had grown up in this tense, stingy atmosphere. Lydia was twenty and needed to enter society to find a husband, but she was plagued by a skin condition on her face and body that marred her appearance. Without his mother-in-law's financial help, which she adamantly refused to give, Forbin was despondent about Lydia's chances. Valentine was sixteen and a beauty. She adored her father, but she was a quiet, passive girl who could never express her affection in a way he understood or believed in. Forbin's wife consistently demanded money from him although all he had was his salary from the Louvre and whatever he could earn from his painting—and his works were no longer selling. His daughters' unpleasant lives and shaky futures bore down on him. He couldn't help them; nor, if his own health failed, could his daughters or his wife help him. But worst of all, Forbin was tortured by the knowledge that this late in life no one took him seriously as an artist or a man. His looks and his social gifts were so overwhelming that, except for Granet, few of his contemporaries could see anything else in him. He was considered a light-weight with artistic pretensions. E. J. Delecluze, an important critic, novelist, and memoirist, who had known Forbin since they were both young art students in Paris, expressed exactly what the world thought of Forbin:

> It is unfortunate for a man when the subtleties of his personality are not deeper than those of the clothes he wears and one will always reproach M. de Forbin for that. He had received some precious gifts from nature, but he neglected to cultivate them in order to seek the appearance of a greatness that his position did not give him, that his varied but puny talents will not acquire for him, and from which the buffoonery of his conversation removes even the idea.

Delecluze was right that Forbin wanted the appearance of greatness, but he did not understand that the key to Forbin's character was that he also wanted greatness itself, greatness as a painter and as a friend of art. Though he squandered time on Pauline Borghese and a succession of other intrigues, and though he became enamored of his own legend—he seems to have been seduced by his own looks and charm—Forbin worked on his painting throughout his life, often for periods of intense concentration. When possible he was in his studio from eight in the morning until after six in the evening. "I'm working like a rabid dog," he wrote Granet. He had conceived of a grand canvas titled *L'Inquisition*. When he finished, he wrote Granet, "I believe I have done nothing that can approach its combination of color and execution." But the rumor spread, as Forbin had feared it would since there had been similar rumors before, that Forbin's painting was really the work of Granet.

Then, late in the winter of 1820, as if in answer to a prayer, a letter came to the Louvre from the marquis de Rivière. He was in Toulon, where he had arrived on the *Lionne* with what he claimed was one of the greatest masterpieces of Greek sculpture wrapped in canvas and carefully stored belowdecks.

D'Urville returns

DESPITE THE turbulence of his mind, and despite a persistent cold that he was treating with leeches, Forbin responded decisively, even bravely, to the letter from the marquis. The letter itself is lost, but from the flurry of internal correspondence it caused at the Louvre, it's easy to guess what it said: Rivière asked for money, and Forbin gave it to him. On January 4, 1821, Forbin sent a letter authorizing the necessary expenses to have the statue unloaded from the ship, crated, and brought to Paris. Forbin had had to dicker with his superiors for permission—this consumed much of his time during the Christmas season of 1820—but he didn't falter, even though he was being asked to invest in a work of art he had never seen.

Six weeks later, in mid-February, the marquis de Rivière and the Venus de Milo arrived in Paris. In a private audience with Louis XVIII on March 1, 1821, Rivière offered the king the statue for the royal museums. The homage was accepted. Consequently, Forbin had to reimburse Rivière the 1,500 francs he had paid for the statue and the cost of the shipping. But now the Venus de Milo belonged to France. Forbin had the statue delivered to the Louvre.

(In 1826 Rivière made another payment from his own funds that has prevented the bitter diplomatic problems that still plague the Elgin marbles. The dragoman Morousi had fined the primates on Melos more than 7,500 piasters for allowing the statue to be carried away. A French admiral in the Aegean wrote to the Ministry of the Marine that the primates wanted reimbursement. After hearing this news, Rivière repaid the primates himself. In return, they signed a quittance to any further claims for money or for the statue, which has been honored. In the early 1980s, when the actress Melina Mercouri, who had become the Greek minister of culture and science, began demanding the return of the Elgin marbles from England, she repeatedly declined to make any claim for the Venus de Milo.)

But this beautiful statue from Melos—what exactly was it? Forbin had acquired it assuming that it was beyond doubt a masterpiece from the classical age of Greece, around 450 to 350 B.C. Rivière's letter to Forbin had quoted the opinion of Fauvel, the French consul in Athens who had seen the Venus aboard ship in the moonlight. According to Rivière's letter, Fauvel said that the statue was a masterpiece "worth at least 100,000 ecus." Forbin knew Fauvel. He had visited him during his recent voyage to Greece and Egypt and considered him "our Nestor of eastern antiquities." Fauvel's endorsement gave Forbin the assurance to go forward. But if the statue was anything but a product of the classical age in Greece, then its value would presumably fall far below 100,000 ecus. Worse, it could not stand with the Elgin marbles in England or the Apollo Belvedere in the Vatican as the great prize whose glory animated, even sanctified, the national identity.

Cautiously, Forbin sequestered the statue in a back workshop of the Louvre, where he allowed only a few trustworthy scholars and artists to see it. The custom at that time was to repair and restore broken statues. That meant the scholars had to determine the original position of the arms. Doing that meant deciding what the statue had originally been. Which goddess was she? What was she doing?

But Forbin couldn't wait patiently for these scholarly investigations to take their course. The first report from the museum needed to express the only opinion that would satisfy Forbin, the king, indeed all of France: that the statue was a Venus from the classical age. Having the right scholar state this opinion in a convincing way was necessary to protect the investment in both money and pride that the French had made in this statue. Forbin had to find that scholar.

Unfortunately, word about the statue had already begun to leak out. Dumont d'Urville had arrived back in France in October 1820 after the *Chevrette* had finished its scientific mission in the Black Sea. Still consumed by the need to create a personal legend, he couldn't wait to take advantage of the opportunity presented to him by the statue from Melos. On November 24, 1820, he read a paper—"Account of an hydrographic expedition in the Levant and the Black Sea by his majesty's ship the *Chevrette* commanded by M. Gautier, captain of the vessel, in the year 1820"—to the Society of Sciences and Arts of Toulon. He then read the same paper to the Academy of Sciences in Paris on January 22, 1821.

D'Urville is the hero of his own paper. He describes the farmer digging for rocks, finding the niche, and taking the upper half of the statue to the cowshed. He talks about going to see the statue himself, but he never explains how he came to do so or alludes to anyone else, although Brest and Matterer were certainly there with him. He does not mention that Brest and the four ships' captains all had seen the statue before he had. He did originally thank the faithful Matterer and some others, but only for their roles *after* the discovery. He deleted these words from his final version.

Since his report was the first news of the statue to be published in France, d'Urville was able to cement the public perception that he had been the sole discoverer of the Venus de Milo. He instantly became what he longed to be: a famous man. As he wrote in his journal in the weeks after reading his paper, "Thus the obscure ensign, thirty and one-half years old, with more than seven years at that rank, is suddenly the one sought out by artists, recognized by experts, welcomed by eminent persons." In August 1821 d'Urville wrote a letter proposing himself for membership in a provincial learned society named the Academy of Caen, the city in Normandy where he had attended school. He boasted, "I owe to a lucky happenstance the opportunity to be the first to visit, describe and make known the celebrated *Venus Victrix* of Melos." Beginning exactly here, his fame would continue to grow until it extended throughout Europe.

An embarrassment appears and disappears

AT LEAST d'Urville had said only that the statue was a Venus and, for once recognizing his limitations, had not hazarded an opinion about when it was made. The damage was not as bad as it might have been, but d'Urville's self-promotion tended to force Forbin's hand. He had to display the statue soon, since public pressure to see it would become greater as the news continued to spread. On March 7, 1821, he had the first official announcement about the acquisition of the statue placed in the *Moniteur,* a government newspaper. It concluded with an assertion that inadvertently expressed both Forbin's hopes and his frustrations: "Experts are busy researching what must have been the position of the arms in order to proceed with the restoration. The very pronounced movement of the torso seems to assure the success of this research soon."

This public confidence was contrary to the confusion the statue was creating deep in the workshops of the Louvre. Unfortunately, each of the sages Forbin admitted there had his own opinion about the original position of the arms.

In truth, they weren't researching so much as groping in the dark. Archeology barely existed as a science then, and the whole world of Greek antiquity was just being rediscovered. Very little reliable information was available, while a great deal of mistaken information was accepted as true. For example, any statue unearthed in Italy was considered to be an ancient original. Then a duplicate would turn up at another site, and yet another at a third place. By 1821 scholars were slowly beginning to realize how many copies of famous statues had been carved in ancient times. A few years after the discovery of the Venus de Milo, even the revered Apollo Belvedere was proved to be a Roman copy.

Since the science of archeology was just beginning to develop, a critic who was writing about antiquities could let his mind range freely, unfettered by inconvenient facts. Papers that at the time were considered learned and scientific seem today like the most indulgent flights of fancy. And the scholars at the Louvre let their fancies soar. Some thought the statue was not a Venus but a Victory. Others thought it was a Venus holding a bow. Or maybe she was holding a shield and gazing at her reflection in it. And, of course, each of their proposed reconstructions would produce a different position for the arms.

But unexpectedly, perhaps even disastrously, the statue presented other problems that were just as difficult as her missing arms. When Forbin's staff unwrapped the parcels of canvas containing the Venus de Milo, they found that four pieces had broken away from the hips. Two came from the right hip and two from the left. These four pieces had first broken away in ancient times and been reattached with plaster. The large piece from the right hip that Voutier had described was the only piece broken when the statue left Melos. The three others must have broken away during the sea voyage to France when humidity or the rocking of the ship loosened the plaster. No surviving record from that period mentions these pieces at all, and we know about them only from events that occurred fifty years later. The restorers in the back workshop reattached the four pieces with plaster, two on one hip and two on the other, assuming that no one would ever discover how much their handiwork had affected the statue.

Nor did the complications stop there. The base of the herm with the young man's head was broken so that its right side formed a jagged wedge. The base of the Venus de Milo was broken on its left side, where there was a jagged cavity. The wedge on the base of the herm slid nicely into the cavity at the base of the statue. It appeared, therefore, that this undistinguished herm and its base once belonged to the Venus de Milo. Worse, there was an inscription in Greek on the base of the herm that read, ". . . xandros son of Menides citizen of Antioch of Meander made the statue." If the base of the statue and the base of the herm were originally the same slab, then an unknown sculptor named Alexandros had carved the Venus de Milo. And worst of all, Alexandros had lived in Antioch, a city in western Turkey that, as the scholars at the Louvre well knew, had not been founded until 270 B.C., at least a hundred years after the classical age in Greece had ended.

According to Winckelmann's theory of the cycles of art, that would have been a time when art was in decline. Had Forbin committed the museum, the king, and all of France to a statue by a nobody who had lived too late to have had any contact at all with the great Greek masters? If so, all Dumont d'Urville's bragging before learned societies and in the salons of Paris would only add to the museum's embarrassment when the real story came to light.

Slowly a solution appeared. The more the experts at the Louvre pondered the problem, the more they thought the base was wrong. The fit wasn't right after all, and the marble wasn't the same. And even if the base *did* belong with the statue, it could not have belonged to it originally. It must be the remains of some later, decadent addition made during the declining Hellenistic era. It was an ugly barnacle on the hull of a sleek yacht. Worse than that, the inscribed base was a threat to the statue's very integrity. Anyone who was jealous of France's prize possession could use this inscription to denigrate it, to cheapen it. Since the slab was not really, truly part of the statue, why give anyone this ammunition to use against France's treasure?

So the slab disappeared. Forbin either had it destroyed or hid it so deeply in some recess of the warehouses of the Louvre that it has never been found. We would not know about it today, and certainly we would have no idea what the inscription said, except for Forbin's loyalty to his difficult, conceited, yet inspiring former teacher David.

David had read the notice in the *Moniteur* about the statue. He was now living in Brussels, where he had fled after the Restoration, certain that the new regime would want his head. In fact, Louis XVIII put aside any malice he may have felt. Through intermediaries he implied to David that if he were to petition to return, he would be granted amnesty. But David, instead of petitioning, which he saw as demeaning to his dignity, remained in Brussels, seething with resentment. But a statue from classical Greece was irresistible for someone with David's

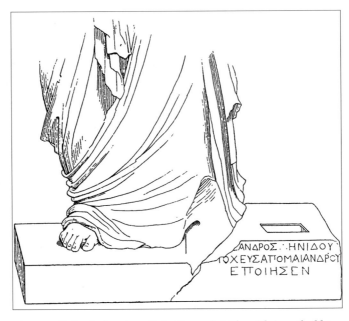

Auguste Debay's drawing of the Venus de Milo with inscribed base

aesthetic, and he wanted to see what it looked like. He wrote to Paris to ask to have a drawing sent to him.

David's request fell to the sculptor J. B. J. Debay, who had been a student in David's school at the same time as Forbin. Now he was the curator in charge of antique restorations at the Louvre. Debay gave the task to his sixteen-year-old son, Auguste, who was an art student. Forbin allowed him into the back workshop in order to make the drawing and this happened to be during the time when the inscribed base was still in place against the base of the statue. Young Debay, either unconcerned by or unaware of the debate over the base and the inscription, drew them both quite clearly. The jagged edge of the inscribed base seems to match the jagged edge at the base of the statue. The Greek letters of the inscription are clear.

Debay made one original drawing and then a tracing of it. The tracing went to David. Debay gave the original to his father. Forbin either forgot or never knew the elder Debay had the drawing until it was too late.

The right scholar

MEANWHILE the Louvre continued to remain silent about the statue. At the time there were two dominating classical scholars in France, either of whom could write the first paper that would establish the museum's thinking about its new treasure. One was Quatremère de Quincy, a Winckelmann disciple who had introduced David to the wonders of antiquity in Naples more than thirty years earlier. The other was Toussaint-Bernard Emeric-David. These two men were bitter intellectual rivals who seem to have disliked each other personally as well. They were about the same age—Quatremère was sixty-six and Emeric-David sixty-five—and as young men had both studied for the law. They both had gotten in trouble during the Revolution—Quatremère was sent to jail on a warrant signed by David—and neither ever shrank from a good scrap. But the resemblances end there. Quatremère was effete and remote, whereas Emeric-David was an energetic man of the world, devoted to his family, who had broad intellectual interests. Those differences alone might have been enough to make them wary of each other, but they became enemies because of their different responses to Winckelmann.

In short, Emeric-David disagreed with Winckelmann, while Quatremère embraced him. Emeric-David did not believe, as Winckelmann did, that art moved in a cycle of four stages from beginning to development to flowering to decadence and decline. He thought Greek art in particular had not declined after the classical period but had a long, glorious history from the time of Phidias until at least the Roman emperor Hadrian in the first half of the second century. And since art didn't move in cycles, there was no reason to think that art in France was in hopeless decline. It could flourish just as Greek art had.

For Quatremère all this was simply a heresy, and a fatuous one at that. European art was clearly in decline after the great flowering during the Renaissance, just as Greek art had declined after the classical age. The only way to revive art was to imitate the ancient masters as Winckelmann had said.

Since Forbin's temperament was closer to that of Emeric-David, and since both men were raised in Aix and had extensive family ties in Provence, he would seem to have been Forbin's natural ally. But Emeric-David, free of the prevailing orthodoxy derived from Winckelmann, didn't believe that the statue from Melos belonged to the classical era of ancient Greece. He thought it was from a later period. Nor did he think it was a Venus. Instead he concluded that the statue represented the nymph Melos, the divine guardian of the island. For Forbin, this would not do at all.

Quatremère, stuffy and superior though he may have been, was at least dependable. He was a dour but impressive man with dark black eyebrows and cropped white hair. He had a long, hatchet nose, heavy bags beneath his eyes, a thin mouth, and a double chin. He used his voice, which boomed from his chest, as a cudgel in debate. Independently wealthy (his family had made its fortune selling drapery to Louis XVI) and inspired by Winckelmann, he had lived in Italy for eight years during his twenties. Since then, the art of the classical age in Greece had become the basis for all his aesthetic theories and judgments. He elaborated his thinking in a blizzard of books, articles, reviews, and papers across a lifetime of ninety-four years. The further art moved from his ideals, the more he wrote and the more his prose became pompous and doctrinaire. In 1816 he had become permanent secretary of the Académie des Beaux-Arts, a position he would hold until 1839. Thus elevated, he was able to toss down his opinions from on high like Zeus raining thunderbolts. His influence on David alone changed the course of French art.

Unlike Forbin, with his mistresses and his charming way with fashionable hostesses, Quatremère found nothing interesting or attractive about women. On the contrary, he disliked them intensely and never married. His closest emotional attachment was a nobleman he met in Italy who was also a painter and sculptor. Otherwise he lived entirely for the sake of his stern ideas, theories, and dogmas.

Just two years earlier Forbin and Quatremère had quarreled rather bitterly. Quatremère wanted the Académie to judge the art in the museum's Salon of 1819 only after the show had been taken down. Forbin wanted the judging done while the show was still up so that visitors could know the winners. The real reason for the argument—carried out in highly formal but steely letters—was that Forbin had accepted the *Raft of the Medusa* by Géricault for the salon. This painting introduced romanticism to French art, and romanticism, which imitated nature directly rather than basing itself on the Greek ideal of nature, and which honored individual feeling over classical rules, rejected everything Quatremère believed about art. He hoped to diminish the effect of Géricault's painting on the public by delaying the judging. Forbin as always was a difficult opponent to outmaneuver, and his views prevailed.

Yet for all his bluster, for all his fruitless determination to bend art in France to his reactionary ideas, for all his humorless severity, Quatremère did have a formidable intellect. And when he was observing a work of art that fit his aesthetic theories, especially one like the Venus de Milo that not only fit his theories but in his eyes *proved* them, he had formidable judgment as well. Best of all for Forbin, Quatremère believed the statue was exactly what the museum wanted it to be. Forbin trusted Quatremère, his former combatant, in the back room of the Louvre and ignored Emeric-David, the fellow son of Provence.

On April 21, 1821, just six weeks after the statue arrived at the Louvre, Quatremère read a paper entitled "Dissertation on the antique statue of Venus discovered on the island of Melos" to a meeting of the Académie des Beaux-Arts. The Académie was the leading official institution concerned with the fine arts, and its members were the best possible audience to endorse the paper's conclusions about the statue. Forbin had known what the paper said—and that it said the right thing—before the meeting. But the result was successful beyond his most ambitious dreams.

Quatremère begins with a simple—for him—statement of why the statue was so important: "The appearance of a new work of Greek genius is always an event in the empire of the arts, above all when unimpeachable testimonies of the authenticity or the presumable originality of this work add the weight of their authority to the judgment of taste." In other words, this is an authoritative statue because it is beautiful and because the evidence proves that it is truly Greek. Of course, he continues, the same is true of the Elgin marbles, so recently arrived in England. Both the scholar and the public can have confidence in them, although not in "most of these antique remnants, that come down to us without a title, without a date, without the name of an author or a country, without any certificate as to their origin." So he loses no time in proclaiming this statue to be the equal of the Elgin marbles, even though it had arrived in France without a title, a date, or any certificate of its origin.

He continues with a brief account of the discovery and a detailed description with special attention to the scrapes, gouges, and other ravages of time. (Few if any in his Académie audience had seen the statue yet.) He does mention the inscribed base, only to insist in a footnote that it was a later addition whose purpose was merely to help support the statue. This block, chosen at random, happened to be inscribed, but "one cannot draw any conclusion relating to the creator of the work from the inscription on the piece of marble." Perhaps it was his conscience that led him to mention the inscription at all. He does not record what the inscription actually said.

Quatremère insists that the statue is a Venus. More than that, upon his very first sight of the statue, the turn of her body and the position and expression of her head made him think that she must have originally been grouped with another statue. By examining more closely the left side, "where the drapes are far less carefully done, in considering the much less happy effect of the face on that side," he became certain that he was right.

But what was the other statue? Quatremère cites several other statues, medallions, and coins that show Venus with her body turned to the left and her left foot resting on some support in a pose similar to that of the Venus de Milo. Next to her stands Mars, the god of war. Venus's left arm is on his shoulder, and her right reaches across to touch his right biceps. She hopes that her beauty will restrain him so he will stay with her instead of going to war. Therefore, Quatremère concludes, the Venus de Milo must also have been originally grouped with a statue of Mars. The missing arms must have been reaching out to him, touching him on the shoulder and arm. The look on her face, turned imploringly toward him, is her yearning for him to stay. Quatremère also argues that the arms of the statue broke off when it was separated from the statue of Mars and that the other pieces found with the Venus—the hand with the apple, fragments of arms, the two herms—were all part of a later, crude restoration.

After this grand moment, the rest of the paper is essentially nicely articulated propaganda for the statue and, by extension, for the museum. He speculates about whether the Venus de Milo was the original statue in this pose from which all the other examples were copied. He admits that it is impossible to know with certainty. "If, however," he adds cleverly, "one wishes to understand [original] in a sense relating to the superiority of merit among the copies of the same work, there will be, I think, no reason to doubt that the Venus de Milo, in the group of which it was a part, was the original of those others that we have cited." He declares that since the statue is clearly not from the decadent period of Greek art, it must have come from the workshop or the school of Praxiteles, the greatest of Greek sculptors. There is no support for this view other than the wishes of Quatremère, Forbin, the museum, the king, and the rest of France that it be true. England might have the marbles from the Parthenon designed by Phidias; but France, courtesy of Quatremère, could claim it possessed a work by the one Greek sculptor who was even greater.

In his final three paragraphs Quatremère directly confronted the problem of restoring the arms. A modern curator would never consider adding whole new elements to an incomplete ancient work, but in the early nineteenth century restoration was the common practice. Quatremère swam against the current by arguing that the statue should not be restored at all. His reasoning was ingenious. He said Venus shouldn't be restored because it would be impossible to create the second statue of Mars that originally went with it. "Even if," he continued, "one were limited to restoring the arms, using the other works as a model for the restitution, that could only make one feel even more the emptiness and the absence of the figure to which she was joined; the statue, remaining always isolated, could only produce an equivocal movement and an action that nothing would explain to the viewer."

In fact, a few restorations to the statue were made at the Louvre. The broken tip of the nose was fixed, as were the nipple of the left breast and the lower lip. The most noticeable and unfortunate restoration was an ugly plaster left foot sticking out from under some even uglier plaster folds of drapery. But the arms were not restored. Often it's said that Louis XVIII himself decreed that the statue should be left as it was. But Forbin made the decision not to restore the arms on the advice of Quatre-mère. It was this stiff, arrogant reactionary who prevented the harm to the statue—possibly severe—that any restoration of the two missing arms would have made inevitable.

Clarac's anger

AT THIS time the conservator of antiquities at the Louvre was the comte de Clarac. The arrival of the statue from Melos, which technically was in his jurisdiction, should have been a crowning event in Clarac's career. Instead it brought him nothing but frustration and grief.

At forty-four, the same age as Forbin, Charles-Othon-Frédéric-Jean-Baptiste de Clarac was an odd, lovable busybody. He liked to spend an hour or two each morning carving fantasy objects in ivory on a lathe. Although he never married and his family line died out with him, he often spent evenings making elaborate jumping jacks for the children of his friends. He was frequently broke, despite his title, since his family's property had been confiscated during the Revolution and he had to live on his meager salary from the Louvre. Yet he maintained the air of a bon vivant who loved good food and wine when he could afford them. Like Forbin, he had a gift for composing comic songs. One was a parody of the "Marseillaise." The chorus of the original says,

> *To arms, citizens!*
> *Form your battalions!*
> *March! March!*
> *Let impure blood water our furrows.*

Clarac's version says,

> *To arms, scullions*
> *Let's uncork the flasks.*

Let's drink, Let's drink
Let pure wine soak our lungs!

(In French it's cleverer: *"Aux armes, marmitons, / Débouchons les flacons, / Buvons, buvons, / Qu'un vin bien pur abreuve nos poumons!"*)

Clarac spoke German, English, Italian, Portuguese, and one of the Polynesian languages. Exiled during the Revolution, an officer in armies that fought against the French republican forces, he returned to France during the Empire. Eventually he became tutor to the children of Napoleon's sister Caroline in Italy. At the same time he directed some of the excavations at Pompeii. That was when he discovered his taste for archeology. Like Dumont d'Urville and most intellectuals of the era, he was also fascinated by botany. On a long voyage to South America he made precise and painstaking drawings of the flora of the Amazon.

Clarac approached his job at the museum rather like a botanist: He cataloged and described relentlessly. His great work, which still has historical value today, was a complete inventory of the statuary possessed by the Louvre. Yet even those who were sympathetic to Clarac did not claim he was a distinguished scholar. Zealous, yes, and generous toward young artists and archeologists with both his time and his money. But finally his many varied interests served him poorly. He simply didn't know enough about art or archeology. A friend wrote a sympathetic sketch of him after his death that declared, "There are antiquaries who are better informed than he was. He had neither the sagacity nor the critical perception of some erudite French, nor the vast knowledge of the Germans; nor did he have elegance and clarity as a writer." And this was the opinion of a friend!

Forbin, like everyone else, felt some affection for Clarac, but the inscribed base and the problems it presented made Clarac's presence at the museum inconvenient. Who could tell what he was going to do or say? And whatever he said could cause a problem. If he said the right thing about the base inscribed with the name of a sculptor from Antioch—that is, that it didn't belong to the statue—Clarac's reputation was not weighty enough to make any difference. But if he said the wrong thing about the base—that is, that it *did* belong to the statue—his position as conservator of antiquities for the museum was important enough to raise questions about the base to the whole world. In any case he couldn't be depended on to keep what the inscription said a secret. So Forbin simply froze him out. Assuming it was his duty, Clarac did write a brief paper on the statue intended for the king, but Forbin, who saw that Clarac's paper did indeed say the wrong thing, pocketed it instead of sending it on.

For all Forbin could tell, this strategy worked perfectly. Now, in late April 1821, with the inscribed base having been secreted away or destroyed and the question about restoring the arms resolved at last, all that remained for Forbin to do about the Venus was to decide where to display her in the Louvre. Meanwhile he wrote to Clarac asking him to have a marble pedestal inscribed with the name of the statue. To Forbin this was simply a routine request, but the letter sent Clarac into a fury. He took it as the most degrading in the series of recent affronts by Forbin. Why was this happening? Clarac couldn't understand it. As conservator of antiquities, he would have been the proper choice to write a paper, not Quatremère. Clarac had suffered patiently, perhaps in deference to Quatremère's august position and reputation. But now, as if everything were normal, here was this letter from Forbin. In response, Clarac wrote:

> I don't really see why you address yourself to me to have the name of the statue inscribed. Ever since it came into the King's possession and I sent you a notice on the subject—which one has not judged proper to bring to His Majesty's attention—one has spoken to me of the statue only as if it was a stranger to me, or rather as if I were a stranger to the royal museum. . . . I am charged with the evaluation of ancient monuments, with their cataloging, with their placement, with their restoration, and

with their casting. How does it happen, then, that it has been decided, without my knowing anything of it, and probably in a secret meeting, where I should have been called, that this statue would not be restored? . . . Also, how is it that I discovered yesterday all the preparations for placing this statue without my having received any notice?

In his reply, which did not come until May 24, a delay of several weeks, Forbin offered no explanation, and certainly no apology, for Clarac's complaints about being excluded. He did say that it was "pure forgetfulness that you have not been informed of my decision." Then he added bluntly, "It was I who ordered the restoration of two Egyptian statues and I believe I remain completely authorized to take a similar measure every time it appears advisable to me."

Forbin simply proceeded with his plans. A few days later, sometime in late May 1821, without any great ceremony to mark the event, perhaps because the king had not yet seen the statue, the Venus de Milo was displayed to the public at the Louvre.

Clarac was appalled. The statue had been put in the Salle de Diane, at the opposite end of the long corridor where the Venus now stands. During the Empire its name had been the Salle de l'Apollon, because this was where Denon had chosen to display the great Apollo Belvedere. The Venus de Milo would assume that statue's former place of glory. But the setting wasn't right for her. Her back was to a wall, so the statue could not be seen from every angle. Indignant artists and connoisseurs complained to Clarac, and he agreed with them. Hadn't the famous Venus of Knidos, the masterpiece of Praxiteles, been displayed in its temple so she could be seen all around?

On the other hand, with the statue now on open display, the curtain of secrecy was drawn aside, and Clarac was free to study her as he wished. In a matter of weeks he published his own paper. Forbin could not pocket this work as he had Clarac's earlier paper for the king. And, as Forbin suspected, Clarac was a renegade. Without mentioning Quatremère by name, he disagreed with the scholar's most important conclusions and rejected the Louvre's orthodoxy about the statue, which Quatremère's paper had defined.

Or, to be precise, he rejected almost all of it. He begins by mentioning the Elgin marbles in England. They "represent an epoch in the history of art," but the Louvre's statue "that recalls to a great degree all their diverse beauty" creates an epoch, too, and one not less important. In fact, he concludes, many think it is an even finer work.

After this nod to French pride, Clarac begins his attack. He criticizes the placement of the statue in the Salle de Diane. Then, facing off directly with Quatremère, he insists that the statue could not be part of a group—"If it is part of a group, why is there no trace of Mars?" Furthermore, the inscribed base did belong to the statue. It was exactly the right size, and the fracture lines at the back and the sides fit precisely. It was not there by chance but was an integral part of the statue. The sculptor was neither Phidias nor Praxiteles, as much as he would like to say it was. Then he gets in a nice little dig. Those who claim it was by Praxiteles seem to be "so familiar with his style that one would be led to believe that they had seen him work." No, the statue was by Alexandros of Antioch, just as the broken base said. The inscription could not be a forgery, because forgers would have carved a name that would have added value, while this is not a famous name. But what difference does that make? The Apollo Belvedere was the work of an unknown sculptor, too. No, in his opinion it is a bad mistake to display the statue without the inscribed base.

Clarac called his paper "On the antique statue of Venus Victrix, with a drawing by Debay the younger." And there on the cover of the pamphlet was Debay's drawing. The fragment of left arm was attached at the shoulder and stuck straight out parallel to the ground. And against the left side of the statue's base, fitting perfectly against the jagged edge, was the broken base with the inscription. The Greek letters were clearly legible. Discord had thrown an apple into the party at the Louvre, although it would be almost eighty years before the trouble rose to the surface.

The statue comes to the king

FORBIN, however, does not seem to have borne a grudge. On June 24, just a few days after Clarac's paper had appeared, Forbin wrote a letter to him about his criticism of the placement of the statue in the Salle de Diane. "I find your ideas very wise," Forbin said, "but if you knew all that stops me, you would approve of the moderation by which I buy peace. However, the statue from Melos will be placed soon in a more favorable setting and with a little patience everything will work out."

Forbin needed to be forgiving, since he had other problems now and he would need Clarac's help; but he could afford to be forgiving as well. He had won, after all. The radiance of Quatremère's paper put Clarac's in shadow. The statue was established as a Venus from the hand, or at least from the school, of either Phidias or Praxiteles. It had filled the tremendous gap left by the return of the Apollo Belvedere to the Vatican and stood as a prize equal to or perhaps even better than the Elgin marbles.

Despite his frosty treatment of Clarac while the statue was in the back workshop, Forbin seems to have been generous by nature. Even his feuds over women, like the one that led to the duel with Constant, were one-sided, born from the frustrations of rivals jealous of Forbin's good looks and charm. Although he had his favored friends among the artists of the day—Granet, of course, Ingres, and a number of others—he was surprisingly free from the vengeful politics that infest the arts in every time and place. The letters he wrote to Granet are filled with his efforts on behalf of many artists. He was virtually their business agent. He was neither doctrinaire in his taste nor snobbish about class. Granet, after all, was the son of a bricklayer.

There were two exceptions to Forbin's general amiability.

One was his miserly mother-in-law. The other was Pierre-François-Léonard Fontaine, now sixty years old and by appointment the official architect of Paris, architect to the king, architect to the duc d'Orléans, and architect of the Louvre.

Since Fontaine lived to be ninety-one and worked incessantly, France is covered with buildings he designed or restored. In Paris those include the Palais Royal, the Théâtre Français, the Arc de Triomphe du Carrousel, and many parts of the Louvre itself. He, like Clarac and Quatremère, never married but had a long personal and artistic association with a fellow architect, Charles Percier, who decorated the interiors of Fontaine's buildings. In fact, as young men Fontaine and Percier made a pact never to marry. Fontaine adopted a daughter, raised her, and, after her marriage, customarily spent evenings with her family. His daily routine never varied. He was at work every morning at five. In the afternoon he visited construction sites and did other necessary business. He dined at six and went to bed at ten.

With most people he was dry, remote, and imperious, although generally not unkind. An artist who had suffered a reversal of fortune once called on him at his office. The artist stammered a few words before Fontaine, understanding what he wanted, cut him off. "I am very busy," he said. "My bureau is in the neighboring room. Here is the key. Do me the courtesy of taking the sum you need, which I do not need to know, and allow me to finish my work." When the artist returned months later to repay the debt and thank Fontaine, the architect again cut him off and said, "I am very busy. Here is my key. Take it, lock up this money, and allow me to finish my work."

Fontaine could not be intimidated or easily moved against his will. He once contradicted Napoleon to his face and refused to carry out a restoration the emperor had just ordered. Napoleon turned and left the room. For three hours Fontaine waited until Napoleon returned and relented.

When Forbin mentioned in his letter to Clarac "the moderation by which I buy peace," he was referring to peace with

Fontaine. This peace was difficult, if not impossible, to maintain, because Fontaine opposed Forbin's ideas simply because they came from Forbin. "The continual buzzing of this skinny administrator is unbearable," Fontaine wrote in his journal. "Always driven by the heat of an ardent ambition, troubled by the consciousness of an incapacity that is difficult to hide, meddling in everything, not accomplishing anything, how many times he has worn us out by his importuning and frustrating presence!"

Since the king himself appointed the architect of the Louvre, the architect wasn't answerable to the director of the museum. Consequently, Forbin had no authority over Fontaine, nor Fontaine over Forbin. In the case of the statue, Forbin as director had the power to determine where the statue should be displayed. Fontaine as architect had the responsibility for moving it and for designing and creating the display. The only way to resolve a dispute between them was for the two men to try to outmaneuver each other.

Fontaine thought the Venus should be displayed in the Rotonde d'Apollon, a round room on the second floor at the top of the grand staircase by which the Winged Victory stands today. Forbin knew he had made a mistake putting the statue in the Salle de Diane, but he didn't want it in the Rotonde d'Apollon either. He thought it should remain on the ground floor near the rest of the Greek and Roman antiquities. In August 1821 Forbin requested that both Clarac and Fontaine make preparations for the move. Fontaine ignored him, stalling. This went on for months until in late October Fontaine conceived of a brilliant strategy for having the statue placed in the Rotonde d'Apollon after all.

The statue belonged to the king, but he had never seen it. In fact, it was difficult to know how he ever could. He was so fat that he couldn't walk and spent all his time in a wheelchair. He lived on the second floor of the Tuileries Palace, which did connect with the second floor of the Louvre, but the statue was on the first floor. The only way to move the king from the second floor to the first would be to lower him like a piano with a crane. The king wouldn't submit to such indignity, even to see his famous treasure.

Fontaine's inspiration was to realize that if the king couldn't come to the statue, the statue could come to the king. Each year in January Louis made a ceremonial visit to the opening of the chamber of deputies. As a courtesy to him, the deputies held that session in the Salle Lacaze on the second floor of the Louvre in the southwest corner of the Cour Carrée. Meeting there made it possible to wheel the king over from the palace. The Rotonde d'Apollon was just a short distance from the doorway to the Salle Lacaze. On his way to the meeting, the king would have to pass right through it.

The minister of the Maison du Roi, a baron and general named Lauriston, controlled the property of the king and was the immediate superior of both Fontaine and Forbin. Innocently, as if the good of the king were his only interest, Fontaine proposed to Lauriston that the statue from Melos be displayed in the Rotonde d'Apollon. There at last, while on his way to open the chamber of deputies, the king could see his precious possession. Forbin must have understood Fontaine's real intent, but he could hardly disagree. To do so would have appeared disloyal, since the plan was so clearly to the king's advantage.

The statue was moved upstairs from the Salle de Diane and installed in the Rotonde d'Apollon. In January 1822, Louis XVIII stopped his wheelchair in front of the statue on his way to the opening of the chamber of deputies. Unfortunately, there is no record of who was present on this occasion or what was said. Afterward, the king rolled on to the Salle Lacaze and performed his official duties. Then he rolled back through the Rotonde d'Apollon and down the whole length of the Louvre to the Tuileries palace. The Venus de Milo remained standing in the Rotonde d'Apollon, precisely where Fontaine had wanted it all along.

Of course that was precisely where Forbin did not want it. He still believed it should be displayed in the galleries on the ground floor. Clarac supported him. The two men had mended their differences, addressing each other now as *"cher ami."* Perhaps Clarac supported Forbin because his plan would put the statue with the other Greek and Roman antiquities and thus under Clarac's jurisdiction.

But Clarac might have supported Forbin because he was right. It seems obvious now, accustomed as we are to museums organized by periods in art history, with the works in each period organized roughly chronologically, that there should be some order to the way works are displayed in a museum, especially one as large and varied as the Louvre. But that wasn't obvious in the early nineteenth century. Denon put some order in his displays, and now Forbin wanted to impose an even stricter order.

He wanted the Louvre to be a tool for learning by artists, connoisseurs, and anyone else who was interested. He wrote that the purpose of the museum was to be "a place consecrated to arts and to study." Forbin jealously guarded his authority over the arrangement of artworks because without it he could not transform the Louvre into the kind of museum he wanted it to be. He had forcefully, even arrogantly, reminded Clarac of his power in the letter he wrote during their quarrel. Now the greatest threat to that authority was Fontaine.

With the Venus de Milo in the Rotonde d'Apollon, Forbin couldn't afford any further delays. The longer the statue remained there, the more it would seem to belong in that spot. In February 1822 he decided it should go into the Salle de Tibre, in the southwest corner of the Cour Carrée on the ground floor.

Forbin's decision sent Fontaine into a rage. Why take the trouble and why risk the danger of moving the statue again? He called the idea a "turbulent uselessness" that was nothing more than one of Forbin's "capricious fantasies." He had had enough of this man's stupidities! The two men argued loudly and publicly. They were often on the verge of coming to blows.

Fontaine insisted on having a plaster cast made in order to see how the statue would look in the Salle de Tibre. He thought the response to the cast proved him right, but Forbin was unmoved. Then, desperate to circumvent Forbin, Fontaine suggested that a jury of knowledgeable artists, including both Forbin and himself, be formed in order to decide whether the statue should remain in the Rotonde d'Apollon or be moved to the Salle de Tibre. Forbin couldn't abide this threat to his authority. He now turned to Lauriston, the minister of the Maison du Roi, who this time sided with him. On April 14, Forbin wrote to Fontaine, "I have the honor to advise you that my orders having been given and my measures taken for the displacement of the Venus de Milo and its replacement [in the Salle de Tibre], I would like the transport of this figure to be accomplished by Tuesday the sixteenth of this month."

Still Fontaine did nothing. Incensed, Forbin wrote him a letter the next day that began, "I am truly displeased that you would force me to repeat to you for the tenth time that I have received the orders of the Minister for the placement of the statue from Melos." Fontaine at last had the statue moved on April 23, 1822. Still furious, that night he made a long, unrepentant entry in his journal: "It was only the personal interest, the ambition, the wounded vanity, and the ardor of a hypocritical zeal that motivated Monsieur le comte and caused the whole affaire."

But Monsieur le comte was right. The Venus de Milo remained where Forbin placed her for more than twenty-five years. Then, during the revolution of 1848, she was moved to the opposite end of the hallway—still among the Greek and Roman antiquities, still on the first floor—and placed in an alcove (behind the room where she stands today). She stayed there until 1870, when another violent social upheaval forced her removal from the museum for safekeeping. That move would reveal that this Venus, apparently solid rock, in fact held secrets deep within.

A cavalier in a corset

BUT A different generation, one that had just been born in 1822, would discover those secrets. As for the generation of adventurers and collectors who had found the statue and acquired it for France, two came to sad ends.

Dumont d'Urville achieved all his dreams. He became an admiral and explorer whose books spread his fame throughout Europe. The French claim with justification that he was the equal of Captain Cook. In 1842 he was living in Paris with his wife and his son Jules (their three other children had all died). On May 8 they took a train to Versailles for a festival. During the trip back the train, which had two engines, began speeding in order to keep to a contracted schedule. The engines went out of control, jumped the track, and burst into flame. The wooden passenger cars behind them, whose doors had been locked for some reason, ran up over the burning engines and trapped the passengers, including d'Urville and his family, in an inferno. Two days later coroners identified his wife's remains by a necklace she was wearing. Some charred bones apparently of a child were assumed to be Jules. A phrenologist who had measured d'Urville's head was able to identify his skull. His monument in Condé-sur-Noireau describes him as the discoverer of the Venus de Milo. A bas-relief, comically inept and inaccurate, shows the moment of his great "discovery."

Despite his efforts for the Louvre, Forbin's paintings never received serious recognition. During his final years he lived with the gloomy belief that he had failed. He continued in his position at the Louvre and kept working on behalf of his friends. He even continued to paint, but he himself knew that his skills had declined. He clung instead to appearances. He became obsessed with trying to preserve himself as the handsome, witty cavalier he had once really been. He took to wearing a tight corset to give his body the form it had had when he was young. In 1827, only six years after the arrival of the statue, he had a stroke. His doctor strictly forbade him to wear the corset any longer. But he did, lacing it even tighter. Enamored of Madame de Castellane, a woman well into her fifties who still attracted lovers, he took to using Spanish fly, hoping to restore his sexual prowess. That brought on another stroke in 1828.

Rumors circulated around Paris that Forbin had gone mad. He hadn't, but he was no longer the same man. He stayed in his post at the Louvre, although he was now powerless and ineffective. He still attended salons, particularly that of Madame Récamier, the woman he had once dueled over, until his death in 1841. Her servants would carry him up her staircase. He looked like a ghastly phantom, but he smiled and saluted the room gallantly. She reawakened the spirit in him, made it worthwhile to attempt a quip or two. When he was rewarded with a smile or laugh, he would say, *"That* is the real Forbin."

I V

Broken Marble

On a Tuesday evening in May 1853 the romantic painter Eugène Delacroix attended a lecture at the Louvre. He described the event as a "big reunion of artists, of semi-artists, of priests, and of women." The speaker, "a certain Ravaisson," as Delacroix wrote in his journal, turned out to be a man of forty with luminous blue eyes, a sad, sagging face, and an air that was both passive and distracted.

Ravaisson was late beginning his lecture, which annoyed Delacroix, and when he did speak at last, it was in a soft, dry voice that was difficult to hear. Ravaisson talked on and on without pause and with no inflection whatsoever. The lecture's main theme, so far as Delacroix could tell, was to link Christianity to the art of classical Greece. Ravaisson, droning on, repeatedly cited Aristotle as an authority. He quoted Greek in the same inaudible monotone he used for speaking French.

Vexed and bored, Delacroix followed the example of several others and ducked out after hearing only half the lecture. Outside the Louvre he reveled in "the magnificent weather and the fact that I could move my legs in freedom, after the captivity I had just endured."

Over time, however, Delacroix changed his opinion of Jean-Gaspard-Félix Ravaisson. He continued to encounter him here and there in Paris and came to admire his "intelligent zeal" and to support various artistic causes that Ravaisson initiated. This pattern of response to the man—boredom and rejection, followed eventually by appreciation and respect—occurred again and again throughout Ravaisson's lifetime. It damaged his career and forced him into years of oblivion before he finally achieved prominence. Although banished from teaching philosophy during an era when philosophical studies were the foundation of a liberal education, Ravaisson eventually became one of the most influential French philosophers of the nineteenth century. And though he was neither an archeologist nor a historian by training, it was Ravaisson who at last determined what had really happened to the Venus de Milo while it was kept secluded in the back workshop in the Louvre.

The sealed room

FÉLIX Ravaisson became conservator of antiquities and sculpture at the Louvre in June 1870. He was appointed by the government of Napoleon III, who was then in the last days of his reign. The emperor had foolishly provoked a war with Prussia. Before the end of August he would be utterly defeated and locked in a Prussian prison while enemy troops streamed across France to besiege Paris.

Ravaisson was fifty-seven and had spent the past thirty-five years in one government job after another concerning arts or education. At the same time he maintained a separate reputation as a critic and thinker. He had just published a tome on nineteenth-century French philosophy. Reflective and ethereal by nature, with no experience in administration, Ravaisson was plunged immediately into weeks of intense activity at the museum.

The French government assumed that if the Germans captured Paris, they would plunder the Louvre and take whatever works they pleased to Germany just as the French armies under Napoleon had plundered art. Before the foreign troops could

Félix Ravaisson, photograph by Pierre Petit

arrive, paintings by Leonardo, Raphael, Titian, Correggio, Rembrandt, and other great masters were rolled up, carefully packed, and sent to Brest on the northwestern coast, from where they could be shipped on to safety in England if necessary. Marble statues presented a more difficult problem because of their size, weight, and fragility. Instead of being evacuated, they were moved into a hallway in the Louvre where the windows were filled with sandbags to protect against artillery shells. The Venus de Milo, however, required more elaborate precautions, since it was a prize the Germans had always coveted.

Félix Ravaisson, in one of his first official acts, had the Venus de Milo packed in a stout oak crate in which interior supports and considerable padding kept the statue immobile. In the dead of night a crew of trustworthy men took the crate to a secret door of the museum where another crew, who were ignorant of what they were hauling, carried it to a building used by the prefect of police.

The basement of this building was a labyrinth of thick walls. Ravaisson had the crate placed at the end of a dark corridor and there constructed a wall that sealed the crate into a secret cubicle. This wall was scraped, nicked, and smeared with dirt to make it look old. Then Ravaisson had a mass of documents, just sensitive enough to make it plausible that they would be hidden, stacked in front of the new wall. A second new wall was built in front of the documents, and that wall too was scraped, nicked, and dirtied. The hope was that any search party that broke through the near wall would assume the documents were the only hidden treasure and not press farther. All this left the Venus de Milo standing in a sealed niche, a faint echo of the sealed niche on Melos where the statue had been discovered fifty years earlier.

The Prussian army arrived outside Paris and began a siege that lasted from September 1870 to February 1871. During those five months the only means of escape was by hot-air balloon. As the siege went on, Parisians were reduced to eating rats—when they could find them. The siege ended only when the provisional government created after Napoleon III's capture signed a humiliating peace treaty with the Prussians. When the new French government moved from Paris to Versailles, the Commune—a loose confederation of extremists, including Marxists, aging Jacobites, anti-clerics, and people from myriad fringe groups—seized control of Paris and brought on civil war. Then, as the government at Versailles tried to recapture Paris, the Commune set fires around the center of the city. The Tuileries palace was burned so badly it had to be razed. The Louvre, the Palais Royal, and the Palais de Justice survived, although they did suffer damage. And the Commune burned the building where Ravaisson had hidden the Venus de Milo. He and the few others who knew the statue's location assumed, glumly, that it had been damaged or even destroyed.

When the Versailles government retook Paris in May 1871, horrifying reprisals followed. Twenty thousand people were executed in only a few weeks. About the same number had died on the guillotine during the Revolution, when the Terror was at its height. But the Terror had lasted a year.

Ravaisson endured all these events quietly and safely in his apartment on the left bank of the Seine, directly across from the Louvre. Then, in June 1871, just days after the defeat of the Commune, he led a group into the basement of the police prefecture to bring the statue, or what was left of it, back to light. Anxiously, they shoveled aside the mass of still-smoking rubbish that had fallen into the basement and discovered, to their great surprise, that the oak crate was intact. By happy accident water from a burst pipe had protected it from the flames.

The crate was carried back to the Louvre, where Ravaisson had it opened. The statue had not suffered any permanent damage, but the stay in the basement had had some dramatic effects. The four broken pieces, two from the left hip and two from the right, which had been reattached to the statue with plaster in the Louvre workshop, had now broken off again. Evidently humidity in the basement had weakened the plaster until it gave way.

Although the missing pieces left a huge cavity on each side of the statue, putting the four pieces back in place with new plaster appeared to be easy enough. But Ravaisson realized that these chance events had given him the opportunity to see into the interior of the statue for the first time since it had arrived at the Louvre fifty years earlier.

Working rapidly, which was not customary with him—normally he was as languorous and dreamy as Delacroix had found him on the evening of the lecture—Ravaisson examined the statue thoroughly, thought through the implications of what he had found, and published a paper just a few weeks later. His titles are as maddeningly quiet and unassuming as he was himself. He called this work "The Venus de Milo." In it Ravaisson proved that the way the statue had been reconstructed in the Louvre in 1821 was so wrong that it had actually changed the way the statue looked. For fifty years the jewel of the Louvre's collections had been presented to the public in a pose that was incorrect.

A look inside

RAVAISSON began by answering a question that had puzzled everyone since the statue was discovered: Had the Venus de Milo originally been carved in two blocks, or had it been one block that was later sawed in two? Now, courtesy of the hole at each hip, Ravaisson could examine the interior of the statue. The carving all along the line where the two blocks met was smooth and precise, so that when the top half was placed on the bottom, the two stones touched on their carefully carved edges and fit together perfectly. That precise workmanship was proof that the statue had not originally been one block that was later carved in half. Instead, the two halves had indeed been carved separately and then united. But why?

It was not unusual for Greek statues to be carved in several pieces, especially when the design was complex or when the statues were carved in a place where it was difficult to obtain marble. But, as Ravaisson says in his plodding, modulated prose, "it is difficult to understand, in a land where marble is easily found in large blocks, particularly the marble of Paros from which the Venus de Milo is made, why an artist such as the creator of this statue did not take the care or did not find the means to procure, for the work that he contemplated, a piece of marble that would suffice for it."

A statue made of two or more pieces creates practical problems that do not arise with a statue from a single block. In an area like the Aegean, where tremors and earthquakes are common, a statue made of two blocks would not last long with one block simply placed on the other. Eventually a tremor would shake the top half off. To prevent this disaster, the Greeks inserted two metal rods, or tenons, between the parts of a statue. In the case of the Venus de Milo, there are holes dug for the tenons about three inches inside each hip. Once the two halves were erected with the tenons in place, the sculptor or his assistants poured molten lead solder down tiny canals that led into the holes with the tenons. When the lead cooled and hardened, the two pieces of the statue were welded tightly together. Peering into the statue, Ravaisson could see the holes where the tenons had been. The metal had disappeared, but there were clear traces of rust and even a few pieces of solder still clinging to the stone.

But there are problems that come with introducing iron tenons into marble. The iron oxidizes, expands, and causes ruptures in the stone. Consequently, tenons should have been a last resort. If the sculptor of the Venus de Milo purposely chose to construct his statue in a way that required tenons, he must have been ignorant, cavalier, or, worst of all, indifferent toward his masterpiece and its preservation.

This subtlety was important, because presumably none of the great masters of Greek sculpture would have treated his work so casually, and Ravaisson was eager to protect the supposed pedigree of the French treasure. In order to acquit the ancient sculptor of such carelessness, he proposed that the statue had originally been carved in one piece. However, an accident of some kind had broken or splintered the lower part of the statue so badly that it could no longer support the upper half. That made it necessary to carve a new lower portion modeled after the original one. This hypothesis absolved the original sculptor of the sin of indifference. Or, as Ravaisson put it, "The present lower part, although from a period not too distant from that when the statue was originally created, would be nevertheless a restoration. It would be then the restorer and not the creator of the Venus de Milo who would have fastened the original upper part to the new lower part by metal tenons."

It's impossible to know whether Ravaisson's conjecture is

true or an ingenious fantasy. He adds as an aside that the lower half is not quite as well carved as the upper, an opinion that many people share and is consistent with the notion that the lower part is a restoration by a second hand. And even a casual observer can see that the marble in the lower half is not as fine as in the upper. The lower stone seems coarser and has a brownish tint that is inferior to the pale luminosity of the marble of the upper block. But none of this can prove whether the lower part is original or a slightly later renovation.

There is, however, one piece of evidence that proves that there was at least one restoration made in ancient times. Evidently, the four pieces near the hips had first broken off not too long after the statue was created. Now that these pieces had broken off again, Ravaisson was able to examine them individually. He found that the upper piece from the right hip could not have been the same piece that had originally broken off in antiquity. It was of the same marble and the same workmanship as the rest of the draped portion of the statue, and it had been carved to fit perfectly in place. But that original piece would have had some trace of a tenon—a groove on the inside and fragments of iron and solder—as the other three pieces did. The piece Ravaisson held had no trace of a tenon whatsoever. This meant that sometime not long after the statue had been carved the tenons had been removed, perhaps to prevent further splintering. This piece from the hip was a replacement made in antiquity after the two tenons had been removed.

That wasn't the only renovation Ravaisson found. The others were more serious, damaging in fact, and they had occurred, as he reluctantly had to admit, in 1821 while the statue was in the workshop of the Louvre.

The protruding edge

WHEN THE Venus de Milo arrived at the Louvre, the four pieces from the hips were detached and needed to be remounted. The two from the right side were attached properly. But for reasons that remain unclear, the restorers at the Louvre were unable to reattach the lower section from the left hip where it should have been. The faulty readjustment made the top edge of the broken piece extend higher than the top surface of the lower block of the statue. The restorers tried to chisel the protuberance down, but they couldn't chisel off too much without causing visible damage. The edge of the broken piece still exceeded the surface of the bottom block by several millimeters, perhaps a sixteenth of an inch. But that small lip sticking up forced a series of readjustments, each one worse for the statue than the last.

The tiny protuberance at the left hip meant that the upper half of the statue could not be placed flush against the lower because it would then be resting on just a few thin millimeters of marble that, sooner or later, would give way under the weight of the upper half. The remedy was to place two wooden wedges about two centimeters wide and twenty-five centimeters long between the two large blocks, one wedge near each hip. That meant that the upper torso rested on the wedges rather than on the thin protuberance at the left hip. But the wedges left a gap between the upper and lower halves of the statue. To keep the gap as small as possible, the restorers made the wedge on the right slightly smaller than the one on the left and beveled both wedges so they were thinner toward the front than at the rear. The result was that the upper torso, leaning toward the front and to the right, met flush with the front edge of the lower block. That hid the line where the two large pieces of the statue met, but the cost was great. The wedges made the upper block incline more to the right front than it should.

That's not all. From Clarac's paper we learn that the line where the two major blocks joined was originally horizontal. But after the restoration, the line between the two surfaces was not horizontal but at least six degrees off the horizontal, meaning the statue was out of plumb and subject, in the case of any shock, to sliding further or even falling. This imbalance came about when the old base of the statue, which was level, was placed inside a new base, which was not level. Although Ravaisson doesn't say this, the new base must have been added in an excess of zeal to disguise the disappearance of the base with the inscription.

Ravaisson blamed all of the faulty reconstruction—the misplaced piece at the hip with the projecting edge, the chiseling of that edge, the wooden wedges, and the irregular new base—on haste and confusion at the Louvre. This was going a little easy on his predecessors, but we can go further than Ravaisson dared. Whether the inscribed base was destroyed or simply hidden—and the fact that it has never been found despite detailed searches of the Louvre's warehouses suggests that the base was destroyed—it was suppressed and then lied about to preserve the identity the museum wanted for the statue.

The piece of left hip that was incorrectly restored is another matter. Reattaching it properly could not have been that difficult. And even if it was difficult for reasons we cannot know, there is no excuse for not finding the solution to the puzzle. It's true that archeology was in its infancy and practices were acceptable then that are considered destructive today. Still, it was obvious that the piece had fit properly once and that it wasn't fitting properly now. Ignoring that and sacrificing the integrity of the statue at the same time was simply incompetent.

Ravaisson, however, chose to look on the bright side. He wrote that "fortunate circumstances"—that is, the humidity in the basement of the police building—had made it possible to understand the mistakes made previously and to return the statue to the "proportions and appearance that she had in the past." He concludes, "Now not only is this thing possible, but, according to the preceding argument, it's a simple thing, too."

Ravaisson may have thought the change was simple, but instead he found himself suddenly trapped where he was most uncomfortable: at the center of a controversy. The notion of making changes to the Venus de Milo instantly attracted the attention of French officialdom. Such a decision could not be left to some conservator at the Louvre. Instead the Academy of Fine Arts was summoned to study whether to remove the wedges and restore the statue to its proper appearance or to leave the wedges in and continue to display the statue in the incorrect position it had had for fifty years. Faced with this "problem," the Academy had two plaster casts made, one in the proper position and one in the false one, and stood them side by side against a background of green drapes.

Théophile Gautier, an author whose prolific writings included art criticism, was a member of the Academy. He concluded that, when properly displayed, the "Venus appears younger and more slender, but she has not the graceful abandon and voluptuous languor imparted to her by the inclined pose . . . she is more of a goddess and less of a woman." This extreme example of French pride contends that the renovations made by the Louvre had actually *improved* the statue. In the end the Academy agreed with Gautier that the wisest course was to leave the wedges in so as not to change the look of the statue and interfere with the public's "habit of admiration."

Habitual passivity

RAVAISSON acquiesced to this decision. He didn't have the wedges removed until twelve years later, in 1883, and then only when some repairs to the antique galleries of the Louvre forced the Venus to be removed from view for a short while. At the same time he had the hideous left foot made of plaster the restorers had added in 1821 taken off. Ravaisson later tried to explain his reluctance to correct the travesty he had exposed by saying that it seemed to him necessary "to give critics time to verify the facts and to get rid of long ingrained prejudices." In other words, he didn't want to cause any trouble.

This was typical Ravaisson. He had great gifts—a superior intellect combined with the eye and the hand of an artist. But he was so passive that his passivity could become a weapon. Henri

Bergson, the leading philosopher in France in the late nineteenth century, a man whose thinking was directly influenced by Ravaisson's philosophical writings, described him precisely: "Never did a man seek less to influence others than did that man. But never was mind more naturally, more tranquilly, more invincibly rebellious to the authority of others: it eluded by its immateriality all attempts to come to grips with it. He was one of those who offer so little resistance that no one can flatter himself that he has ever seen them yield."

In 1833, when he was twenty, Ravaisson won a contest sponsored by the philosopher Victor Cousin for the best essay about Aristotle. Five years later he published *Habit,* a work of barely a hundred pages that was his doctoral thesis and his only work of original philosophy until the last years of his life. *Habit*—and note his predilection even early in life for the quietest possible title—is little known outside France, but it deeply influenced Bergson as well as many German philosophers, including Heidegger. It's still important in France, still easily available in bookstores, and still read.

Despite its brevity, *Habit* contains a whole philosophy of nature. What, Ravaisson wonders, is concealed beneath such natural laws as the regular working of cause and effect? The key to the answer lies in habit. Habit is an activity that by degrees has passed from a conscious act to an unconscious one, from will to automatism. But aren't cause and effect and all the other workings of nature the same thing: the unconscious, automatic repetitions of habit? These repetitions must have begun with some will, then little by little become automatic, which means the laws of nature are the remains of a spiritual force. That is how, for Ravaisson, the presence of habit in our lives reveals the existence of God.

After publishing *Habit,* Ravaisson lived in Paris, where, despite the passivity of his nature, he managed to cut an impressive figure. He dressed with élan, favoring brightly colored checkered vests. His uncle, a famous explorer who wrote popular books about his adventures deep in the jungles of Senegal, introduced him into the best salons, including that of Madame Récamier. There he met Balzac and Lamartine and perhaps even Forbin, who was then entering his dotage. At the same time Ravaisson was painting and exhibiting at the salons. He was good enough to earn compliments from Ingres and the two men became close friends.

The natural course of his career would have been to become a professor of philosophy at one of the leading universities. But Victor Cousin, the philosopher who only a few years earlier had given Ravaisson the prize for his essay on Aristotle, disagreed with the spirituality in *Habit*. Cousin was an uninspired philosopher but an adroit politician who, thanks to a government position, now controlled the appointments to every philosophy faculty in France. He denied Ravaisson a chair. Ravaisson accepted the rebuke without complaint and quietly waited twenty-eight years for the opportunity to take his revenge.

Through his uncle's influence, he obtained a government sinecure in the education bureaucracy. He wrote little until 1867, when, as part of a jubilee celebrating the fifteenth year of Napoleon III's reign, Ravaisson was commissioned to write a history of French philosophy in the nineteenth century. After a feverish period of reading and study, he wrote a huge volume that contained a brilliant and devastating attack on Victor Cousin. Cousin's preeminence and power were immediately broken, and he never recovered.

After being appointed to his post at the Louvre in 1870, Ravaisson retained it until his death in 1900. He had a wife, two daughters, and a quiet, self-effacing son named Charles, who worked for him at the Louvre. Ravaisson's thirty years at the museum were a period of what was for him almost frantic activity. He wrote on Pascal, on funereal vases and bas-reliefs of antiquity, on Leonardo da Vinci, on the history of religion, on the French civil code and factory workers, and on the one subject about which he knew less than any other man in the world:

military strategy. In his philosophical writings, which became more frequent toward the final years of his life, he continued his consistent theme of linking Christianity with ancient philosophy and art. And he became a surprisingly skillful sculptor, taking up the chisel because of his continued, almost obsessive interest in the Venus de Milo.

The story of the fight on the shore

IN 1874, just three years after Ravaisson's paper revealed the addition of the wooden wedges, a series of articles began to appear in the newspaper *Le Temps* in Paris. They contained the sensational news that when the Venus de Milo was discovered, her arms were intact. The author of the articles was a young writer named Jean Aicard, but the source for this inflammatory information was a minor character in the drama of the discovery, the faithful Amable Matterer, the old naval officer who had befriended the young Dumont d'Urville on the *Estafette* and remained loyal to him for the rest of his life.

When d'Urville died in the train wreck with his wife and son in 1842, he left no heirs. Around 1860 a box of his papers turned up at an auction in Toulon. It was bought by an unnamed collector, who found in it a handwritten version of the paper d'Urville had published in 1821, proclaiming himself the discoverer of the Venus de Milo. However, there were certain small but interesting differences between the manuscript and the paper as it was published. One was that in the manuscript d'Urville had mentioned Matterer, called him a man "of great merit and one of my good friends," and said he would never forget his kindness. D'Urville had deleted this short passage from the published version of the paper.

By the 1860s Matterer was eighty years old. He was living in Toulon, retired for many years. The unnamed collector took d'Urville's manuscript to the old man, who was deeply moved by the tribute to himself. D'Urville had written it when he was only an ensign, but after all this time Matterer took those words as coming from the famous admiral d'Urville had become.

Matterer's affection for d'Urville was real and constant. While the great admiral was off on his journeys to Polynesia or Antarctica, Matterer paid visits to his lonely wife and son and maintained these visits even after Madame d'Urville became so peculiar that their other friends began to avoid her. Shortly after d'Urville's death, Matterer, who always claimed that he was nothing but a rude seaman, nevertheless wrote a dignified memoir that he called *Notes nécrologiques et historiques sur M. le contreamiral Dumont d'Urville.* He published it in the *Annales maritimes et colonials* of October 1842.

As Matterer returned d'Urville's manuscript to the collector, he said, "The whole truth about the Venus de Milo is not known, but I know it." After some prompting and after obtaining a promise of secrecy, Matterer told the collector that the statue's left arm was still attached when he and d'Urville had first seen the statue. It was raised and held an apple in its palm. Later, the comte de Marcellus had arrived on the *Estafette* to buy the statue just as the evil monk Oconomos, leading a troop of marines who had arrived on a Turkish warship, was taking it away. On Marcellus's order fifty armed French sailors immediately went ashore to rescue the statue from the Turks. During the fight, the Venus de Milo, bound by ropes, was dragged across the beach, where small rocks pitted its surface and the arm was broken off. Finally, the French sailors prevailed and saved the statue.

The collector, with more promises of secrecy, insisted that the old man write his story down, which he did. Matterer died in 1868, when he was eighty-seven years old. Several years later, assuming that Matterer must have wanted his story to be known after all—otherwise why consent to write it down?—the collector took the manuscripts by both d'Urville and Matterer to Jean Aicard in Paris.

In 1874, when he began publishing his stories on the Venus

de Milo in *Le Temps,* Aicard was twenty-six. He was quite visible on the Paris literary scene, where he reveled in his role as the conquering provincial. He was handsome, wore his dark hair and beard long, and was blessed with a seductive, theatrical voice with which he entranced the audiences who crowded into his readings.

He had just published *Poèmes de Provence,* a series of lyric poems about the life and countryside of his native region. The book became a spectacular success. For the rest of his life, his childhood in Provence continued to inspire his many poems, plays, essays, and novels. Eventually he was admitted into the Académie Française. He wrote rapidly while lying in bed and refused to rewrite. When friends urged him to use more care, he said, "It's useless. I can't. You have to take me as I am."

Aicard expanded his articles in *Le Temps,* added some new information uncovered after they had appeared, and quickly published the result as a book called *The Venus de Milo: Investigations of the History of the Discovery according to Unpublished Documents.* Being by Aicard, it is sloppy, shallow, and a long way from presenting a rational argument. He often refers to both arms being intact, although his sources mention only the left arm. But the book is also passionate and readable. Aicard gives a stirring account of the supposed battle on the shore. That, in addition to his glee in revealing what he believes is a long-hidden secret, has given his book an influence out of proportion to its merit.

Aicard's *Venus de Milo* reproduces a number of original documents concerning the statue that are difficult to find elsewhere. For that scholars owe him some thanks. Otherwise, he attempts to prove that the fight occurred and that the arms of the statue were lost by quoting Matterer's written recollections; by a careful parsing of d'Urville's paper; by reading between the lines of Marcellus and Clarac; and by the later claims of Brest, Brest's son, Yorgos's son, and Yorgos's nephew, all as quoted in a letter from a former French ambassador to Greece. Unfortunately for Aicard, each of these arguments is easily refuted.

Aicard accepts Matterer's story of the fight as true in every detail. But when Matterer wrote his *Notes nécrologiques* about d'Urville in 1842, he never mentioned either an intact arm or any fight on the shore. Why not? Matterer says he did not commit this "imprudence" because "I would have incurred the wrath of the great men of Paris, especially that of the minister of the navy. Undoubtedly, this minister would not have printed my notice and might have even forced me to retire, for I was still in service as a ship's captain." Matterer is trapped by his 1842 reminiscence, and this clear prevarication was nothing more than his way out.

Neither d'Urville nor Marcellus nor Clarac mentions any fight in his account of the events. To Aicard that doesn't mean there was no fight; on the contrary, it is absolute proof that they are all complicit in the cover-up Marcellus began in order to make his diplomacy more impressive. Aicard doesn't propose to tell us what Marcellus could have said or done to keep all fifty sailors on the winning side of a fight from ever bragging about it even years later.

After his newspaper articles appeared, Aicard received a letter from Jules Ferry, formerly France's ambassador to Greece. Aicard includes this letter in his book. As ambassador Ferry had visited Melos in 1873. There he met Louis Brest's son, who, like his father, grandfather, and great-grandfather, was France's vice-consul on the island. In the fifty years since the affair, local legend had greatly amplified Brest's role. Bitter because he thought the French government had neglected him and diminished his role in the discovery of the famous statue, he himself was the source of his growing local reputation. Just a few years after the discovery, he began telling stories about his role to anyone who would listen. Supposedly, he had purchased the statue long before any of the French ships arrived; when he bought it, the statue had its left arm; there was a fight on the shore. Brest, old and fat, would get a laugh by posing as the statue, with his left arm raised in the air.

The ambassador also met the son and the nephew of the farmer Yorgos. They both claimed to have been present at the discovery, and they too insisted that the left arm was intact. It extended straight out to the left and held an apple in its palm, exactly the pose that Matterer describes in his final recollections. They had seen the fight on the shore as well.

Unfortunately, Brest seems to have forgotten the letters he himself wrote at the time of the discovery. For instance, he wrote to Pierre David, the consul in Smyrna, "She is a little mutilated; the arms are broken." And d'Urville's paper, which does say that there is a hand holding an apple, also says that the arms "have been mutilated, one and the other, and are presently detached from the body."

The drawings reappear

AICARD's case collapsed from its own weight, but the popularity of his book brought the proofs that would clinch the case against him to the surface. The most important person to emerge from obscurity was Olivier Voutier, the dashing Bonapartist and revolutionary soldier in Greece who had been digging nearby when Yorgos first uncovered the statue. When Aicard's book appeared, Voutier was seventy-eight years old and living in his château on the Côte d'Azur. (This beautiful property later belonged to Edith Wharton.) After fighting for Greek independence and winning a hero's medals, Voutier found his later years something of a disappointment. Like Forbin and Ravaisson, he had been a friend of Madame Récamier's, and he had written her long, intense letters about the fighting in Greece. He had known Napoleon III when they were both young men, and Voutier expected to be rewarded for his lifelong Bonapartism with an important position in the government or military. But the new emperor inexplicably shunned his old friend. Wounded, Voutier retired to his château, married, and quietly raised two daughters.

In 1860, prompted by having come across one of Marcellus's books, Voutier wrote him a long letter expressing fond memories of the count and their voyage around the Levant on the *Estafette* with the Venus de Milo on board. Voutier also explained for the first time his role in the discovery. He even told Marcellus about the drawings he had made on the spot and added that, despite the vicissitudes of the years, he still had them in his possession.

Marcellus, who had married the comte de Forbin's beautiful younger daughter, Valentine, had had a distinguished career as a diplomat. He had left government service in 1830 when Charles X was overthrown and retired to his wife's estate. Presumably Valentine's miserly grandmother had either died or loosened her grip on the family fortune. Marcellus occupied himself by writing a series of popular memoirs about his years as an ambassador in the Levant and in England. He responded to Voutier with a joyful letter. He reminisced happily about their voyage together. He even remembered the comic sacrifice of the chicken when they were hungry and their ship was becalmed near the mouth of the Nile.

Marcellus died in 1865. The only other person who knew of this correspondence was his widow, Valentine. When Aicard's book appeared in 1874, she was insulted because it imputed lies and an unattractive careerism to her husband. She wrote Voutier asking him to tell Ravaisson all he knew about the discovery of the statue. Voutier, responding to the request of his friend's widow, but perhaps also aware that here was his final chance to secure at least a small place in history, at last broke his silence about his role in the discovery. He published a short pamphlet that told the story of finding the statue with Yorgos and making drawings at the site. Then he sent tracings of the drawings to Ravaisson. They show both halves of the statue and the two herms, each one standing on an inscribed base. The base of the herm with the young man's head is inscribed with the name of the sculptor from Antioch. The base of the bearded herm also has an inscription, which had by now been completely lost. These two inscriptions proved the validity of Voutier's draw-

ings, since he could not have known about them except by seeing them with the herms when the statue was discovered.

The most important detail in the drawing is this: At the time
of the discovery the statue had no arms. It looked just as it does
today.

Now, just months after the 1874 publication of Aicard's
book, Ravaisson had proof that its revelations were false. But
the ethereal philosopher had spent all his life avoiding conflict,
and he avoided it once again. Eventually, he did write a paper in
which he published Voutier's drawings. And he used them to
attack Aicard's book directly. But that was eighteen years later,
in 1892.

This long delay had its consequences. Many people read
Aicard's book with its fight on the shore, but only diligent scholars read Ravaisson's refutation so many years later. Meanwhile,
the story about the fight between French sailors and Turkish
marines rallied by the evil priest Oconomos became an established "fact," and, sadly, it has remained part of the lore about
the Venus de Milo ever since. Here is Matthew Kangas writing in
the November–December 1990 issue of *Sculpture*: "It seems
clear that the statue was found in two parts in a cave on the
Greek island of Melos and then reassembled, and that later, during a battle between French consular officials and Turkish
agents trying to prevent its export, the arms were broken off."

In 2001, the generally savvy Mary Beard and John Henderson wrote in their *Classical Art from Greece to Rome* that after "a
scuffle on the beach between some Turkish and French soldiers
(who were both claiming the prize), she fell into the hands of
the French."

The fight on the beach is an article of faith among certain
academics whose political beliefs almost demand that a fight
have taken place. Here is Olga Augustinos, author of *French
Odysseys: Greece in French Travel Literature from the Renaissance to
the Romantic Era* (1994): "Years later, Marcellus's account of his
feat was contradicted by eyewitnesses, some of whom main-

tained that when the statue changed hands, force was used and there was an armed confrontation between the Greeks and the crew of the *Estafette,* who won in the end." She admits that the "evidence surrounding this episode is conflicting." Nevertheless, she concludes:

> The conduct of the whole affair shows clearly that in European eyes the modern Greeks had no right to the monuments of antiquity because they could be of no use to a people who had neither enough culture nor sufficient means to appreciate and safeguard them. So pervasive was this patronizing and arrogant attitude that even philhellenes such as Marcellus subscribed to it implicitly.

She is wrong about more than just the fight, since the alleged battle was against Turks, not Greeks, and the Turks certainly had no respect for Greek antiquities. The Europeans saw themselves, often correctly, as protecting the Greek heritage from the hostile Turks.

Augustinos has a light touch, however, compared to Caroline Arscott and Katie Scott, both of the Courtauld Institute in London, who write in *Manifestations of Venus: Art and Sexuality* (2000):

> Though Marcellus never admits to a fight, the *Souvenirs* repeatedly invoke strife between the contending French, Greek, and Turkish parties for possession of the Venus. . . . More particularly, the distribution of the means and use of force in the text in a pattern that contrasted the French (heavily armed but choosing rather to persuade by force of reason) with the Turks and Greeks (poorly equipped but willing in their ignorance and greed to seize the statue by force, though damage was certain) crudely and predictably put into play a set of reinforcing oppositions between West and East,

Christian and Muslim, reason and passion, civilization and barbarism. As such the violence of the narrative also had something to say about the origins of Western culture.

"Something to say about the origins of Western culture"? What, exactly? Here again, these authors get more wrong than the fight on the shore, and they are guilty of the cultural stereotyping they pretend to oppose. For instance, the Turkish military of 1820 was not poorly equipped. On the contrary, it controlled a vast empire, including all of southeastern Europe, that once stretched from the Caspian Sea almost to Budapest. For these authors the fight simply must have happened. If there was no fight, the facts of the discovery and acquisition would not support their political theories. Such are the results of Ravaisson's delay in closing Pandora's box.

The Venus of the Gardens

RAVAISSON'S refutation of Aicard in 1892, although arriving too late to be effective, was at least convincing. He trotted out Voutier's sketches, explaining how he obtained them so as to establish their authenticity, and rested his case. Then Ravaisson spent the remainder of his essay describing and defending his reconstruction of the statue. Here, too, his long delay—the best excuse is that these were to be his final words on the Venus de Milo after twenty years of study—proved self-defeating. He lived so much in his own mind that he had not noticed the new generation of archeologists who had come of age. They were different. They knew more than their counterparts in the past, and they played rough.

Ravaisson, like Quatremère de Quincy, had always thought that the Venus de Milo had been paired with a statue of Mars. In his paper of 1871, where he began by describing his discovery of the two wooden wedges and the faulty restoration at the Louvre, he even identified the second figure as being like the Borghese Mars, a sculpture showing a nude Mars with a helmet, a shield on his left arm, and a short sword in his right hand.

Ravaisson never wavered from his belief that these two statues belonged together, although he eventually came to believe that the Borghese statue was not Mars but Theseus, the legendary king of Athens who as a young man had killed the Minotaur on Crete. The clue was a band on the statue's right ankle, a reminder of the time when Theseus was taken to Crete as a slave in chains.

Ravaisson sculpted many versions of the Venus de Milo and the Borghese statue standing together. He tried them turned at different angles to each other and with Venus's arms in different poses. He had a plaster cast of the most convincing arrangement made in the true size of the two statues. The male stands straight while Venus is in three-quarter profile to his right. Her left foot is behind her right. Her right arm comes over to his right side, her fingers separated. Her left hand holds the apple and rests lightly on his right shoulder.

All his life, from the time Delacroix heard him speak at the Louvre until his final philosophical writings in the year before his death, Ravaisson wanted to show that the ancient world could be reconciled with Christianity, that the Greeks themselves were almost Christians even though they lived before Christ. By grouping the Venus de Milo with a statue of Theseus, Ravaisson could show that the Venus, as he had reconstructed it, with the immortal woman and the mortal man in a moment of tender intimacy, was an "image expressing a divine grace that is going to look for humanity in order to unite with it—a conception that was not foreign to Judaism, where Jehovah seems to seek out the elected nation, and that the Christian religion was to carry, after paganism and Judaism, to a new height."

From here Ravaisson passes even further into the imaginary. He tries to determine the prototype for the Venus de Milo and chooses a statue known as the Venus of the Gardens by either Phidias or one of his pupils. It was created in the fifth century

Ravaisson's reconstruction of the Venus de Milo
with the Borghese Mars

B.C. in Athens. We know of it only through references in ancient writings. Ravaisson surmises that the Venus de Milo together with Theseus was a version of the Venus of the Gardens done during the time of Alexander—the fourth century B.C.—specifically to grace the theater in Melos.

Ravaisson weaves an elaborate rationale for his choice, although it is undoubtedly wrong. For one thing, no ancient author mentions either Mars or Theseus together with the Venus of the Gardens. Ravaisson himself dismisses this objection airily, but the point remains.

Ravaisson was too isolated from the world to understand or even to suspect that during his lifetime archeology had changed. It was no longer an avocation for scholars with an appreciation for ancient art and some knowledge of classical languages; now it was a profession that required training and experience and that aspired to become a science. Salomon Reinach, who by 1890 had become the leading archeologist in France, reviewed Ravaisson's paper. He treated the old man gently and praised him for disproving the still current story of the fight on the beach in Melos. But, Reinach says, the grouping with the Borghese Mars derives "less from proven facts than from personal impressions and judgments." Even worse, there "are errors, slight no doubt, but too numerous to allow the critic to conceal them." He then lists, in a withering footnote, some twenty errors.

Adolf Furtwängler, Reinach's counterpart in Germany, also reviewed Ravaisson's paper. He saw no need to be gentle with a man, no matter how aged or distinguished, whom he thought to be simply wrong. Furtwängler gives Ravaisson credit for proving that the fight on the shore was a myth, but the rest of the paper had "only the value of a dilettante's fantasy." The grouping with the Borghese Mars is "certainly one of the most absurd and unfortunate of all restorations." And he thought Ravaisson's ignorance was staggering: "A large role is played in Ravaisson's conjectures by the ring that Theseus wears on two famous vases. Ravaisson unites it with the ring of the Mars Borghese, but overlooks the fact that the ring was a fashionable touch during a particular period of vase painting, even occurring on some figures of Silenus, so it has absolutely no special significance."

RAVAISSON was eighty-one in 1892 when he wrote his final paper on the statue. He lived for eight more years. He was lucid to the end, but his interests had returned to metaphysics. He retreated increasingly into his speculations, to the point that he couldn't recognize his two adored granddaughters at first if they surprised him on the street as he returned home from his office. He still had his luminous blue eyes and dressed in bright colors, and his work in philosophy had influenced the next generation of French and German thinkers. As an archeologist, however, he had thought himself into irrelevance. His archeological papers were based on deduction from a few premises—the way a philosopher reasons—rather than on research and deduction from the proven facts, as a scientist reasons. In the end, his only permanent contributions to archeology are not his theories or his reconstructions but the important facts fate placed in his way: the wedges between the two halves of the Venus de Milo and Voutier's sketches.

The future belonged to the next generation, specifically to Salomon Reinach in France and Adolf Furtwängler in Germany. Furtwängler had concluded his critique of Ravaisson's paper by saying, "I must decline further comment on questions addressing the Venus de Milo itself, because an essay by me on the subject is currently on the press." When that essay appeared a few months later, the future had arrived. Reinach responded with papers of his own, and classical archeology, once the domain of titled art connoisseurs and gentle philosophers, became a contact sport.

V

Two Geniuses

O<small>F ALL</small> the peoples of Europe, the Germans of the nineteenth century were by far the most obsessed with classical Greece. And they had a particular, almost proprietary interest in the Venus de Milo, in part because they thought it was rightfully theirs. In 1817 Prince Ludwig of Bavaria, who was passionate about classical antiquity, had bought the ruined theater in Melos. After the discovery of the Venus de Milo in 1820, he claimed the statue. He was not convinced by the French government's reply that his claim was invalid because the statue had been found near—but not on— his property. After that, the statue had an aura of lost love for the Germans. It was still visible, yet forever out of reach. The romantic poet Heinrich Heine used to talk to her in the Louvre. During his last visit to see the statue before leaving Paris he burst into tears.

But Heine was a poet. German archeologists, disappointed that Germany couldn't have the statue, became skeptical of its real value. As a group they put the date of the statue in the first century B.C., during the supposedly inferior Hellenistic times, and not during the fourth-century classical period, as the French insisted. The Germans were in effect devaluing the jewel of the French collections, although that didn't stop German scholars from proposing various reconstructions. Christoph Hasse, a fellow at the anatomical institute of the University of Breslau, tried to determine the position of the missing arms by close observation of the muscles in the back and shoulder. He concluded that she was removing her robe with her right hand and loosening her hair with her left as she was about to enter the sea. Other scholars proposed that she was holding a shield or a mirror and was lost in her own reflection. A scholar named Viet Valentin, after pondering every square millimeter of the statue, decided that she was recoiling while warding off a male god who had surprised her at her bath.

These reconstructions all seem unlikely today, but they were dutifully discussed until Adolf Furtwängler appeared. His career had the effect of shoving all that had come before into the distant background.

In 1872, when Furtwängler was nineteen, his father sent him to study at Leipzig, an important intellectual center at the time. Furtwängler was bored with his classes, but he did discover a Leipzig museum with plaster casts of classical statues. In those days, before photographs and widespread travel made seeing art relatively easy, museums everywhere in Europe filled their rooms with plaster casts of masterpieces from the classical age. Wandering among these casts made Furtwängler feel ignorant and uncomprehending of even their basic forms. He couldn't stand that feeling and, as it turned out, spent the rest of his life trying to eradicate it.

In 1873 he transferred to the University of Munich, where he studied with Heinrich von Brunn, a venerable founding father of German archeology. Brunn found himself with a student who had a feverish enthusiasm, immense energy, an unrivaled capacity for work, high intelligence, and, best of all, a visual memory so vast and so acute it was unique in the history of archeology. As Brunn put it, "He is all fire."

While studying with Brunn, Furtwängler began what was to become the bedrock of his work throughout his career. He

Adolf Furtwängler

was by instinct a great cataloger. He began by creating detailed personal files containing entries on every piece of antiquity in the collections around Munich. He cataloged large items, such as statues and urns, as well as the smallest pottery shards, coins, and carved gems. His thesis under Brunn in 1876—*Eros in Greek Vases*—had also been a kind of catalog. But he began to understand the real potential contained in his systematic sorting two years later in a dusty storeroom in Athens.

Furtwängler, who had been traveling and studying in Italy and Greece on a stipend from the German Archeological Institute, had immersed himself in a daunting project involving pottery found during Heinrich Schliemann's excavations at Mycenae. Schliemann was the flamboyant self-proclaimed archeologist who, convinced of the literal truth of Homer's *Iliad,* had discovered the ruins of Troy in northwestern Turkey, along with a hoard of golden objects he called the treasure of Priam. He then turned to Mycenae in Greece, where, to the amazement of the world, he found graves at the bottom of deep shafts, including a death mask he called the mask of Agamemnon. Neither the attribution to Priam nor that to Agamemnon was accurate, but there was no questioning the importance of the finds or the vast popular interest they created.

At Mycenae Schliemann had found a huge amount of pottery that was sent to a storeroom in Athens, where it was piled indiscriminately. Furtwängler confronted this wasteland of old clay early in 1878. With nothing to go on but his energy, visual memory, and genius for seeing parallels and connections among even widely separated objects, he began to sort the pottery by such simple criteria as color, shape, and firing techniques. After that initial classification, other more subtle and interesting connections began to emerge. Finally, some years later, as he continued to study the pottery—Furtwängler always had eight or ten difficult projects going at the same time—he was able to establish what he called the "evolutionary stages of ornamentation," which proceeded from clearly drawn natural objects to intricate abstractions. This timeline of designs made it possible to date later finds and to see a changing flow of taste, ideas, events, heroes, and divinities.

While Furtwängler was still working in Athens, Ernst Curtius, the most famous archeologist in Germany at the time, sent for him to join the German excavations at Olympia. The ruins at this site of the ancient Olympic games beckoned to lovers of Greece, and excavating there had been a dream in Germany since Winckelmann. Surely here, where for centuries the Greeks had met for the sacred games, the greatest artifacts of the Greek genius must lie buried in the rubble. The Germans hoped that the sculpture in the temples at Olympia might surpass even the Elgin marbles and the Venus de Milo.

Curtius had recruited Furtwängler to Olympia to help with

an awkward situation. It wasn't that the excavations had come up dry. On the contrary, many thousands of objects had been found. A similar discovery today would be in newspapers and magazines with dazzling photographs and ecstatic quotes from scientists about their good fortune. But for Curtius and, more important, for the royal family and the German government who sponsored the dig, and for the German people who had taken Curtius's romantic history of Greece to their hearts, the finds were not of the right sort at all.

In nineteenth-century Germany, unlike in France, classical philology was the foundation of scholarship about the ancient world. Philology, which involved deriving conclusions and interpretations from a close reading of the ancient texts, originated in the early Middle Ages when monks pondered Latin religious texts letter by letter. The reliance on philology to learn about the ancient world meant that artifacts from the past, whether a shard of pottery or the Venus de Milo, had little importance for scholars compared to the written record, such as it was. For them the goal of an archeological dig was to find writing, manuscripts if possible, but inscriptions at the very least.

For the German public, however, whose professional classes had been steeped in Greek and Latin, the goal of a dig was monumental sculpture, because it was beautiful and inspiring and because it competed with the possessions of the English and French. After statues, wall paintings or mosaics were acceptable, barely, but pottery shards, small figurines, tools, and the detritus of everyday life held no interest for either scholars or the public.

Unfortunately, shards, tools, figurines, and ancient trash are what archeological digs usually find. Certainly that was the case at Olympia. Despite the assumptions of the glories that would be found there, the digs had produced only one spectacular discovery: the Hermes by Praxiteles. This beautiful statue was at the time taken to be original, and that made it the only positively identified original work still extant by any of the major Greek sculptors. (Beautiful though it is, subsequent research has shown that it, too, is a copy.) Otherwise, the discoveries at

Olympia were not inscriptions or monumental sculptures or even mosaics but, rather, a teeming multitude of small, common objects. That was all Curtius had to show for three years of support from the German government. He had to make some sense of it in order to justify all the time, effort, and expense. This was where Furtwängler was supposed to help.

And he did. After moving from the storeroom in Athens to the excavations at Olympia, even he was disappointed at first in the finds Curtius showed him. He called them "the rubbish of ancient times, small worthless things or single fragments of larger ones." But if the quality was low, the sheer quantity was overwhelming. The army of diggers found one hundred to two hundred objects every day. By now they had accumulated some 1,300 stone sculptures, 7,500 bronzes, 2,000 terra-cottas, and 3,000 coins. Furtwängler shrugged his shoulders and happily dug in. As he wrote to his beloved teacher Brunn, "I have to say that I feel quite satisfied. If the cataloging of many small bronze objects, coins, and the like is truly onerous, I am learning so much which one otherwise would have no opportunity [to learn]."

To a layman, creating catalogs like this sounds mundane, and indeed it is often the worst kind of work—tedious, demanding, and endless. Hundreds of objects, or more often thousands upon thousands of objects, need to be handled one by one, measured, described, sketched or photographed, and then filed by style or date or some other kind of classification. Today, no matter how tedious, it is standard practice in archeology, because the accumulation of all this detail, properly organized and then intelligently analyzed, can lead to the most important conclusions about a society's political and social organization, economy, religion, and daily life. Without a detailed catalog of objects, none of these conclusions could be supported scientifically or even discerned.

At Olympia Furtwängler also described the strata of the site in detail. That in turn allowed him to date the finds according to the level where they were found. Then, combining that information with methods of dating as he had done with the pottery from Mycenae, he was able to arrange the 7,500 bronze artifacts into groups and then arrange the groups chronologically. His methods for dating Greek bronzes remain the standard.

This was a tremendously important moment, not just in Furtwängler's career but in the history of archeology. Furtwängler was not working with texts, so he had made a break with philology. He was working with artifacts, but these artifacts were not isolated objects of great beauty like the Elgin marbles or the Venus de Milo. Instead they were thousands upon thousands of undistinguished, often unlovely objects he had not chosen and didn't necessarily like. Faced with this overwhelming flood of things, Furtwängler developed methods of grouping them, comparing them, dating them, and then drawing conclusions from them. Some precedents existed, and there were others involved in a similar process of discovery, but Furtwängler played an important part in the invention of modern archeology. He created a philology based on objects rather than words.

In 1879 Furtwängler left Olympia for Berlin, where there were two collections of Greek and Roman antiquities. But the director of the collections so despised the young man's arrogance—Furtwängler was twenty-six—that Ernst Curtius took him in at the Antiquarium, where he was director. Furtwängler, who attributed his troubles to anti-Catholic bias, immediately began cataloging more than four thousand disparate items in the Berlin collections, describing each one in painful detail. He also cataloged the Antiquarium's collection of twelve thousand engraved stones, gems, and cameos.

Here again he found this tedious work congenial. "I am already in the museum at half past eight," he wrote to a friend, "and working hard on vases. It is pleasant to be able to work undisturbed on such great material. I have three servants at my disposal who obey all my orders."

But even these monumental tasks absorbed only a fraction of his boundless energy. He published a torrent of papers and articles. He feuded constantly and was often vicious in his printed remarks about scholars with whom he disagreed. He called one a "complete ignoramus." He relished swooping down uninvited and unwanted on some museum's prized artifact and declaring it a fake, particularly if the museum was French. And yet Furtwängler could not endure being attacked in the kind of brutal phrases he himself used habitually. It hurt and bewildered him. "One of my fundamental failings," he once remarked, "is my constant readiness to believe that another is hostile to me or despises me."

In 1886 Furtwängler met Adelheid Wendt, whose father was the headmaster of a gymnasium just as Furtwängler's had been. A gymnasium was a secondary school for boys. These schools had been established across Germany early in the 1800s in order to wrest control of education away from the Catholic Church. German civilization at the time was so enthralled by classical antiquity that the students took Greek and Latin, studied classical writers, and learned little else. The intention was to teach the boys not how to do anything but how to be something. The gymnasiums were prestigious because only their graduates could enter universities, and a university degree was the only path to careers in the state bureaucracy or the professions. The headmasters made a good living and had a highly respectable social position.

Brash and quick-minded in all things, Furtwängler proposed to Adelheid the night they met. She objected that it was too sudden. He agreed, so they waited until the next night to announce their engagement. She had some sort of birth defect on the right side of her face—even casual family photographs always show her in left profile—and grew up slightly wounded, since both her sisters were considered beauties.

Adelheid was typical of the shy but benevolent women who marry interesting but self-absorbed men, and the couple seems to have been very content. Furtwängler liked rural areas more than cities. In Berlin and later in Munich they lived in pretty countryside near the edge of town. He was a tall, lithe, handsome man with bushy hair and a swashbuckling mustache who adored physical activity. Life with him was almost a self-parody of constant hiking, sailing, and swimming. His idea of the ideal existence was to be an English gentleman living in the country and riding to hounds. He even sprinkled his speech with Anglicisms.

By the time he was at the Archeological Institute in Berlin, Furtwängler could afford books, a fine house, and travel. Archeology had become a mighty force in Germany. There were museums of antiquities that had an important role in the cultural life of German cities, and in the universities the classical departments attracted eager students. Furtwängler's father had raised him to believe that a true modern hero was one who devoted his life to the Greeks and Romans, and that was exactly what Furtwängler had chosen to do.

And apparently all Germany felt the same way. Furtwängler's lectures became so popular that seats had to be reserved in advance. Too busy to prepare, he spoke extemporaneously. His voice was thin, and his bushy hair became a distraction as it shook with his exertions. But he spoke beautiful German with precise diction as hard-won knowledge and brilliant ideas flowed out of him like a river. As one student said, "The influence that radiated from him was overwhelming, because he always spoke from the abundance of his own experiences and his own work, with its continually new perceptions and discoveries, and because his enthusiasm was genuine." Furtwängler had no time for students who didn't rise to his standards, but he was fond of those who did and treated them with respect. He welcomed and encouraged women and allowed them to read for a doctorate even though the German universities did not formally admit them.

In Berlin he wrote his great work *Masterpieces of Greek Sculpture,* which contained his long essay on the Venus de Milo. Yet, comfortable and well situated as he was, when Kekule von Stradonitz, a virulent opponent, was appointed to a post in Berlin that Furtwängler coveted, his wounded pride caused him to leave for Munich, where he lived for the rest of his life.

He and Adelheid had four children, two boys and then two girls. Wilhelm, the older boy, born in 1886, was a musical genius. As a conductor he was one of the foremost interpreters of Beethoven and Wagner in the twentieth century. During the Nazi years he continued to conduct in Berlin for audiences that included Hitler, though Wilhelm was not a party member or even in sympathy with Nazism. After the war he was formally exonerated of complicity. Nevertheless, public sentiment didn't agree, and in 1949 hostile protests caused his appointment as conductor of the Chicago Symphony Orchestra to be canceled.

The island

THE ONLY contemporary archeologist who approached Adolf Furtwängler in stature was French. Salomon Reinach and he were united by their intellects and their passion for classical antiquity. Otherwise they were opposites who, disagreeing about almost everything, disagreed most about the Venus de Milo. While Adolf Furtwängler loved his wife and children and his family remained close all their lives, the Venus de Milo was the only woman Salomon Reinach ever understood, and he may not have understood her.

Reinach had become famous as a genius when he was still in secondary school. Salomon and his two brothers—Joseph, the oldest of the three, and Théodore, the youngest—won so many scholastic prizes that their accomplishments were heralded in the national press. In fact, the brothers were not awarded all the prizes they deserved, because they were Jews; their total domination would have caused political trouble. Later, when Joseph and Théodore were in the Chamber of Deputies and Salomon was a famous scholar, a cabaret singer in Montmartre christened them the "Know-it-all Brothers," which may have been an anti-Semitic jibe.

Their father, a brilliant commercial trader who moved first from Germany to Switzerland and from there to Paris, pos-

Salomon Reinach, photograph by Roger Viollet

sessed one of the five or six largest fortunes in France. Despite their wealth, the three brothers all chose to work hard in careers that combined public service and scholarship. Salomon worked hardest of all. He wrote so much that his bibliography runs to 262 pages, including more than ninety lengthy works and at least seven thousand articles. But this list is certainly incomplete, because he often published his articles unsigned or under a variety of pseudonyms.

The sheer volume of his writings is staggering, but so is the breadth of his subject matter. In addition to detailed, lifelong work on the archeology of the Mediterranean and several hundred pages on the Venus de Milo, he wrote a history of religion and a history of art that were reprinted in edition after edition in both French and English. He wrote French, Greek, and Latin grammars as well as histories of Renaissance art, the Spanish Inquisition, and the trials of Joan of Arc. He wrote a history of the Celts. He translated the German philosopher Schopenhauer into French. He wrote a manual of philology, a study of Albrecht Dürer, a treatise on the way galloping horses were represented in art, and a tome called *Cults, Myths, and Religions* that is well over a thousand pages and influenced Freud while he was writing *Totem and Taboo.*

This almost inconceivably vast output left little time for much else, and his obituary in the *Revue Archéologique* says that he knew nothing of the pleasures of life, had little taste for society, and preferred to work. That assessment seems rather dour, since others' recollections make it clear that he enjoyed interesting people and was very good company himself. He visited friends such as the Rothschilds and others at the top of Jewish society, and he was welcomed at the best intellectual and artistic salons of the era. Although he was diabetic and often appeared pasty and overweight from the disease, was a heavy smoker who developed a persistent cough, and easily became excited, which caused him to stammer, he was known—and liked—for launching into dizzying monologues that leapt from topic to topic in a display that was part erudition, part shrewd perception, and part playfulness. His charm was that it became impossible to know which was which. He once insisted to the art critic and historian Bernard Berenson that it was an important scholarly challenge to establish the exact moment in history when the back of a woman's neck came to be recognized in art and literature.

This was only a spur-of-the-moment improvisation, but the subject is revealing. Reinach had the fetishist's obsession with the parts of a woman's body as well as with their representations. He once wrote a paper proposing a method of dating Greek statues of women based on the variations in the distance between their breasts. But he also had the fetishist's confusion when confronted with the woman's body in the flesh. Liane de Pougy, a beautiful former courtesan and actress who occupied much of Salomon's time and imagination during the last decade of his life, once lifted her dress while in a feline mood to show him a scar on her thigh. This sort of thing was how she had made her living when she was young, so she knew the effect it would have. Reinach was confused, tormented, attracted, repelled. She later remarked, "It's said that the only nakedness he has ever seen is that of statues."

This observation may not have been literally true, but it was accurate in its way. Reinach tried to conceal his fears and confusion by adopting a pretentious courtly manner with women. He made a display of elaborately kissing their hands. Afterward, given the slightest chance, he liked to play the role of an all-knowing instructor to women, particularly if they were young and pretty. He once pulled Bernard Berenson's wife aside with an air of mystery and said to her, "Tell me then, these things that your husband has written, are they things you believe one could explain to young girls?" He even wrote a series of instructional manuals, each of which was addressed to a teenaged girl: *Eulalie or Greek Without Tears, Cornelie or Latin Without Tears, Sidonie or French Without Pain,* and *Letters to Zoe on the History of Philosophies* (in three volumes!). Although Reinach could lecture charmingly in person or in print—*Eulalie, Cornelie, Sidonie,* and *Letters to Zoe* all sold so well that new printings were constantly in demand; in fact, except for *Zoe,* they are still in print—this social strategy preserved a professorial distance between him and women. Berenson, who saw what Reinach was doing to himself and how it made him unhappy and even ridiculous, said in a letter to a friend, "Much more romance, and yearnings, and even passion hides behind his pedantries than many a professed ladies' man has ever known."

Reinach did have a wife. In 1891, when he was thirty-three, he married a woman named Rose Morgoulieff, whose family had fled Russia. She had a life of her own as a doctor who directed a hospital for unwed mothers. She worked so selflessly for the hospital and its patients that she was awarded the Legion of Honor. Although she was proper, solemn, and admirable, she seems to have been entirely out of her husband's erotic range, whatever its exact nature may have been. They had no children. The reason—or the excuse—was that he had been influenced by the theories of Malthus and worried about overpopulation. But some connection existed between them. They were married for forty-two years. He donated massive sums to Jewish causes in Russia because of her. Just weeks after he died, in his own home in 1932, Rose too passed away.

There were, however, three women whom we know he deeply loved. They all shared two characteristics: a taste for literary artiness and a passionate lesbianism. In 1914 he became obsessed by the poet Pauline Tarn. She was an English-American woman who wrote in French under the name Renée Vivien. Five years earlier, she had died of alcoholism and anorexia at the age of thirty. Love between women is the principal theme of her poetry. After reading all of her work—nine volumes of poetry, including translations of Sappho and variations on some of Sappho's poems, a novel, and two volumes of prose—Reinach became convinced that Pauline Tarn had been a genius. He began placing letters in literary journals in England and France asking for information about her, and he made diligent, if not annoying, inquiries among people who might have known her while she lived in Paris.

Pauline's first great love, a Parisian girl named Violet Shilleto, had died when Pauline was twenty. After that, living on an inheritance from her deceased father, Pauline had wandered the world aimlessly with a succession of lovers or lived alone in a shuttered room in Paris. Her sad life, her love for Greek culture, her sexuality, even her recourse to a pseudonym all fascinated Reinach. He placed the material he gathered—reminiscences, letters, and so on—into files left in a library in Aix-en-Provence that were to be sealed until the year 2000. To those friends who found this obsession just the least bit odd, he replied that if someone had preserved similar material about Sappho after her death, wouldn't we be thankful today?

One day a friend took an excited Salomon Reinach to meet Natalie Clifford Barney. Although she came from Cincinnati, where her father had made a fortune manufacturing railroad cars, Natalie Barney had attended school in Paris and lived there most of her life. Known for her beautiful, slightly archaic

French, she was a voluptuous, charismatic woman, a writer, and the hostess each Friday afternoon of a salon at her house at 20 Rue Jacob. Everyone important in arts or literature went there, including Auguste Rodin, Colette, James Joyce, Gertrude Stein, Anatole France, Count Robert de Montesquiou (on whom Proust patterned Baron Charlus), Isadora Duncan, Ezra Pound, Max Jacob, Jean Cocteau, and many others.

But for Reinach all that paled beside one fact: Natalie had had an intense love affair with Pauline Tarn. That, together with Natalie's powerful physical presence and formidable personality, overwhelmed Reinach. He arrived at her house on the Rue Jacob in love with one unattainable woman, the dead poet. When he left, he was in love with another.

"She reads nothing, knows nothing, intuits everything, this wild girl from Cincinnati," he said of her. When she was young, she had a huge mane of blond hair that fell in waves well below her shoulders and a full, athletic figure that exuded sexuality. She had never been interested in men, although she attracted many suitors. Instead she became a predatory seductress of women, often arriving to court them dressed as a page. She liked to pose for photographs kissing another woman or reclining completely nude in a forest. Now, in 1914, she was thirty-eight to Reinach's fifty-six and had begun to appear blocky and mannish. But her eyes were still radiantly blue, her manner was free and enthusiastic, and she had a pointed wit. What excited Reinach most of all was that she was an open, unapologetic lesbian.

Reinach saw her often. At a party at his house he introduced her to Bernard Berenson, saying, "Surely the wild girl from Cincinnati and the sauvage du Danube were meant to meet!" Berenson fell for her too, attracted by what he called her "physical radiance." And Natalie, who indulged and teased Reinach more than she really liked him, was taken with Berenson. "I was madly in love with you," she told him, "until I suddenly woke to the realization that you were a male."

When he was with Natalie Barney, Reinach constantly tried

to turn the conversation to her sex life. He called lesbianism "the island," and he could never seem to get enough of the details. Years earlier, when she was just twenty-one, Natalie had seen a radiantly beautiful woman, just a few years older than her, riding in an open carriage in the Bois de Boulogne. Natalie learned who she was, began sending flowers and gifts, and came to call in her page's costume. Without too much difficulty the woman succumbed; afterward, she wrote a barely disguised novel about the affair called *l'Idylle Saphique,* which was a scandalous success when it was published in 1901. Natalie, whose character in the novel is named Flossie, told Reinach about the book, and he, of course, devoured it.

But even its explicitness did not satisfy his curiosity. He wanted to know still more. He wanted to meet the author, Natalie's former and still occasional lover. He pressed Natalie until at last, in 1918, just after the war ended, she took him to the Majestic Hotel in Paris to meet Liane de Pougy. She too had known Pauline Tarn, and as Natalie's lover she knew the most intimate details of life on "the island." Reinach could not resist her. She became the third of his great unattainable loves.

Madame Reinach admitted Natalie to her home, but she would not allow Liane de Pougy there until one afternoon shortly before Salomon's death. Liane had been one of the most notorious women in Paris at the turn of the century, but now, by marriage to an epicene Romanian noble many years her junior, she was the Princess Ghika. Reinach had seen her during her years of blazing glory in the theater. She had no talent as an actress, which even she admitted, but she was so beautiful that she could command an audience, especially the men, simply by appearing onstage in a daring costume. She lived off a succession of lovers and admirers, who competed for her by giving ever more expensive presents. The press chronicled the splendor of her jewelry, the luxuriousness of her homes in Paris and the French countryside, the extravagance of her carriages. Sometimes she received her lovers wearing a sumptuous, transparent negligee and lying on a polar bear rug. (At the height of their affair, she gave the rug to Natalie, of whom she wrote, "We were passionate, rebels against a woman's lot, voluptuous and cerebral little apostles, rather poetical, full of illusions and dreams. We loved long hair, pretty breasts, pouts, simpers, charm, grace; not boyishness. 'Why try to resemble our enemies?' Natalie-Flossie used to murmur in her little nasal voice." The rug was still on the floor in Natalie's apartment in Paris when she died in 1972 in her ninety-sixth year.)

Although Liane was not above a joke or two at Reinach's expense when he was not around, she developed a genuine affection for him. She was in her early fifties when they met, and she enjoyed his talk and admired his knowledge and intelligence. "Torrents of rain all day yesterday," she wrote in her diary on July 6, 1920, "broken by a pleasant but too-short interlude: Salomon's visit. What an agreeable talker! What a charming reader! He read us Bossuet and tried to read Cocteau but threw the book aside, laughing." Liane even pitied him a little for his erotic confusion. After giving him some letters she had from Pauline Tarn, she wrote, "No doubt he will bequeath them to posterity, fully annotated, according to his habit. I don't think I could possibly give a greater pleasure to Monsieur Reinach, in love with a ghost."

Occasionally he wearied her—she once wrote:

> *Deserving a smack*
> *how he does annoy*
> *neither girl nor boy*
> *Salomon Reinach*

—but generally Liane didn't mind when he obsessively turned the conversation to "the island." In particular he enjoyed bringing her gossip about Natalie Barney, whom they always called Flossie. "A charming note from Salomon," she wrote in her diary, "commiserating with my sorrows and scolding Flossie who is still tucked away at Samois with 'someone.' Mystery and discretion. It enrages Salomon who loves our Flossie more than he admits—perhaps more than he realizes." And sometimes she treated him as if he belonged on the island after all: "I received Salomon like the Queen of Sheba, reclining in a mass of mauve and blue chiffon, lace, scent, cushions, and silk with the Italian greyhound lying at my side. We sipped beverages from China, nibbled sweetmeats from the South and pastries from the Ile de France. I read him some poems by Verhaeren. We talked about Renée Vivien and Flossie."

In addition to Reinach's frequent visits to her, the two also carried on an intense correspondence that began in 1920 and lasted until 1932, when Reinach died. (She did the same with the surrealist poet Max Jacob, who, although homosexual, also fell under her spell.) There is plenty of gossip about Flossie in the letters, but there is also high-minded and erudite discussion of religion, art, and history. And there are moving personal moments when Reinach confesses his fatigue or loneliness: "I blame myself ceaselessly for my life in a shell."

They aren't love letters; Salomon Reinach could not have written a love letter. When in one letter he did write *about* love, he said that love was essentially an illusion and quoted Theophrastus, a student of Aristotle, who said, "Love is the passion of those who have nothing to do." But if they aren't love letters, they are at least letters of a profound friendship. Liane admired his intellect while he admired her taste. His own was deeply conservative. She had him read contemporaries like Max Jacob and Jean Cocteau, whom he had considered "charlatans" and "literary Bolsheviks" but who, he grudgingly admitted, had some value. And there was an emotional bond as well. Liane had, after all, revealed to him her alluring life of sensuality, a life he longed for but could not escape from his shell to enjoy.

A mystical crisis

THOSE WHO knew Salomon Reinach only professionally or who were not inclined to speculate about his relations with women would have been surprised to know he thought he lived in a shell. He was by far the most public archeologist and critic of his time. His lectures at the Louvre were always filled with a faithful following of adoring matrons. His writings appeared everywhere. And he often wrote on current politics, joined activist committees, and contributed to a variety of political causes. He was made to seem even more open and public by his brothers' positions as members of the Chamber of Deputies.

Joseph Reinach in particular was prominent. While the Rothschilds represented the height of Jewish economic power, he was at the height of Jewish political power. He was also the most virulently attacked Jew in the scurrilous, anti-Semitic press of the day, and when he publicly defended Colonel Dreyfus, the Jewish army officer wrongly convicted of treason, the attacks became even worse. He was called a "microbe," a "Jewball." One paper said, "While his monkey face and deformed body bear all the stigmata, all the defects of the race, his hateful soul swollen with venom sums up even better all its malfeasance, all its deadly and perverse genius." Each day Joseph was caricatured as some kind of animal, usually an ape. Once he was assaulted by a mob shouting, "Death to the Jews! Down with Reinach!"

Salomon, who had no political office, had little of this ugliness directed at him personally. Instead he found himself at odds with some of the Jewish community. The Reinachs were not religious Jews. In fact, they favored assimilation based on what they saw as the affinity between revolutionary France and the Jewish race. Consequently, they were anti-Zionist. Salomon was vice president of the Universal Israelite Alliance, which was pro-assimilation, and the founder in 1913 (with the composer Darius Milhaud and the poet Gustave Kahn) of the Friends of Judaism, whose goal was to have both Jews and non-Jews study Judaism as a moral philosophy. But Salomon was attacked by the Zionist press and had to resign these positions.

Reinach had an antipathy for all religion. That and the shell that he drew around his erotic compulsions seem to have begun during several months of personal crisis in the summer of 1877, when he was eighteen.

The previous fall he had entered the Ecole Normale, an elite public all-male college. It was highly intellectual and competitive, and it was where Reinach began to concentrate less on philosophy and more on archeology. But the combination of youth and disorienting intellectualism made the years at the Ecole Normale a turbulent time for most of the students. They formed factions, and there was a lot of roughhousing among them. The dormitories were riddled with venereal disease, and the air reeked of testosterone.

Reinach was torn. He was then a short, slight young man who hardly filled out his clothes. His head was rather large for his body, and his eyes, beneath a large shock of curly black hair that fell over his forehead, looked sad and weary and made him appear older than he was. Searching for a higher world in art, in books, in his writing, and in his studies, he was, by his own avowal, at the same time desperate for friendship and tormented by the thought of homosexuality. Then too, lurking behind the lines of his letters from the period are oblique references to a devastating disappointment in love with a girl named Alice Kohn.

At last, at the beginning of the summer of 1877, Reinach, succumbing to all that was swirling around him, suffered what he called a "mystical crisis" and converted suddenly to Catholicism. This was something of a fad at the time; several other classmates did the same thing. Depressed and frustrated by the intellectualism of the university, they idealized the simple faith of humble people. At Mass they gathered around the organ, singing loudly. Reinach took to ending his letters with "in Jesus Christ." All of this left him even less popular with his classmates than before. He took refuge in Saint Augustine and Pascal, to whom he would return from time to time for the rest of his life, even long after he had lost the faith of his adolescent conversion. But the scars from this desperate period remained. Having once embraced religious belief only to lose his faith, he emerged not just skeptical of religion but feeling superior to it. And he continued to long for Alice Kohn. Ten years later, while writing a brief autobiographical sketch, he mentioned without any introduction or comment that she had just gotten married.

In 1880 Reinach graduated first in his class. Almost immediately he left for Athens despite a bout of bad health from his diabetes. In Athens he met Charles-Joseph Tissot, France's ambassador to Greece and president of the French Hellenic Institute. He was thirty years to the day older than Reinach (they had the same birthday), but the two immediately became close. They were both melancholy men who shared a passion for antiquity, languages, and art. This trip and his virtual apprenticeship with Tissot would be the beginning for Reinach of four years of travel, study, and digs in Greece, Asia Minor, and northern Africa. He continued to publish books and papers on diverse subjects, but his main vocation as an archeologist had been set.

In late September 1880, Reinach visited Melos. He was surprised and offended by the remarkably high prices the local people wanted for antiquities, much higher than on other islands. Three years earlier an oversized statue of Poseidon had been discovered. In a burst of enthusiasm Tissot had proclaimed the statue the "brother of the Venus de Milo." He tried to acquire it for France but failed. It went instead to the museum in Athens, where it remains today. But the Poseidon statue had become linked in Reinach's thinking to the Venus de Milo.

While at Melos, Reinach sought out the son of Louis Brest, still in his position as French consul. He gave Reinach his biased account of the discovery of Venus with its inflated version of his father's role. Reinach later did enough detailed research to learn not to credit the son's account, but the visit shows Reinach's great curiosity about the statue even here at the beginning of his career. Of the great scholars who wrote about the Venus de Milo, he was the only one who ever visited the island where she was found.

A tiara for 200,000 francs

SALOMON REINACH and Adolf Furtwängler developed an unlikely friendship. It began in 1893 when Reinach prominently reviewed Furtwängler's magisterial *Masterpieces of Greek Sculpture*. In the *Gazette des Beaux-Arts* he proclaimed that *Masterpieces* was the book "the most rich in new ideas and the most provocative that has been written in our century on Greek art." In the *Revue Critique* he called the work "the most important that has yet appeared on the history of antique art. One admires on almost each page the vast erudition of the author, the independence of his judgment, the incisive clearness of his style."

Furtwängler was ecstatic that such glowing words had been written by a Frenchman and had appeared in French journals. He wrote to Reinach, and the two men became friends.

Furtwängler was five years older than Reinach, but they were both at similar places in their careers. Each was the leading archeologist in his country at a time when the field was still rather new, and archeologists were romantic and popular figures. Furtwängler had a lucrative position in Berlin. Reinach, with his mountain of publications rising almost daily, with his wealth and his prominent family, was on his way to becoming the conservator of national museums, director of the museum at Saint-Germain-en-Laye, a professor at the school of the Louvre, a member of the Academy of Inscriptions and Belles Lettres and other learned societies, and the director for more than forty years of the *Revue Archéologique,* the leading journal of its kind in France.

Reinach and Furtwängler were frequent and indefatigable battlers in the scholarly journals, and even when they were together socially, neither could resist seizing an opening to prod the other. One pleasant summer evening in Paris in 1901, they were strolling along the Seine. Reinach, speaking in German, began explaining the latest English theories about the history of religions. Furtwängler knew little about the subtleties of English anthropology, but he was enthralled, at least according to Reinach, and felt "as if, leaving a dark room, he had suddenly been flooded with light." Reinach, not missing a beat, expressed no surprise at his effect on his listener. With no pretense of modesty, he replied that he always spoke "with the clarity which the superior education in France makes habitual."

For his part, Furtwängler was ready to pounce whenever Reinach made a mistake, and in 1896, while the two men were in the heat of their disagreements about the Venus de Milo, Reinach made a colossal blunder.

Reinach was part of a committee of experts who advised the Louvre to buy the tiara of Saitapharnes, an ornate cap of gold covered with chains and scenes from Homer in bas-relief. It was represented to be a Greco-Scythian relic from the third century B.C. The price was 200,000 francs, an extravagant amount for the time. The purchase was financed in part by a loan from Salomon Reinach's younger brother, Théodore, who had left politics and was now an archeologist himself. Salomon, alone among the members of the committee, had expressed some doubts about the authenticity of the tiara but had voted for the purchase nonetheless. The committee had been forced to decide in a hurry, since the seller used the clever ploy of announcing that if there was any delay, he would leave for England and sell the tiara to the British Museum.

Reinach had seen Furtwängler at the Louvre while the purchase was being considered and asked his opinion of the relic. Furtwängler was evasive. After the purchase was completed and the seller had retreated back to Russian Georgia, Furtwängler published a polemical paper claiming that the tiara was a blatant forgery. Both Salomon and Théodore Reinach defended the tiara vigorously and were able to refute the specific arguments Furtwängler had made. But the extravagant price and the heat of the controversy attracted the interest of the press. In the end, although his arguments weren't convincing in themselves, Furtwängler's intuition was right. The tiara was a forgery. The forger himself, a man from Odessa named Israel Rouchomowsky, who had received only a fraction of the seller's fee of 200,000 francs, arrived in Paris and proudly demonstrated his skill at creating what appeared to be ancient treasures.

The Louvre lost its money. Since the forger and the tiara's two strongest defenders had been Jewish, the anti-Semitic press seized the opportunity to add their repellent attacks to what had already become an overwrought debate. They chose Salomon as their specific target. Reinach, who had been known since his teenage years as a genius, was ridiculed as an imbecile. Although his friends on the committee urged him to defend himself by revealing the doubts he had had, Reinach refused and took the abuse in silence. He did not want to appear to be shifting the blame from himself to others. This admirable conduct cost him dearly. Because of his silence, he never quite lived the incident down. The affair of the tiara of Saitapharnes was played over again even in his obituaries more than thirty years later.

A goddess in a limekiln

REINACH wrote about the Venus de Milo not long after visiting Melos in 1880, but his first important essay on it appeared in May 1890 in the *Gazette des Beaux-Arts*. He began with a statement, emphasized by his own italics, that Furtwängler would later quote slyly in his own work on the statue: "I repeat today what I wrote ten years ago: *The Venus de Milo is a mystery*." The rest of the article, in which he summarized the story of the discovery as well as the various restorations that had been proposed over the years, is important for one reason: Reinach placed himself exactly in the mainstream of French thinking about the statue by insisting that the Venus de Milo was created in the fourth century B.C., during the classical age of Greek art. He too had been seduced by the desperate desire of the French, as strong in 1890 as it had been when the statue was discovered seven decades earlier, that the Venus de Milo was classical and *not,* as some heretical voices with German accents liked to argue, Hellenistic.

The most dramatic piece of evidence that the statue was

Hellenistic was the base with the inscription ". . . andros son of Menides citizen of Antioch of Meander made the statue." Reinach denied that this inscription belonged with the Venus de Milo. His reasoning was both original and peculiar. He said that he had concluded that the place where the statue was found was an ancient limestone kiln. Reinach makes this supposition without any proof. It was merely his ingenious means of explaining away the inscribed base: It and the Venus were there to be burned as random pieces of marble.

With the base disposed of, Reinach directly confronts the question of the date of the statue. He says that from political history we know that Melos was an Athenian colony from 416 to 404 B.C. From art history we know that "the style of the Venus de Milo is that of attic sculptors of the same period, that is to say of the students and successors of Phidias." He knows, he says, that "today it is fashionable in Germany to attribute the Venus to a much more recent era," but this is due to a bias for denigration "from which even our masterpieces themselves do not escape." No, he says, the "analogy of style, of execution, of sentiment that one notes between the Venus de Milo and the sculptures of the pediments of the Parthenon [i.e., the Elgin marbles] suffice to refute every hypothesis that would place the artist of our statue more recently than the first half of the fourth century B.C." Though he admits he can't prove that mathematically, "taste has its truths, like reason and the heart." This is not science or even art history. It's wishful thinking, exactly the same sort of wishful thinking displayed more than two generations earlier by Quatremère de Quincy when he wrote that the statue must have come from the hand or the school of Praxiteles.

Meisterforschung

FURTWÄNGLER had Reinach in his sights from the beginning of his chapter on the Venus de Milo in *Masterpieces of Greek Sculp-*

ture, published three years later. To a modern reader, *Master-pieces* is a bit like an archeological ruin: an impressive, inspiring, even intimidating relic of an age now past, an age that believed that with enough hard work and a little inspiration it was possible to know everything. Furtwängler, ever the brilliant cataloger, here attempted nothing less than to write a history of the development of Greek sculpture by examining detail by detail the individual innovations of the greatest masters of antiquity. It was a conscious attempt to write a book that would rival and supplant Winckelmann.

Such a sweeping endeavor had always been considered impossible, because the works of the great masters had all disappeared. They were known only through Roman copies or from descriptions in the writings of ancient travelers. Furtwängler tried to prove that these Roman statues were often direct copies of Greek originals, not just loose versions of them, and that they were copies of the most esteemed works of ancient times, for why would a status-conscious Roman commission a copy of an inferior work? As Furtwängler wrote in his preface, the Roman copies

> have preserved that pick from the masterpieces of the classical epoch which pleased ancient taste and connoisseurship in the times of highest culture. It is the pick of the best and the most famous that antiquity possessed. Among these copies it is that we must look for the masterpieces mentioned by the authors, for the statues that made epochs or initiated movements. Were we to possess only copies of the noble creations of a Raphael, a Michelangelo, or a Rembrandt, these would certainly be better worth one's study than the hosts of other originals of the time.

Furtwängler believed that his precise, systematic analysis of the form and style of these Roman statues, when compared with descriptions of lost masterpieces in antique texts, could lead to identifying Roman statues as copies of specific lost masterpieces of specific Greek masters. More than that, the copies could then be used to discover the individual contributions from each master to the evolution of Greek art. German, a language always ready to invent a new word, calls this process *Meisterforschung*—master research. By *Meisterforschung* Furtwängler wanted to show that the Greek genius, which had always seemed monolithic and anonymous, could be completely recast as a historical sequence of identifiable works by certain specific individuals.

Many of the reconstructions and conclusions Furtwängler made have been discredited, and *Meisterforschung* is a method that is considered doubtful today. Yet *Masterpieces* lives on. It was reprinted in English translation as late as 1964, and its most spectacular reconstruction has often been attacked without being disproved. Furtwängler, in a display of his astonishing visual memory and ability for synthesis, recognized that a head in Bologna belonged to a statue in Dresden, and that the properly reconstructed statue was a copy of the Lemnian Athena of Phidias, a work previously known only by written descriptions. Ancient writers identified twenty-one works by Phidias, all now lost, including the giant statue of Athena in the Parthenon. Furtwängler had, as if by magic, brought one back to life.

He begins the chapter entitled "The Venus of Milo" with a warning shot at Reinach: "The Venus of Milo is still a center of eager controversy, and only recently a distinguished archeologist pronounced the whole question to be an insoluble riddle. Before resigning myself to this conclusion, I should like to be sure that no means of solution has been left untried."

Furtwängler believed that the hand with the apple, the fragments of a left arm, and the inscribed base that were found in the niche all belonged to the statue and that "Alexandros son of Menides citizen of Antioch" was the name of the true sculptor. As evidence that the base belonged, Furtwängler cites Debay's drawing, which does in fact show the inscribed base fitting perfectly to the base of the statue. And he reads between the lines of earlier accounts to make a telling point:

> When the statue and the separate pieces were brought to the Louvre and the first attempts (quite unbiased by preconceived theories) were made to put them together, it was at once noticed that the inscribed fragment exactly fitted the breakage on the right side of the plinth, nor did any of the witnesses present—savants like Clarac, Quatremère de Quincy, and Saint-Victor among them—ever express the smallest doubt as to this, or suggest that the inscribed fragment did not fit. It must therefore have appeared quite obvious that the inscribed piece belonged to the statue.

So now, Furtwängler concludes, "it is very easy to see why the piece was not fastened on, and why it disappeared. . . . Since the statue was to be presented to the king as a work of Praxiteles . . . it would naturally be inconvenient to have to affix to it the name of an unknown sculptor." Then Furtwängler fearlessly proceeds to the logical conclusion of what he has just said: "The disappearance of the inscription, in my opinion, is only a proof of its genuineness. It was an awkward witness, and had to be quietly got out of the way." These are words that still raise temperatures in the hallways and back offices of the Louvre.

Furtwängler scoffs at Reinach's notion that the niche that held the statue was in reality a limekiln. He had helped excavate many former kilns, he stated, and the statues had always been broken into small pieces before burning, so the litter of broken marble made the kilns unmistakable. "Not even the most ignorant person," he said in his typically politic way, "could ever mistake such a limekiln for an architectural 'niche.' Reinach's supposition has no foundation in fact."

Furtwängler turns to Ravaisson, who in his last paper also wrote that the inscribed base was a later addition.

Therefore [Furtwängler says] he too must believe that the piece belongs to the statue. He does not, however, deign to explain how it happened that the Mars or Theseus grouped with the Venus came to disappear (without, however, the hand with the apple that rested upon his shoulder also disappearing!), and to be replaced by a little terminal figure with an inscribed basis picked up anywhere.

Furtwängler relegates this observation to a footnote, but it's still a crushing blow. How *could* the male figure disappear and the hand with the apple that was supposedly resting on its shoulder still remain? This direct and obvious objection, which no one else had thought to make, completely destroys the reconstructions of Venus beside a warrior that both Quatremère and Ravaisson had proposed. To see her as part of such a group, where she gently turns the man's attention from war to her, is appealing and in keeping with so many statues in a similar pose. Unfortunately, that reconstruction cannot be true.

Unfortunately for Furtwängler, the reconstruction he proposed cannot be true either. Since he had argued that both the hand with the apple and the inscribed base belonged with the statue, he had to use them in his reconstruction. And since Debay's drawing shows a square hole in the top of the inscribed base, he had to use that, too. Furtwängler concludes that a rectangular column, tall enough to rise just above the goddess's waist, fit over the hole. Her left elbow rested on top of the column while the hand holding the apple extends forward, palm up.

That makes a graceful composition. Similar images exist in Greek art and, quite provocatively, on coins from Melos. But there is one devastating objection: Voutier's drawings, published by Ravaisson the previous year, clearly show the beardless herm, not a column, standing inside the inscribed base. Furthermore, although there was no trace of a statue of Mars to support Quatremère's and Ravaisson's reconstructions, a fact Furtwängler

Furtwängler's reconstruction of the Venus de Milo

had gleefully noted, no trace of his proposed column was ever found either.

Furtwängler, cornered by his own argument, decided that Voutier's drawing was "quite arbitrary," because he had put the herm in the base where it didn't belong at all for purposes of his sketch. Clearly, though, it's Furtwängler who is being arbitrary. There's no reason to believe that Voutier stuck a random herm into the inscribed base just to bedevil a German archeologist seventy years later.

In conclusion, Furtwängler returns to *Meisterforschung* to try to establish the antecedents for the Venus de Milo. He contends that a statue by Skopas showing Venus admiring herself in a shield resting on her left knee was one inspiration. The second came from images of Tyche, the patron goddess of Melos, holding an apple. Although Furtwängler thought this combination was "not altogether happy," he considered the artist to be "at least a man who could make a traditional type his own, and reproduce it with all the freshness of a new technique."

This conclusion, as opposed to Furtwängler's reconstruction, is quite convincing. To a modern reader it's curious that Furtwängler—and how he would recoil in rage if he were to hear this—is most convincing when he is least scientific. He's at his best when he looks closely at the art and describes it as a connoisseur. Here, for instance, he describes the changes the artist had to make because he had removed the shield from the composition by Skopas. It's a long passage, but worth quoting because it reveals the exquisite sensibility beneath all Furtwängler's bluster:

> The main lines of the composition—the raised foot, the turn of the nude torso to the left, the gesture of the arms—are all meaningless when the shield is removed, and are adopted here only because they form a graceful pose. Yet the artist was no slavish imitator, like those Roman copyists who grouped together at random and without alteration traditional types of Ares and

Aphrodite. He was one who knew how to subject the composition to a thorough remodeling for a definite purpose. All the movements that had the shield for center might be made less pronounced now that the shield was removed. Thus the inclination of the body and head to the left and forward being lessened, the whole figure becomes more erect, and the eyes look straight into space. The right shoulder droops less and the right arm falls more perpendicularly—all this evidently because the goddess is no longer looking at her image in the bright surface. . . . The drapery too has been altered. As the shield is not there to keep up the left side of the cloak, and there is accordingly no reason why one side should be higher than the other, both sides have been allowed to slip down as far as they can without falling off. The torso, especially from a back view, gains in sensuous charm by the change, but the drapery would always produce an impression of insecurity even were the right hand still intact to keep it in place.

In this passage, where Furtwängler leaves his theories behind and becomes pure connoisseur, he has out-Frenched the French. None of them—not Quatremère, not Clarac, not even Ravaisson—ever wrote about the statue with such precision, intensity, and good sense. But he had made an implied boast at the start of his paper that he would succeed where the French had failed and settle all the mysteries of the Venus de Milo. For all Furtwängler's imposing intellect and erudition, the mysteries remained.

An inscription reappears

WHEN Reinach reviewed *Masterpieces,* he did not accept Furtwängler's dating or reconstruction. He simply asserted that Furtwängler was wrong. Over the next few years, though,

Reinach produced a series of papers scrutinizing the roles of Voutier, d'Urville, Marcellus, Brest, Rivière, and the rest. He also considered the proposed reconstructions of other scholars, and then proved their impossibility one by one. Then, in 1897, aided by a lucky discovery in a forgotten gallery in the Louvre, Reinach was able to create his own reconstruction and—sweet victory!—to prove at last that Furtwängler's reconstruction was wrong.

Voutier's drawings showed two herms and two inscribed bases. One was the herm with the youth's head standing in the base inscribed with the name of a sculptor. The Louvre still possessed this herm, although the base, of course, had been lost. The second herm, a bearded man, was still in the Louvre as well, but its inscribed base had also disappeared; in fact, the base's existence seems to have been entirely forgotten until Voutier's sketches reappeared. He had copied the inscriptions on both bases clearly enough to be read. The disputed base clearly showed ". . . andros son of Menides citizen of Antioch." The second inscription, the one on the base supporting the bearded herm, read enigmatically, "Theodoridas son of Agesistratos."

Reinach initially took this to be the name of another sculptor, and published that conclusion in January 1897. Only a few days later a German scholar named Hiller von Gaertringen visited Reinach. Von Gaertringen's current task was collecting inscriptions from the Aegean islands for the Academy in Berlin. When Reinach showed him the inscription in Voutier's drawing, von Gaertringen was reminded of another inscription he had recently seen, and after a few minutes of research the two men found it. Charles Tissot, Reinach's mentor from Athens, had copied it in 1878 on Melos. It read, "Theodoridas, son of Laistratos, to Poseidon." The scholars immediately saw that "Agesistratos" in Voutier's drawing was a mistake; he had incorrectly repeated two Greek letters. If the extra letters were removed, Voutier's drawing would also say "Laistratos." Both the inscription Tissot copied and the inscription on the base of the bearded herm referred to the same Theodoridas, son of Laistratos.

How Tissot came to copy the inscription made it even more interesting. He had seen it while trying to buy the newly discovered statue of Poseidon on Melos for France. Several other statues, originally grouped with the Poseidon, had been found at the same time. One of these was a robed man missing his head, set on a base with the inscription "Theodoridas, son of Laistratos, to Poseidon." This statue must have been of Theodoridas himself. He must have been the one who built this elaborate shrine to the god of the sea. And he had also dedicated the bearded herm found with the Venus de Milo. Therefore—and Reinach found this so exciting he put it in italics in his paper—*"if the Venus is contemporary with this herm, she is thus also contemporary with Poseidon."* He had reason to be excited. The lettering on the two inscriptions was carved in a form that dated to the fourth century B.C., exactly the period into which French scholars had always longed to place the Venus de Milo.

There were other reasons beyond the two inscriptions to link the Venus and the Poseidon. Both statues had been sculpted in two halves that joined just below the waist, and in each case the line of juncture was concealed by drapery. Both had been discovered in a kind of niche, and although the Poseidon was taller than the Venus, just as gods were always taller than goddesses in Greek sculpture, the two statues were carved in the same scale. They were not by the same sculptor. The Poseidon was artistically inferior to the Venus, but otherwise the similarities were too strong to overlook.

Buttressed by the two inscriptions to Theodoridas in fourth-century characters, Reinach persisted in dating both statues to that period, but he was uneasy about this conclusion. The headless statue of Theodoridas was similar in style to the Poseidon. Other scholars, French scholars among them, thought both these statues came from the Hellenistic era, around 100 B.C. or, maddeningly, exactly the period in which Furtwängler placed the Venus de Milo.

Reinach couldn't see his way out of the confusion. "The question of the date of our statue," he concludes somewhat lamely, "must be entirely left to the judgment of historians of art."

The following year, 1898, Reinach had progressed far enough in his thinking to publish his own reconstruction of the Venus de Milo. He still insisted that the statue had been found in a limekiln, and he believed that the evidence of the two inscriptions mentioning Theodoridas meant that the Venus was originally in a group with Poseidon from the fourth century. Placing the statue with Poseidon meant that the Venus de Milo wasn't Venus at all. Instead, Reinach said she was Amphitrite, the wife of Poseidon. Since the statue of the god shows him standing with a trident in his right hand, Reinach places the Venus to his left, holding a trident in her left hand. This, he says, explains the direction of her gaze—she is looking out to sea "as if she wanted to sound the horizon."

Two years later, in 1900, Reinach got an unexpected confirmation for at least some of his conjectures. The base of the bearded herm with the name Theodoridas inscribed on it, as Voutier had drawn, suddenly reappeared. It had been in the Louvre all along.

For almost seventy years the base had been attached to a small, insignificant funerary monument. This absurd reconstruction had been stuck under a staircase along with other presumed junk from antiquity. There it rested until two conservators, who had taken it upon themselves to put some order to the mess under the stairway, realized to their great surprise that here was the base inscribed to Theodoridas that Salomon Reinach had been writing about.

The base confirmed every one of Reinach's suppositions. The lettering was in a fourth-century style. And Voutier had indeed mistakenly duplicated two letters in the inscription when he made his sketch. The inscription did read "Theodoridas, son of Laistratos" and was identical to the name on the base of the headless statue found with the statue of Poseidon.

And the base offered a spectacular proof that Furtwängler was wrong. He had insisted that Voutier had stuck the two herms into the bases for purposes of his drawing. Why, Reinach had always demanded in his papers, would Voutier do such a thing? Now that one of the inscribed bases had been found, it was a simple matter to place the bearded herm inside it to see if it fit. If it did, that would prove that the two belonged together and that Voutier had not arbitrarily, as Furtwängler claimed, put them together.

The result was so important that when the discovery of the base was announced at a meeting of the Académie des Inscriptions, plaster casts of both the bearded herm and the Theodoridas base were on hand. At the dramatic moment, after the conflicting theories of Furtwängler and Reinach had been carefully explained, a curator from the Louvre slid the cast of the bearded herm into the cast of the inscribed base and—*voilà!*—the fit was perfect.

The patience of a saint

FURTWÄNGLER did not meekly submit to this trouncing. In a paper he wrote for the Academy of Bavaria in 1902, he came roaring back full of assurance and contemptuous of anyone who would question him. And now that Reinach had had his day, there was new information that supported Furtwängler's theories.

In 1900 and again in 1902 the French scholar Etienne Michon, adjunct conservator of antiquities at the Louvre, published articles in the *Revue des Etudes Grecques* that were the result of many months of diligent research in maritime records, Louvre archives, published memoirs, and private family papers concerning the discovery of the Venus de Milo and its transportation to the Louvre. In the course of these researches he discovered information about the purchase of a statue of Hermes, signed by a sculptor named Antiphanes, found on Melos in 1827. The statue came from one of three niches in an ancient wall. The first was the one in which the Venus had been discovered; at its entrance an inscription said that a man named Bakkhios had dedicated the niche to Hermes and Hercules. The second niche, about twenty paces away, contained the statue of Hermes signed by Antiphanes. In the third niche, another twenty paces down the wall, only the feet remained of the statue that once stood there, but an inscription revealed that it had been a statue of a man named Hagesimenes, whose father and brother had dedicated the niche to Hermes and Hercules.

These two gods were the patrons of gymnasiums. According to Furtwängler, their ubiquitous presence made it clear that this had once been the wall of a gymnasium, and that the Venus de Milo had been displayed in her niche as part of the decorations. Thus, he concludes in triumph, she had been found in situ, as he had maintained from the start, and not in a limekiln, as Reinach continued to believe.

The fact that the bearded herm fit in the newly rediscovered base didn't impress Furtwängler at all. "These two little herms," he said, "simple offerings to the god of the gymnasium, derive from an époque older than the gymnasium of Melos. Later, when the niches had been constructed and provided with large statues from the second to the first centuries B.C., the herms were employed as decoration of the niche dedicated by Bakkhios." And he continued to insist that Voutier had put one of the herms in the base with the signature where it didn't belong. That base, Furtwängler still defiantly believed, belonged to the statue and gave the name of its sculptor and, because of the reference to Antioch, its true date.

Salomon Reinach took all this as a direct, personal affront. He could hardly control his rage. "I admit," he wrote in a paper he published in response a few months later, "that I sometimes have trouble arguing coolly with Mr. Furtwängler. Even when he is wrong, he has a passion to be always right that would put the patience of a saint to a harsh test. That said, I am going to be very objective." Reinach, it's fair to say, failed to achieve this goal.

Furtwängler now dated the bearded herm with the Theodoridas inscription to the end of the fifth century B.C. Reinach wrote,

"He was previously content to say that it was 'older than the Empire'; I am the one who determined the date." Furtwängler now put the two herms in different eras. Reinach retaliated: "He thought formerly that the two herms were contemporary; I am the one who corrected him." And when Furtwängler repeated his belief in his reconstruction with Venus resting her left forearm on a pillar ("Of which," Reinach added in a parenthesis, "no one has found the slightest fragment!"), Reinach smugly added a footnote: "Mr. Furtwängler, however, must know that I have demonstrated the impossibility of this tendentious restitution." But he could not stop there: "What a shame that the tribunal in The Hague does not settle scientific disputes! I would readily agree to a meeting before judges, who wouldn't be archeologists but rule by the simple lights of common sense and by what is most likely. He would be given a grueling time."

With all that out of his system, Reinach then calmly explained the crux of their differences. They agreed that the statue of Poseidon was Hellenistic, which means it dated from the first or second century B.C. Furtwängler thought the Venus came from the same period but that the Poseidon had no relation to it. For him, they were two separate works. Reinach thought that the Venus was really an Amphitrite from the Greek classical period, the fourth century B.C., and was part of a group with the Poseidon.

But then how could Reinach agree that the Poseidon was Hellenistic? By pure invention. He contended that the original Poseidon had indeed been created in the fourth century, but it had been damaged or destroyed and "replaced by a mediocre copy from the Roman era." He had dropped his limekiln theory without a word; the three niches with statues in a row and the dedications to Hermes and Hercules were too strong proof that the location had been a gymnasium.

Reinach concluded by saying he hoped someday to convince Furtwängler, whom, in a conciliatory spirit, he calls his "eminent friend and contradictor." Reinach failed in this goal as well. Neither man ever retreated from his position.

Lilacs and tulips

INSTEAD they apparently agreed to disagree about the Venus de Milo. Since each was hyperactively busy and each was confident he had solved the mystery, the men resumed other projects. Furtwängler's second great work after *Masterpieces of Greek Sculpture* was *Of Antique Gems*. He was attracted to ancient carved gemstones because enough had survived to allow a thorough historical analysis. The first two volumes reproduce and discuss thousands of carved stones, which are cataloged according to content, form, and chronology. The third volume is a historical survey that one critic called the "phenomenal achievement of its marvelously productive century."

In 1900 Furtwängler had also begun re-excavating a temple on the island of Aegina that had been bought by the same King Ludwig of Bavaria who owned the theater on Melos when the Venus was discovered. Furtwängler made important finds, and the digs continued. In the fall of 1907 he traveled to Aegina again despite suffering from a fever. When his condition deteriorated, he was taken to a hospital in Athens, where, after several days of intense pain, he died on October 11, at age fifty-four. The city of Athens dedicated an honorary grave to him over which a Sphinx found on Aegina stands watch.

Reinach never again found such a worthy combatant among archeologists. In the obituary he wrote for the *Revue Archéologique,* he called Furtwängler "the greatest archeologist of our times. . . . We remain, almost incredulous, by the side of this prematurely opened grave, astonished, even after so many proofs, that an untimely death was able to strike down this superb athlete and to make him so soon what he will always remain for our science—a hero." Later he added, "No one has inherited his great and legitimate authority."

Reinach lived until 1932. In the *Revue Archéologique* he continued to report on any new papers or theories about the Venus de

Milo. To his dismay, the story of the scuffle on the beach on Melos continued to live, and Reinach continued dutifully but wearily to contradict it. Nor were any of the more responsible scholarly papers of any great interest.

His later years were marred by what became known as the Glozel affair. Numerous carvings and tablets, apparently from the Iron Age, were found near the French village of that name. They bore little resemblance to other Iron Age discoveries, and most experts believed they were fakes. Reinach, however, visited Glozel. Convinced that the finds were genuine, he became their most prominent and vocal champion. Eventually, though, as his health declined and he saw so much other work going unfinished, the Glozel controversy wearied him, and he complained about it sadly to Liane de Pougy. (The question of Glozel remains unresolved. Most archeologists still believe the artifacts are forgeries, although some modern chemical dating techniques tend to support their authenticity.)

As his health deteriorated, mostly because of complications from diabetes, Reinach could walk only with help, and even then his pain was agonizing. Still, he attended scholarly meetings when the discussion was something he considered important. Finally he was confined to his bed. Bernard Berenson visited him. "Old Salomon," he wrote, "looked like a dying eagle, really beautiful, but very sad, and I fear not resigned."

One day in the spring of 1932 he sent his car for Liane de Pougy. It was the one time she was permitted in the home of Madame Reinach. Liane "saw him lying on a sofa, depressed, unhappy, his fine prophet's face scarred with pain. When I came into the room he could hardly restrain his tears." The room was tidy, fresh, bright, and lined with books in perfect order. Salomon had covered his legs, which were now completely useless, with a woolen rug. His forced inactivity made him frustrated and angry. Occasionally the pain that shot through him made him groan despite himself. After a short while Madame Reinach joined them. When Liane left, Salomon managed a smile and secretly blew her a kiss from his fingertips. Outside

Madame Reinach gave her a bouquet of lilacs and tulips. In September he wrote to Liane, "I can say that, for the first time, life itself is a burden to me and I would happily take a ticket for another sphere."

SALOMON REINACH died on November 4, 1932. With his passing, more than a century of scholarship about the Venus de Milo came to a close. No one since has written anything approaching the importance of the work of Quatremère, Ravaisson, Furtwängler, or Reinach. And certainly no one has matched the passion of those men. Confronted with the questions inspired by the Venus de Milo—what is it? who made it and when? what was the original position of the arms?—scholars of the nineteenth century were eager to confront the void and propose answers.

Such audacity carries risks with it, and in one sense the work of these venerable scholars was a failure, partly because their thinking was clouded by nationalism, French or German. But it is fair to say that those same scholars would be dismayed by the work of their modern counterparts: It would seem cool, analytic, even timid when compared to theirs. Nationalism has dropped away from contemporary scholarship, only to be replaced by other political agendas based on gender, sexuality, or, as we saw in the contemporary writing about the supposed fight on the beach in Melos, a desperate desire to discover victims of Western culture. The older scholars had an enthusiasm for the statue, almost a gratitude for its presence in their lives. Their appreciation shone through their prose even at its most academic. Contemporary scholars curb their enthusiasm, if indeed they have any. They want to appear superior to what Geoffrey Grigson in *The Goddess of Love* called "that rather chill giantess in the Louvre, the Venus de Milo; by whom most of us now are vaguely unmoved, I suspect, or even repelled." The result is that little of originality or of particular importance has appeared since Reinach and Furtwängler's Olympian quarrels in the scholarly journals of their day.

Contemporary scholars, when they need to confront the Venus de Milo with more than a snide remark, turn to the authoritative source closest to hand, and that turns out to be Furtwängler. His reconstruction, with the goddess resting her left arm on a pillar, appears repeatedly, sometimes credited and sometimes not, to the exclusion of any other reconstruction. His triumph over his rivals in France—and in Germany, for that matter—is complete; but it is a triumph by default rather than by carefully considered judgment of the evidence.

With all the evidence taken into account, it becomes clear that Furtwängler's contribution *was* immense, although he made his share of errors. But, free of nationalism and of modern academic politics, and with all the evidence at hand, perhaps we ourselves can assume some of the nineteenth-century vigor and boldly risk confronting the statue and its mysteries.

V I

A Goddess with Golden Hair

I N   H I S   dialogue *Protagoras,* written around 360 B.C., Plato mentioned sculptors briefly:

> "And suppose your idea was to go to Polyclitus of Argos or Phidias of Athens and pay them fees for your own benefit, and someone asked you in what capacity you thought of paying this money to them, what would you answer?"
> "I should say, in their capacity as sculptors."
> "To make you what?"
> "A sculptor, obviously."

About five centuries later, while the Roman Empire was at its height, the satirist Lucian, who had been a sculptor himself as a young man, warned against such a life:

> If you become a sculptor, you will be no more than a workman, tiring yourself physically, receiving only a meager wage, a common laborer, a man lost in the crowd, bowing and scraping to the rich, humble servant of the eloquent, living like a hare and destined to become the prey of the strong. Even if you were a Phidias or a Polyclitus and created a thousand master-

pieces, it is your art that would be praised and, of those who admired your work, there would not be one, if he had any common sense, who would wish to take your place. Skillful as you might be, you would always be regarded as an artisan, a mere mechanical, a man living by the work of his hands.

In Greek and Roman times, despite the taste for sculpture in both societies, sculptors as a group hovered on an ill-defined plateau among skilled tradesmen. There was such a thing as art in the ancient world, but there wasn't really such a thing as an artist in the modern sense. A sculptor might be considered more elevated than a sandal maker, say, but he was still a trades-man and part of that social group. A Greek seeing a sculptor, sweaty and covered with flakes of marble, his hands rough and gnarled from his work, would have the same reaction Lucian had so many years later. However much a sculptor's work might be admired, few in ancient times would want to change places with one.

There were exceptions. Phidias, for example, was both a masterful sculptor and a successful building contractor. He oversaw the construction of the Parthenon in Athens and the temple of Zeus at Olympia, and created the massive statues of Athena for the Parthenon and Zeus for Olympia. Although his talent as a sculptor was supreme, he owed his wealth and pow-erful position to his friendship with the great Pericles, who then dominated Athens and placed him in charge of the construction of the temples. That position in turn gave Phidias the power to let lucrative contracts. Unfortunately for him, his exalted status didn't last. In time the enemies of Pericles accused Phidias first of embezzlement, then of impiety, and he died in prison.

References like these from Plato and Lucian have become part of a large but patchy fabric of similar written references from across the centuries of antiquity. Scholars labor over every detail of that fabric, because what we know of Greek sculptors comes from occasional and often offhand references in the ancient texts that have survived. Some of these texts are histories or travelogues from writers such as Herodotus, Pliny, Plutarch, and Pausanias, and some are inscriptions, such as those on the bases for statues that have long since disappeared. Without this written record we would know nothing about the work of Phidias, Skopas, Polyclitus, Praxiteles, or any other great artist of the classical age, because none of their works, not even a single fragment of a single statue that we can identify, has survived.

The only way we can get an approximation of what their work looked like is by basic, obvious *Meisterforschung*—that is, by linking a description in one of the texts to one or more surviving statues that appear to be later copies. Sometimes the correspondence between text and copy is exact and the identification can be absolute. One of the most famous Greek statues both then and now was the Diskobolos (Discus Thrower) by Myron. Lucian happened to describe it this way:

> Surely, I said, you do not speak of the discus thrower, who is bent over into the throwing position, is turned toward the hand that holds the discus, and has the opposite knee gently flexed, like the one [that] will straighten up again after the throw? Not that one, he said, for the *Diskobolos* of which you speak is one of the works of Myron.

And enough statues that match this description have been unearthed to show how widely copied the Diskobolos was and to let us see its shape.

At least we see its general shape, since the copies are not identical. The way the knees are bent, the way the hand holds the discus, the angle of the head, and many other details may all be different from one copy to another. Occasionally, some misguided scholar will try to reconstruct the original by taking the feet from one copy, the head from another, and so on, but this is a useless, misleading exercise, since the resulting mélange must inevitably show the taste of the modern restorer rather than that of the antique sculptor.

Furthermore, it's a good possibility that *none* of the copyists duplicated the statue exactly and that they didn't really care whether they did or not. There is a slight chance that one or another of the copyists could have been working from a cast, but more likely they were working from a copy and were not trying to make an exact replica. Instead they wanted to make their own version of what had become a standard subject, just as an early Renaissance master might paint an Annunciation in much the same style and pose as other Annunciations but with his own distinctive touches.

The inexactness of copies is the weakness in *Meisterforschung* as Furtwängler used it. He pushed the connections too hard and made bold but insupportable assumptions, as did Reinach, Ravaisson, and other archeologists before him. It's an easy thing to do. In the quotations above, Plato and Lucian both mention the same two sculptors, Phidias and Polyclitus. We know from a number of other sources that indeed their work was revered in the ancient world. But suppose that the reference in Plato was the only source for the names. One's impulse would still be to assume that these two sculptors were considered masters in ancient times. Why else would Plato mention them? But without corroborating sources, it would also be possible that through some quirk of taste Plato happened to like the work of these two while few others did. Or, since Plato's passage clearly concerns paying a sculptor to become his apprentice, perhaps Phidias and Polyclitus were known more for their teaching than for their own work.

To complicate matters further, we tend to assume that the ancient world valued the works that have come down to us the same way we do, but that may not be true. The Venus de Milo, never mentioned in any surviving text, stuck in a niche in a gymnasium on a minor island, is a perfect example. Marble sculpture itself, though certainly important, was less important to the Greeks than all the marbles in our museums would indicate. It appears that the Greeks considered painting a higher art than sculpture and painters the greater craftsmen; but since so little Greek painting survives, its role is much diminished in our thinking about the ancient world. Although sculptors ranked below painters, they probably ranked above those who made mosaics. Sculptors at least signed their work while the creators of the glorious ancient mosaics did not.

There were even other forms of sculpture that were considered superior to marble. The most highly prized was a technique called chryselephantine, in which a wooden core was covered with plates of ivory representing flesh and worked gold for clothing. Because of its expense, it was rarely used except for cult statues in temples like Phidias's Athena in the Parthenon. The presence of these precious materials made chryselephantine statues a constant temptation to ransackers, and only a few fragments of the technique have survived. Next in importance came bronze, and few bronze statues remain because that metal is easily melted down for other purposes. Then at last came marble. It was used most often for works of less importance— funerary reliefs, copies of bronze statues, and carvings on the pediments of temples. The Elgin marbles, which come from the pediments of a temple, reside at the center of our thinking about Greek art. But the Greeks themselves thought so little of these temple decorations that they rarely bothered to record the names of the men who carved them.

Part of the appeal of classical marbles is the pure whiteness of the stone, yet that pure whiteness isn't at all what the original audience for these statues saw. The statues were painted, often in colors that would seem garish to us, and given metal weapons or loaded with jewelry that might be mere trinkets in some cases but real gold and gems in others. The Venus de Milo had a band around her right biceps—the hole for the pin to hold it in place is still clearly visible. She had earrings valuable enough that robbers broke off her earlobes to get to them. We know she had a choker around her neck, since the slight groove where it rested is clear, and since the goddess loved necklaces, the statue was most likely adorned with them, too. And she probably wore a tiara, and bracelets around her missing wrists. The drapery around her hips and legs might have been painted in a pattern with varied hues. Ancient authors often describe Venus as "golden," so her hair was probably painted yellow or perhaps even gilded. Greeks liked to paint lips bright red, so she would have seemed to us to be wearing lipstick. They liked to paint eyes red, too. Probably her flesh was left unpainted, but the exposed marble would have been polished to a high shine and might even have been waxed. All this paint, jewelry, and polish, which to the modern eye seems extraneous and in the worst possible taste, made statues appear more lifelike to the Greeks. If we could see marble statues as they were in antiquity, adorned with jewels and bursting with radiant color, we might feel the same way.

Aesthetics aside, the loss of these baubles can make identification of statues difficult or impossible. A bronze of a bearded god from about 460 B.C. was recovered from a shipwreck. His left arm is extended and his right is cocked to throw a long weapon, which is missing. If the weapon was a spear, the god is Zeus; if it was a trident, then he's Poseidon. That's the best we can do. Another beautiful bronze, this one from the fourth century B.C., shows a handsome young man holding some missing object in his outstretched right hand. If it was a Gorgon's head, he's Perseus; if it was an apple, he's Hercules; or perhaps he was holding something entirely different that would make him some other character. The missing arms of the Venus de Milo have complicated her identification. Most likely she is a Venus, but if the statue had been found with intact arms holding a trident, as Salomon Reinach believed she was originally displayed, then she was an Amphitrite. That would have settled any question of her identity, but her fame would have been reduced. It's difficult to imagine the phrase "Amphitrite de Milo" becoming part of the popular vocabulary.

Foam-born

APHRODITE is the Greek goddess the Romans knew as Venus, which is what Europeans have called her since Roman times. Venus/Aphrodite is sometimes called the goddess of love and of beauty, which is true enough but not the full story. She had two natures. In one, Aphrodite Urania, she was the goddess of pure, exalted love. As Aphrodite Pandemos she was the goddess of lust and sex. In some of her temples, such as the one in Corinth, the priestesses were prostitutes. In certain Greek cities of Asia Minor a young woman had to offer herself for sale at the temple to have sex with a stranger one time, with the money going to the temple, before she could marry. Aphrodite was less important during archaic times, but her significance grew with the years. By the time the Venus de Milo was created, the goddess was widely revered.

One clear account of her origin and adventures is in *The Greek Myths* by Robert Graves. Mother Earth emerged from Chaos and gave birth to a son, Uranus. He in turn fathered the twelve Titans. Cronus, the youngest, urged on by Mother Earth and armed by her with a flint sickle, castrated Uranus. Cronus held his father's genitals in his left hand—considered the sinister hand for eons afterward—before he threw them into the sea. Foam gathered around them, and from it, fully formed, sprang Aphrodite.

In addition to her beauty, she had a girdle that made men fall in love with whomever wore it. Other goddesses asked her to lend it to them, but she seldom did.

Zeus, the son of Cronus who in turn overthrew his father to become king of the gods, gave Aphrodite to Hephaestus (Vulcan to the Romans) as a wife. Hephaestus was lame and worked constantly at his forge. Aphrodite began a long affair with Ares (Mars) and had three children by him, although Hephaestus thought they were his own.

One day the two lovers tarried too long in bed in Ares's palace, and the sun saw them as he rose. He told Hephaestus, who immediately forged a net of gold chains. These chains were so fine they were invisible but still strong enough to be unbreakable. Hephaestus draped the net on the posts of his bed. When Aphrodite, happy and smiling, returned home from Ares's bed, Hephaestus told her he was leaving for a short holiday. She wished him well and, once he had left, immediately sent for Ares.

The lovers spent the night in the booby-trapped bed and awoke to find themselves entangled in the net. When Hephaestus returned, he called all the gods to come see them lying there, naked and embarrassed. He said he wouldn't release them until the gifts he had given Zeus in return for Aphrodite were repaid.

Hermes, lusting after her beauty, said he would marry her if Ares would pay back Hephaestus. Of course, in order to get free, Ares promised he would pay. He was released but never had to pay because Hephaestus did not really want to let Aphrodite go—he loved her too much to do without her.

After she was set free, Aphrodite reveled in her voracious sexual appetite. She slept with Hermes, who fathered Hermaphroditus, who was both man and woman. She had two sons by Poseidon, and her union with Dionysus produced Priapus, a horribly ugly son with huge genitals. Despite her frenzied lust, Aphrodite could restore her virginity again and again simply by immersing herself in the sea.

Throughout all this, Zeus, under the influence of her magic girdle, also found himself longing for Aphrodite, although he restrained himself because she was his adopted daughter. In time his suppressed desire made him want to make her suffer. He caused her to fall in love with a mortal, a king named Anchises, who was a member of the royal family of Troy. She visited him one night disguised as a princess. As she left him at dawn, she told him who she really was and made him promise not to reveal her visit.

That promise lasted only a few days. During a drinking bout

a friend asked Anchises if he wouldn't rather sleep with a certain man's daughter even than with Aphrodite. Anchises replied, "Since I've slept with them both, I find that a silly question." Zeus heard him bragging and threw a thunderbolt that would have killed him except that Aphrodite used her girdle to deflect it into the ground. Even so the shock waves from the thunderbolt crippled Anchises, which made fickle Aphrodite lose interest in him. She did bear him a son, Aeneas, who escaped after the defeat of Troy carrying his father on his back. After years of wandering, he arrived in Italy and founded the dynasty that came to rule Rome. Among the Romans, worship of Aphrodite, their purported ancestor, became more prevalent than it had been among the Greeks.

When she fell in love with a second mortal, Adonis, in a fit of jealousy Ares changed himself into a boar and gored Adonis to death. His soul went to the netherworld, ruled by Persephone, but Aphrodite pleaded with Zeus to let him spend the spring and summer months with her.

To a modern reader all these stories may have their fascination, but they also seem to be a confusing hodgepodge about a flighty, ill-defined goddess. The stories are indeed a hodgepodge. The Greeks derived Aphrodite from a mother goddess in Asia Minor called Astarte, among other names. Stories about this goddess were mingled with Greek stories and altered as they traveled west across the islands in the Aegean and to the Greek mainland.

Another, more telling reason for our confusion is that we have a different expectation about the nature of a goddess than the Greeks did. To us it seems impossible for as compulsive and unapologetic an adulteress as Aphrodite—and she is the only Greek goddess who is promiscuous—to be, along with Zeus's faithful wife, Hera, a goddess of marriage and family life. Or if she is both Aphrodite Urania, goddess of sacred love, and Aphrodite Pandemos, goddess of profane love, we assume that some moral value must be part of this dual nature. Sacred love must represent the good side of her nature while profane love comes from her evil side. But considering any part of Aphrodite or any other immortal god or goddess as representing good or evil never occurred to the Greeks. To them, the gods had no moral dimension at all. They did not necessarily reward you when you were good or punish you when you were bad, although they might choose to do so. They would certainly punish you if you forgot to honor and respect them. The religious rituals and sacrifices intended to gain the favor of this god or that, or at least to prevent the god's disfavor, had nothing at all to do with sin, redemption, or forgiveness; they were more like elaborate bribes. Nor should mortals draw any moral conclusion from the stories of the gods and their deeds. The gods were immortal and more powerful than humans, but they were not models of conduct. They acted the way they did because they were gods, not because they were perfect humans. They were like the wind or any other force of nature. The wind blows because it is the wind. It may gently waft the sweet perfume of flowers, or it may blow down a house filled with people. Either way, the wind is indifferent. It's in its nature to do both, and it can't be blamed.

As mortals we are trapped between the power of the gods above and the chaos of nature all around us. The Greeks tried to manage the power of the gods by ritual, sacrifice, and other religious celebrations. But against nature, with its brute forces and beasts with their brute needs, the only defenses mortals had were custom, laws, institutions, art, philosophy, and the other creations of the mind. In other words, civilization itself is our defense. Nature wasn't beautiful to the Greeks. It was frightening. They had no romantic poets for whom rivers or mountains or the west wind contained great lessons that could sustain our souls. Odysseus, for example, can't wait to escape from Calypso's island even though it is a natural Eden of beauty and comfort. "Nature is primal power, coarse and turbulent," Camille Paglia wrote, speaking of the Greeks in her book *Sexual Personae*. "Beauty is our weapon against nature; by it we make objects, giving them limit, symmetry, proportion. Beauty halts and freezes the melting flux of nature."

But beauty, and even civilization itself, can be fragile, since mortals are part of nature, too. The Greeks worried endlessly about this conundrum. Are we, after all, born to be part of nature with all its chaos and brutality? Or are we meant to be, or can we learn to be, part of a civilized order of our own creation—and if so, what should that order be? Pondering these questions produced virtually the whole of Greek art, philosophy, poetry, and laws. And embedded within those great achievements we find their opinions about sex and the nature and position of Greek women.

Although the Greeks thought a man's sexual attraction could turn toward a woman or toward another man indiscriminately, sex for them was a union not of equals but of unequals. The lover who was penetrated was the lesser of the two. Since women were subservient to men in every aspect of Greek life, it seemed fitting that nature had made women to be the subservient partner in sex as well as in marriage and society. The kind of homosexuality that Greek society condoned and encouraged was what we would call pederasty. Mature men courted and seduced boys who were just on the verge of puberty. Once boys began to show beards or body hair, their sexual appeal vanished. The sex between the man and the boy was also a meeting between unequals, but one that had an added subtlety. Certainly, the kind of buggery Winckelmann lied about to Casanova did occur; but the implications for a male who was penetrated were so strong that often the boy would refuse and sex would take place between his thighs as the two stood facing each other. Although the boy might happen to enjoy this, there was no expectation that he would. It was a matter of complete indifference to the older male. Homosexuality between two mature men offended Greek scruples. A man who allowed himself to be penetrated lost all status and became an object of ridicule. He had become the worst a man could be: womanly.

Greek men usually didn't marry until they were about thirty, when as a rule they left boy love behind. The brides were much younger. Fathers married off their daughters soon after they reached puberty because the girl's awakened sexuality made men uneasy. A woman's libido, like Aphrodite's, was a destructive force and needed to be quickly confined by marriage, where it could benefit society by producing legitimate children. Women appeared in public only during certain religious festivals or while doing mundane errands like getting water from the public fountain. Otherwise they remained inside the home (or on its roof), where they ran the household, raised the children, and performed other tasks relegated to women, weaving in particular. Women were so seldom seen, and their appearance was so circumscribed, that a man might not recognize his neighbor's wife or daughters.

That was the pattern in classical times. Women were given at an early age to a man they had probably never seen and then were expected to spend the rest of their life indoors, subject to his authority, his passion, and his whims. They had secondary status in all things, no political power, no choice in the life they were to lead, not even a forum from which to make anything known about themselves or their discontents or their dreams.

A modern woman in the West, whose culture derives directly from the Greeks, could not and would not endure such a life. But we do not know what Greek women themselves thought about their lives. Nor do we know directly from a woman what life was like in a Greek household or what went on inside a Greek marriage. The diaries and letters that are the best sources for these matters in later ages do not exist for classical Greece. All we can do is draw inferences from what does exist: plays, histories, poetry, Plato's dialogues and other philosophical writings, and, perhaps most important, vase painting, since the vases were usually intended for use in the home. All these sources are the work of men, of course, but—without apologizing for the social system that prevailed, without extracting too much meaning or only the rosiest meaning from the sources that do exist, and while recognizing that we will never know what Greek women might have wanted and could never have—it's possible to say that Greek women did find ways to create power in their lives and, having gotten it, did know how to use it.

One source of a woman's power in Greece was her position in the home. The Greeks had evolved beyond a strictly tribal society, but the importance of clans and bloodlines still remained. The home was where those bloodlines were both preserved and extended. Its obligations regarding hospitality, order, protection and sustenance, and raising children all made the home the single most important institution for the preservation of the entire community. And the woman, not the man, ran the home.

Greek literature is rich with wives, but the most famous real one is Xanthippe, wife of Socrates. Plato portrays her as a nag, but in her defense Socrates, who was constantly disheveled and preferred his talk and speculations to any real work, was not an ideal husband. Xenophon, who has the misfortune of being the second-greatest author of Socratic dialogues, doesn't dispute that she was a nag, but he gives her intelligence and competence among other admirable qualities that Socrates both recognized and respected.

The other road to power for a woman was sex. Despite the orthodoxy that cast women in the submissive role, Greek men were terrified of a woman's sexuality. Sex is an apparently simple and natural yet eternally confusing subject, as the numerous sex manuals in our bookstores attest. But Greek men knew little or nothing about women's bodies. Since there was never an occasion when women appeared nude, a Greek man may never have seen a naked woman unless he went to prostitutes or was married. This accounts for the frequency of men spying on women in Greek myth and literature. A vase painting from the sixth century B.C. shows a nude man sitting on the ground, phallus erect, with a woman, perhaps a prostitute, standing before him. Her lips are frozen in a straight line. He has lifted the hem of her gown above her hips and is blithely peering in just to see what's there. The vase painter is ribbing this inept lover, but how else was he to find out? It's impossible to imagine what terrifying and tantalizing misinformation went around among the soldiers in a camp or the boys in a gymnasium.

Greek medicine was better than that, but only marginally so. Doctors, who were male, did treat women patients, but the patient stayed behind a screen. If any examination was necessary, another woman or the patient herself did the examining and reported to the doctor what she felt or observed. This secondhand research led to frightful mistakes and wrong assumptions, including long lists of fanciful diseases women were prone to suffer. Among these was "wandering womb," in which, just as the name implies, a woman's womb was supposed to wander about inside her body, thereby bringing on hysterics among other maladies. Midwives and other women attended to labor and childbirth; men had no role at all.

Nevertheless, Greek men did get one thing right: They understood that a woman's sex drive could equal their own and that a woman's pleasure in sex was equal as well. One myth had it that women enjoyed sex not merely as much as men but ten times more. Explicit vase paintings show what must be married couples having sex, and the woman is clearly enjoying herself. In *Lysistrata* by Aristophanes the women of Athens refuse to have sex with their husbands until the men negotiate peace with Sparta. This strategy would make no sense, nor would the play make sense to its all-male Greek audience, if men in Athens could just as easily and with no social opprobrium get sex from boys or from prostitutes instead of from their wives. Much is made among the women in the play about how difficult their own lives will be without sex. And the women prevail as the play ends with a peace between the two cities.

Surely not all of this is male fantasy. It must have been common enough for Greek married couples to enjoy their lives together and for the women to find emotionally richer lives than the bare circumstances of their existence might imply. And in some cases, we cannot know whether it was in many or few, the moment must have arrived when the former frightened four-teen-year-old bride matured and began to understand and use the power that flowed from her sexuality. Aphrodite was the goddess of that power.

The nude goddess

FROM ITS distant beginnings and for centuries afterward, Greek sculpture showed men nude and women clothed. Men's genitals were rendered in accurate detail, their pubes delicately carved in a style that changed from era to era. Even herms had erect phal-luses halfway down the otherwise bare pillar. Occasionally a large statue might reveal a woman's breast, but no statues revealed a woman's pubic area. We don't know why. The rea-sons were so obvious to the Greeks that in the writing that remains to us no one saw any need to comment on it. It could not have been the result of prudery in Greek art. Greek vase painting showed nude women, often in lascivious poses, but vases were used in private, and most statues were displayed in public. Perhaps the reason is simply that male public nudity was common and female public nudity was not. Athletes competed entirely in the nude, whether in the Olympic games or in friendly contests at local gymnasiums, and all athletes were male, except in Sparta, where lightly clothed women competed. Outside Sparta even a glimpse of a woman's leg was rare. A woman who exposed herself would shock and scandalize a community.

In time sculptors who wanted to show a woman's body came to circumvent this convention by showing women covered by wet drapery. These statues preserved public decency while the appearance of cloth clinging to flesh gave them an erotic charge. Then, around 350 B.C., Praxiteles of Athens, in an act that combined inspiration, genius, and audacity, invented the female nude in sculpture. In that moment he changed Western art forever.

The people of Kos, an island near the southern coast of Turkey, commissioned Praxiteles to make a statue of Aphrodite. He created two, one draped and the other nude. On Kos the people made the sober and proper choice of the draped statue, a work that seems to have immediately faded into obscurity. The people of Knidos, a city near Kos on a long, narrow peninsula that projects for miles into the Aegean from southwest Turkey, elected to buy the nude statue. It was an immediate sensation. The statue drew travelers from around the known world to Knidos, an obscure seaport until then, where the statue was first displayed in an open circular shrine so that it could be seen from every angle. One can imagine craftsmen outside the shrine selling replicas to the tourists just as the Louvre sells replicas of the Venus de Milo. The Aphrodite was such a lucrative attraction that later, when a wealthy king offered to pay the city's enormous debt in return for the statue, Knidos refused.

The Aphrodite of Knidos survived until A.D. 476. By then it had been moved to Constantinople, the capital of the eastern Roman empire, where it was destroyed by fire. But the many copies that remain, as well as coins from Knidos with the statue's image, give a reasonable idea of her appearance. Life-sized or somewhat larger, the goddess is standing with most of her weight on her right leg. Her left knee is bent slightly inward. This uneven distribution of weight—known as contrapposto—was one of the great innovations of Greek art. It creates dynamic curves as well as dramatic motion. At the same time the statue seems more natural, since it is easier to stand this way than rigidly with the weight divided equally on both legs.

Beside the goddess is a large urn that holds water for her bath. In her left hand she holds the robe she has just removed. She looks slightly to her left as her right hand hovers in front of her pubic area, which has the effect of both concealing and emphasizing it.

After the nudity, the position of the right hand was the most provocative element of the statue and has endured in Western art through the centuries. The Italian Renaissance artist Masaccio repeats it in his *Expulsion,* where Adam's genitals are exposed, as in ancient Greece, but Eve covers hers with her hand. Recently this pose, known as the *pudica* gesture, has become a subject of much discussion by feminist critics trying to explain why the Greeks showed males as unashamed of their genitals while the Aphrodite of Knidos covers hers. As Nanette Salomon writes in a collection called *Naked Truths,* devoted to this and similar problems in classical art, "Woman, thus fashioned, is reduced in a humiliated way to her sexuality. The immediate and long-term implications of this fiction in the visual arts are incalculable." She may have a point about some Greek works of art, but not this one. Without the actual statue for reference we have no way of being certain how she was represented, but in the copies and coins that remain she appears to be anything but humiliated. On the contrary, she is serene and confident.

The belief was that a mortal seeing a goddess nude would instantly be incinerated by her glory. Perhaps, as Christine Mitchell Havelock, another contemporary critic, has suggested, the goddess is trying to keep the mortal viewer from harm and to protect the source of her divine authority. "I question," Havelock concludes, "whether [the viewer in Greek times] was expected to feel privileged to have chanced upon a naked woman at her private bath."

But there is no doubt that the fame of the statue was due to its erotic charge, which derived from the beauty of the statue, from the tantalizing *pudica* pose, and from its flouting of convention. One pathetic admirer hid in the shrine overnight, and the statue, Pliny says, "thus bears a stain, an indication of his lust." Lucian (or perhaps it was a later writer whom scholars call the Pseudo-Lucian) traveled to Knidos to see the statue. By then it was no longer displayed in an open shrine but in a temple with one door for seeing her from the front and another for seeing her from behind. That way, presumably, admission could be charged twice. Lucian says that in seeing her he was seized by "unforeseen amazement." She had "a look of proud contempt and a slight smile which just reveal[ed] her teeth." A poem from the time has Aphrodite herself coming across the sea to Knidos. After gazing at the statue from every angle, she demands, "Where did Praxiteles see me naked?"

Of course, from prehistoric times there had been images of fertility goddesses that embodied a female principal. Among the Greeks there had been other statues of Aphrodite and many of other goddesses. These statues, however, even the ones with wet drapery, were seldom entirely concerned with a woman's sexuality. As only the greatest art can do, the Aphrodite of Knidos seemed to arrive entirely without warning and changed everything that came afterward. Praxiteles had made mere stone show the Greeks a living force.

Roman taste

AFTER this startling departure by Praxiteles, statues of Aphrodite appeared frequently in a variety of poses. Generally she was nude, but when there was drapery, it was intended to enhance the statue's sensuality by what little it concealed. Scholars have given most of these poses specific and highly descriptive names, including Aphrodite Kallipygos, which means Aphrodite of the beautiful buttocks.

Four principal poses were repeated endlessly in large sculpture for public display, as well as in smaller figures for votive purposes or for household decoration. One type, the Sandal-Binding Aphrodite, shows her balanced on one leg, with the other crooked across her knee so she can readjust her sandal. The sexual wattage seems a little lower to us in this pose than in the others. That may have been true then as well, or perhaps for Greek males, seeing a woman fiddle with her sandal was an illicit pleasure like a glimpse of lingerie. The second type is the Aphrodite Anadyomene. Here she has just risen from the sea or from her bath and is twisting her long hair to wring out the water. A painting by Apelles, whom the Greeks considered their greatest painter, may have inspired this pose. We know nothing of this work (which, like his others, has not survived) except that its beautiful rendering of the goddess's nudity made it famous and exciting in the manner of Praxiteles's statue.

Less common and more provocative, although the pose is concealing, is the Crouching Venus. She is bent down until her buttocks rest on the back of her ankle. Her body is bent slightly forward and twisted, causing rows of wrinkles across her stomach. This pose looks forced and improbable to us, but in reality she is simply having a bath. Greeks bathed by kneeling down while someone, a slave perhaps, poured water over them from a large jar. Just as the jar at the side of the Aphrodite of Knidos implied that she had just bathed or was about to bathe, the crouching pose implies bathing and gives a rationale for the goddess's nudity.

The last common pose is that of the Venus de Milo. There are several other statues in a similar pose—the Venus of Arles in the Louvre and the Venus de Capua in the Archeological Museum in Naples, to name two. They all seem to be from the same era and probably derived from an earlier statue, now unknown and lost. The goddess is nude from the waist up. She is standing with most of her weight on one leg while the other is slightly elevated and resting on a step or stone. In some versions she is holding a mirror or a polished shield and gazes at the beauty of her reflection. That would account for her nudity—she has let down her gown so she can see all her glory—and also gives a reason for her blank and distant stare. This is why some scholars proposed reconstructions of the Venus de Milo holding a shield supported by her left leg, although there is no sign of any disturbance on the drapery of her left thigh where a shield would have to have rested.

This pose became especially popular after about 150 B.C., a curious and unexpected moment in the history of Greek art. It was both the height of the Hellenistic age and the beginning of its end. After the death of Alexander the Great in 323 B.C. his generals had carved up his empire into separate kingdoms. In

150 B.C. these kingdoms still dominated the eastern Mediterranean. However, once Rome had finally defeated Carthage, Romans and Roman power began arriving from the west and would in time conquer the Hellenistic kingdoms one by one. The last to fall was Egypt, when Octavian defeated Anthony and Cleopatra at the battle of Actium in 31 B.C.

Hellenistic art, though still Greek, had not produced any renowned artists, as the classical period had, and Hellenistic sculptors chose subjects that would never have been considered by Phidias, Myron, or their peers: old women with wrinkles, old men with potbellies, savage Gauls in the throes of death, boxers after a fight sitting swollen, scarred, and exhausted. (Pliny, writing around A.D. 100, dismissed all Hellenistic art as inferior, a judgment that held almost until modern times. Certainly that was the accepted opinion in France in 1821 when its scholars were so desperate to place the Venus de Milo among classical statues and not in the degraded Hellenistic age.) But around 150 B.C. there was a change of taste in the Hellenistic world, a reaction against the new subjects and styles. Some of this change may have been due to a growing influx of Romans, who were enamored of classical Greece and wanted art in that manner. They commissioned copies of ancient statues, as Romans would continue to do throughout the empire, but they also wanted new works in the classical manner, and a retro style imitating classical sculpture became fashionable.

Gods and goddesses reappeared amid the potbellies and scarred fighters. Inevitably, copies of the Aphrodite of Knidos and of Aphrodites in the different poses it inspired began to reappear throughout the eastern Mediterranean. One of these was the Venus de Milo. It was carved in conscious imitation of the classical manner. When the French scholars in the nineteenth century insisted that the statue was from the classical period and not the Hellenistic era, there was enough ambiguity in style to make their case plausible. The sculptor himself hadn't wanted his statue to look Hellenistic.

Contrary to the general opinion

BUT IT DOES. The pose, with drapery wrapped around the hips and legs, which was rare before 150 B.C. but popular afterward, is the most obvious sign. Other statues in this pose can be dated by inscriptions or the context of where they were found, and the similarities between them and the Venus de Milo make it clear that she is their contemporary—though whether the Venus de Milo or the Venus of Arles or the Venus de Capua or another statue entirely was the first of this type is impossible to tell.

This form was appealing because the drapery around the hips was a concession to modesty that helped avoid the problems full nudity might provoke even two hundred years after the Aphrodite of Knidos. But there were both aesthetic and structural reasons for the drapery. The human body is an aggravating shape for sculptors. The head, fairly large, sits above a massive torso, but the massive torso sits on human legs, which tend to be two rather spindly supports. Wrapping the legs in drapery adds weight and solidity to the bottom of the figure and gives a stable and appealing support for the torso above.

The statue also reveals its Hellenistic origins by exhibiting two different styles, a fact that some critics have used against it. The torso is that of a beautiful woman, but it is realistic rather than ideal. The hips are thick and wide, and the stomach— "Immense like the sea," as Rodin said—is huge. This realism is akin to the realism that defined so much of Hellenistic art: the scars on the face of a boxer, the sagging flesh of an elderly man. The head, however is classical, inspired by Praxiteles's Aphrodite of Knidos, and even in the body there are bows here and there to the classical rules of proportion. The distance between the tips of the breasts—twenty-eight centimeters—is the same as the distance from the tip of the right breast to the navel and the same as the distance from the navel to the place beneath the drapery that would be the lowest point of the groin. It is this mixture of classical idealism with realism, which appeared during the Hellenistic era and not before, that to the practiced eye, unprejudiced by political necessities, reveals the statue's late date.

No one today challenges the dating to the Hellenistic era, not even the French. In 1951 Jean Charbonneaux, then the conservator of Greek and Roman antiquities at the Louvre, calmly wrote, "Beginning in 1893, contrary to the general opinion, Furtwängler had set 150 and 50 B.C. as the limits of the period where [the statue] belonged." Here we have evidence of Furtwängler's triumph, posthumous but complete, over Ravaisson, Reinach, and the rest of the French who so desperately wanted the statue to be from the classical age. By 1951 even an official at the Louvre could dismiss the impassioned work of his countrymen with the phrase "contrary to the general opinion."

There is one final piece of evidence for dating the Venus de Milo to Hellenistic times. It is conclusive, and Furtwängler was correct here as well. That evidence is the broken base inscribed with the name of the sculptor from Antioch. Quatremère de Quincy, Félix Ravaisson, and Salomon Reinach aside, that broken base did belong to the statue. To see why, we must return to the scene of the discovery and, step by step, reconstruct the Venus de Milo, arms and all, as it appeared when it was first displayed.

A poet and sculptor from Antioch

THE STATUE was discovered in a niche with an arched entrance and an arched ceiling. A few years later, as we have seen, a Dutch trader discovered two more identical niches in the same ancient wall, each holding the remains of a statue. The three niches were twenty paces apart from one another. Greek gymnasiums had walls built just this way, with regularly spaced niches to hold statues.

By the Hellenistic age gymnasiums throughout the Greek world were places for athletic training as well as private preparatory schools for boys. In that regard they were rather like the gymnasiums of nineteenth-century Germany—which had been created after the Greek model—where Furtwängler's father was a headmaster. Surviving inscriptions show that there were footraces, races in armor, races with torches, wrestling, and box-ing, among other contests, all divided into divisions for boys, young men, and men. For boys and young men there were also competitions in music composition, lyre playing, singing, paint-ing, and arithmetic.

The teachers, like sculptors, had the social status of trades-men, but the gymnasiarch, equivalent to a modern headmaster, was a wealthy man with great prestige and great obligations. He was supposed to endow funds for the proper religious sacrifices, for prizes in contests, and for keeping the buildings of the gym-nasium in good repair. In small or remote communities like Melos he might even double as a sort of magistrate for the town.

Gymnasiums all looked much the same. There was a large, open rectangular area in the center known as the palaestra, where the sports and games took place. A covered colonnade ran beside the palaestra. Here men could lounge and watch the athletes, or the young students could attend their classes.

Behind the colonnade were walls with niches at regular intervals for statues, which might be of gods or goddesses, of mythical heroes, or even of local heroes who had triumphed in the various competitions. Every gymnasium had statues that honored Hermes and Hercules, the patrons of gymnasiums, and, beginning in the second century B.C., Venus. This was the start of a tradition that would continue to expand among the Romans, who honored Venus as the patroness of places for con-tests and spectacles.

The niche where the Venus de Milo was found had an engraved stone over its entrance. This stone arrived at the Louvre with the statue. Evidently Rivière acquired it when he stopped at Melos on his voyage back to France with the Venus in the hold. It has since disappeared, but fortunately Clarac carefully copied the inscription. It said, "Bacchios, son of S[extus] Atius, having finished his term as assistant gymnasiarch, [dedicates] both the exedra and the [missing word] to Hermes Hercules." Here we have the assistant gymnasiarch fulfilling his obligations by dedicating statues for the gymnasium. Furtwängler thought that the missing word, which had been obscured by a crack in the stone, mentioned a statue. Assuming that he is correct, the inscription over the niche mentioned Hermes, Hercules, and a statue. Inside, on that April day in 1820, Voutier and Yorgos found a herm of Hermes, a herm of Hercules, and a statue. All this fits together too neatly to be merely coincidental. The Venus de Milo must have been found in the place where she was originally displayed. And the two herms were part of the same display.

The base of the herm representing Hercules, missing from the Louvre since 1821, was the one with the inscription that read "[Alex]andros son of Menides citizen of Antioch of Meander made the statue." The long battles over whether or not this base belonged with the statue were fruitless, motivated entirely by the French insistence on dating the statue much earlier than the Hellenistic era. Since Antioch wasn't founded until about 280 B.C., after the classical age had already passed, the French could not admit that the inscription belonged with their revered work of art. Quatremère, Ravaisson, and Reinach all fought valiantly but in a futile cause. The legs wrapped in cloth, along with the mixture of realism with classicism in the carving, date the Venus de Milo to Hellenistic times anyway. That means that the inscription and the date it implies are perfectly in keeping with the statue. In fact, Antiochus Epiphanes, a Hellenistic king who reigned in Antioch and was famous in the Bible for trying to force Greek religion on the Jews, was so enamored of Greek culture that he made Antioch a center of Greek art. He died in 164 B.C., but for generations after him Antioch was famous for its wealth and luxury, its devotion to pleasure, and its love of the arts. If a patron anywhere in the Greek world wanted to hire a sculptor with skill and training, Antioch was a place where one could be found.

Two more points make it certain that the inscribed base of the beardless herm and the base of the Venus were connected. One is the inscription itself. Since it says that Alexandros of Antioch "made the statue," the base must have belonged with *some* statue or the inscription would make no sense. The Venus de Milo was the only statue found near this inscribed base. More importantly, at the Louvre the broken edge of this inscribed base was placed in the jagged cavity on the left side of the Venus de Milo, and the two fit together perfectly. Debay's drawing shows them matching. Clarac is explicit about how well the statue and the base matched. He says the inscribed base fit perfectly with "the alignment of the front surface of the ancient plinth [that is, the base of the statue] and it also fits exactly both at the rear and at the side with the fractures." In other words, not only do the fractures of the two pieces fit, but the inscribed base is the same depth and height as the base of the statue. The statue and the inscribed base were created at the same moment.

Unknown to the nineteenth-century scholars, the name of the artist from Antioch that is on the broken base is also on an inscription from Thespiae, a city near Mount Helicon on the mainland of Greece where an important contest of poetry and theatrical arts was held every five years. In an inscription from around 80 B.C., Alexandros of Antioch is mentioned twice, as a victor at singing and at composing. Evidently he was the composer and singer of songs as well as a sculptor. The Thespiae inscription also allows us to date the statue closer to 80 than 150 B.C.

The life we can read from these inscriptions is typical of an artist of the time. Leaving his home in Antioch, wandering wherever his commissions took him, he managed to create some ephemeral fame by singing songs here and carving sculptures there. He may have been a great poet and musician, but all we know is that he was good enough to win the contest in Thespiae. As a sculptor, however, he was indisputably a genius whose name deserves to be mentioned in the same breath as Phidias, Praxiteles, and the other ancient masters. Alexandros, son of Menides, citizen of Antioch, was the artist who created the Venus de Milo.

The arms restored

THE POSITION of the right arm is not difficult to determine. It extended down across her stomach and bent toward the left. The stump of the right arm precludes almost any other position. And a hole beneath the right breast, now filled with plaster but still visible, once held a tenon to support the right arm as it bent across her stomach.

The position of the left arm is more mysterious. The solution to the mystery depends on understanding how Alexandros intended his statue to be displayed.

Since the inscribed base that held the herm of Hercules was part of the original statue, the herm stood at the goddess's left. That means she could not have been grouped with a statue of Mars as both Quatremère de Quincy and Félix Ravaisson had supposed, since there is no place for the warrior to stand. Furtwängler's restoration with her left arm resting on a pillar is also impossible, since there is no place for the pillar either. The Venus de Milo standing beside an undistinguished herm of Hercules, a figure that is too short and too narrow for the large statue next to it, is another indication that the Greek aesthetic was not the same as ours. It's an ugly, ludicrous composition, and neither the French scholars nor Furtwängler believed that a sculptor with the skill and sensibility to create the Venus de Milo would have joined his masterpiece with something so trivial. But Alexandros of Antioch did exactly that.

Perhaps he had his reasons. It was rare for a large statue to stand beside a small one, but not unknown. Salomon Reinach's own *Index of Greek and Roman Statuary* of 1908, a revised version of a work by Clarac, shows several statues of Venus with small figures standing almost underfoot and one, from a collection in Berlin, of a Venus standing beside a herm.

Or perhaps Alexandros had no choice. The passage from Lucian about a sculptor's life laments the way sculptors must be subservient to their patrons. This unsightly coupling might have been what Bacchios, the assistant gymnasiarch who dedicated the niche and therefore could have commissioned the statue, insisted on having. Even during that distant era, it wouldn't have been the first time that an artist's patron proved to have unfortunate taste.

Much of the statue's power derives from the contrasting dynamics between the draped and undraped portions. The motion of the lower half of the statue is toward the right. Her hips are turned slightly to the right, and her bent left knee turns inward, a movement that draws the drapery tight against her left leg and reveals its shape. The folds in the drapery begin high on the left hip and thigh and fall dramatically down toward the right. All this powerful movement ends abruptly at the right leg. Straight and firm, it supports most of the goddess's weight. Its rigidity resolves all the motion to the right in the drapery and gives the statue a stable foundation in the midst of so much dynamism.

By contrast, all the motion in the upper part of the statue is to the left: The chest, shoulders, and head all turn to the left as the goddess stares into the distance. Originally, this leftward motion must have appeared even more pronounced, since the right arm must have extended down across her stomach and to the left. That would strongly emphasize yet again the movement in that direction.

But in the statue as we see it today all this motion is unresolved. There must have been some reason for it. The herm is too small. The answer must lie with the left arm and what it was doing.

The carving on the left side of the statue is less careful and refined than on the rest. Both Quatremère de Quincy and

Ravaisson thought that was because she was standing next to a warrior. But if the statue was displayed so that it was seen in three-quarter right profile—and its shape makes it clear that this is how Alexandros wanted his statue to be seen—then the left side of the statue wouldn't be visible either. In the gymnasium wall niche, enclosed on three sides, the sculptor could place his statue exactly at the angle he wanted.

At the time of the discovery a left hand holding an apple was found in the niche with the statue. This hand was even more roughly carved than the left side of the statue, but it was carved from identical marble and had the proper proportions to belong to the Venus. A portion of the upper left arm, also in the correct proportion and of the same marble, was found as well.

The upper arm fit in the left shoulder of the statue. It stuck out directly to the left. Debay's drawing shows that as clearly as it shows the perfect fit between the base of the statue and the broken base with the inscription. So the left arm, most likely bent somewhat at the elbow, extended directly to the left with its hand—the hand holding the apple—held aloft. The Venus de Milo was holding up the apple in her left hand as she serenely contemplated the symbol of her victory over Juno and Minerva.

A Venus with an apple is a common motif in Greek sculpture, but it is particularly appropriate for the Venus de Milo. The Greek word for apple was *melon*. The island was named Melos because to the Greeks its shape resembled an apple. An apple became the symbol of the island. A sculptor who was commissioned to carve a Venus for the island of Melos could hardly resist a pose that emphasized this double meaning.

Displayed as she was in those days, the Venus de Milo, whose image we know so well, would have been barely recognizable to us. She stood in the shadows of the niche, competing for attention with the pattern painted on the walls. She wore jewels on her head, ears, and arms. The marble of her torso was polished. Her hair was painted gold; her eyes and lips were red. Her drapery was painted in a pattern. Turned to a three-quarter right profile, she looked away from the men and boys who saw her. All her attention was on the apple she held in her raised left arm, which extended obliquely back into the shadows of the niche.

That was the statue that Alexandros created for the gymnasium on Melos. The passing of centuries, which wore away the paint and the polish, which saw the jewels purloined and the arms broken off, created the statue we know. But some shadow or ghost of the original seems to have survived and at the moment of discovery was still capable of making its presence felt. The early witnesses—Olivier Voutier, Dumont d'Urville, the captains from the French ships—all assumed that the statue showed Venus holding the apple from Paris. It never occurred to them that the statue was anything else. The shade of the statue in its original glory led these mariners closer to the truth than all the hard work, contaminated as it was by national rivalries, of the sage scholars who came after them.

V I I

The Last Chapter

IN 1886 a German anatomist named W. Henke and his colleague Christoph Hasse found themselves in an intense dispute over the Venus de Milo. As German scholars were prone to do, Henke had studied the statue in minute detail. In a paper that year, he concluded that imperfections in the statue's anatomy meant that the sculptor had worked from a live model and that this live model was deformed! Noting that the legs were of different lengths and that the pelvis was tilted off the horizontal, Henke believed that the model must have limped. An even greater flaw, according to him, was the asymmetry of the goddess's face. The line that connected both pupils and the line that connected the two ends of the lips were not parallel to each other. And neither of those lines was perpendicular to the nose. These asymmetries did occur in life, Henke admitted, but always as an abnormality.

That last conclusion aggravated Hasse, a fellow at the anatomical institute in Breslau. In his paper on the Venus de Milo, published in 1882, he had praised the statue's naturalism. Now he decided that Henke's paper was simply wrong, because he didn't believe that an asymmetrical face was at all abnormal.

To test his assumption, Hasse created a square grid and photographed the face of the statue and the faces of a number of friends behind it. Measuring by the grid, he could see that every face was asymmetrical. The more Hasse studied the grids, the more asymmetries he found. Among the most important was that in every case—including the statue—the left eye was closer to the center of the face than the right eye, and a line connecting the two pupils was not horizontal.

Hasse suspected that the asymmetry of the pupil line in the statue and in people compensated for the tilt of the pelvis. He had long been aware of a slight bow in most people's spinal cords that shifts the head to one side or the other. In 1888 Hasse and a colleague published a study of the pelvises of women showing that they had the same asymmetrical tilt of the hips as the Venus de Milo. In 1893 he published a study of the backbones of 5,141 men, which found that only one third of the backbones were completely straight. All these asymmetries had the effect of canceling themselves out so that the line between the eyes was parallel to the horizon. With this research Hasse had disproved the centuries-old prevailing wisdom of both anatomists and artists that human features were symmetrical. Asymmetry was the norm; symmetry was abnormal.

Hasse's work was the beginning of what has become a fertile and fascinating branch of research in psychology, one that concentrates in particular on how people display emotions. As a simple example, cover one side of a face in a photograph, then the other. The two sides will often appear to show different emotions. Paul Erkman, author of *Emotion in the Human Face* and *Telling Lies: Clues to Deceit in the Marketplace, Politics, and Marriage,* is one well-known researcher in this area. Research methodology has progressed far beyond photographing the face of the Venus de Milo behind a grid, but that is where it began. A meticulous examination of the statue, followed by a dispute over the results, led to a wholly unexpected and unexplored path toward comprehending the human psyche. It's unusual for a work of art to inspire a new field of scientific inquiry, but the Venus de Milo did.

The statue has inspired many artists who, like the scientists, use it for their own purposes. It's not so much the anatomical detail that they respond to but something true—true in the deepest sense—in the form of the sculpture that makes the accurate anatomy matter. Cézanne sketched the Venus in the Louvre and used her pose in his paintings of bathers. Magritte painted a small replica, making the head white, the body the color of flesh, the nipples pink, the drapery deep blue, and the base black. These colors, he said, "restore the Venus to an unexpected life." Dalí sculpted and painted her in a variety of ways. Seeing that her neck is quite long, he created a giraffe Venus with an elongated neck as tall as her body. He also sculpted a Venus with drawers coming out of her breasts, stomach, and left knee. A photograph of the statue wedged into Ravaisson's oak crate could have been his inspiration here. More recently, Jim Dine obsessively returns to the statue in paintings and sculptures. Three of these, cast as massive bronzes, stand on the Avenue of the Americas in midtown New York. Clive Barker has shown her wrapped in rope, locked in chains, and impishly, with her tongue stuck in her cheek. These are only a handful of the many works of art whose inspiration began with the Venus de Milo. All this shows that the truth within her can take many forms. It can even put its tongue in its cheek and pretend it's only kidding.

Artists are seekers after truth, but the Venus de Milo also inspires those who seek something else: increased sales. Advertisers use the statue either to associate its beauty and truth with their product or to get a laugh. In 1996 a Mercedes ad showed a photograph of the statue across the page from their new Class E sedan. None of the type in the ad referred to the statue. Its presence spoke for itself. Leaving aside the appeal to classic beauty, a mid-eighties ad for the French retailer Darty has the statue saying, "When I see Darty prices, it makes my arms fall"; that is, she is dumbfounded.

And then there are the many cartoons and parodies in which low culture gives a gleeful raspberry to the high. A Greek sculptor in his workshop with the Venus de Milo complains to a friend, "I just can't do arms." As Charlie Chaplin's Great Dicta-

Vénus de Milo aux tiroirs, *by Salvador Dalí*

tor rides past her, she suddenly raises a right arm in salute. In a publicity still from 1957, Jayne Mansfield in a tight sweater and tight skirt stands next to her at the Louvre. The poster for Robert Altman's *Nashville* shows the Venus in a cowboy hat and dark glasses.

Venus with Tongue in Cheek,
by Clive Barker, 1990

But the statue's success as a cultural icon has worked against it among scholars and critics. Throughout the nineteenth century and well into the twentieth, writers on the statue were uniformly admiring. The rhapsodies of romantic poets in her praise became almost a cliché. Back then it was the artists and the intelligentsia who were leading the masses toward appreciating the statue. Today the masses don't need to be convinced, while the intelligentsia have lost interest. Although there are scholars who still see the statue as a great work of art, for an ambitious critic who wants to demonstrate his or her discernment, there is no point at all in simply agreeing with the popular taste. We've seen how Geoffrey Grigson, an eminent British scholar, says he is "repelled" by the statue. R. R. R. Smith, a professor of classical

La nouvelle
Mercedes Classe E
est équipée d'airbags*
latéraux de série.

4 airbags de série.*
2 airbags frontaux et 2 airbags latéraux.

Mercedes-Benz

Mercedes-Benz ad, 1996

archeology and art at Oxford, calls her "matronly," "heavy," "blank," and "solemn." In 1975 Martin Robertson wrote in his *A History of Greek Art* that the statue's "mild merits hardly justify the figure's extraordinary reputation, which started by propaganda has become perpetuated by habit."

These dour opinions can only be in reaction to the statue's fame, since the descriptions of other Greek statues, even inferior ones, use noticeably milder language. In a sense these opinions don't matter, since scholarly tastes will change, as they have in the past, while the statue will remain the same. These negative opinions are occasionally based on the presumed superiority of statues of Aphrodite that no longer exist. For instance, R. R. R. Smith says that, "placed beside the original of the Crouching Aphrodite, [the Venus de Milo] would probably have seemed rather dull." But since neither he nor anyone else in the past two thousand years has seen the original of the Crouching Aphrodite, how could he possibly know?

Feminist art historians tend to look askance at the Venus de Milo as well. For the past thirty years they have usually been concerned with art since the Renaissance. Now they are begin-

"Quand je vois les prix Darty... les bras m'en tombent!"

DARTY

TV. ÉLECTROMÉNAGER. HIFI. VIDÉO

Darty ad, 1984

ning to look at the classical world. Feminist interpretations of classical art and life have caused a conservative backlash in some classics departments. The conservatives are generally the better writers, but the books and articles on both sides—the lethal salvos in this arcane fight—make entertaining reading once you know a little about the combatants and become inured to the jargon.

However, the feminist approach strikes me as potentially fruitful. Scholarship about the statue is in a rut. Adolf Furtwängler wrote the last original and convincing interpretation using all the evidence—and that was in 1893!

The problem is that there is so little new information and so little new interpretation. If there is a spectacular archeological find—another statue signed by Alexandros, let's say—that would certainly tell us more about the Venus de Milo. Unfortunately, such a lucky event is unlikely. That leaves new interpretation as the only road to discovery, and looking at the statue with new eyes is exactly what the feminists are trying to do. As Shelby Brown wrote in an essay titled " 'Ways of Seeing': Women in Antiquity," "Authors writing on nude classical sculptures, for example, have tended to ignore completely the gender relations implied by the body language, or to point out their titillating aspects without considering in any depth the social construction of modesty for women and voyeurism for men." Feminist critics are uneasy with the Venus de Milo, the best-known sculpted image of a woman in our culture, because a man created it to be displayed only to other men in a gymnasium. "What does that tell us?" is the question they seek to answer, and answering it adequately will require seeing the statue in ways past scholars never attempted or even imagined. A feminist critic who was backed by solid scholarship and an expert eye and had a mind supple enough to discern whether there is a pattern behind all the subtleties and contradictions could be the next Furtwängler.

WHATEVER opinions modern scholars may have, a visit to the Louvre is enough to show that the Venus de Milo is in no danger of losing its place in the public consciousness. It isn't just the sheer number of people in the crowds that arrive in her alcove, although that is impressive enough. Most visitors listen to their guide, look at the statue quizzically, pose for a picture in front of her, and then move on. They have had the experience they wanted. But a significant minority linger, walk slowly around the statue, look at it from each angle, and try to extract everything from the moment that they can. They get the experience they want, too. It's rare to see someone go away disappointed. People accept that the statue is great art, that it has nobility and truth that are unaffected whether she has drawers coming out of her breasts or wears a cowboy hat and shades.

This lofty place in our culture is exactly what the French wanted for the Venus de Milo so that her glory would reflect onto them. As we've seen, they actively promoted the statue from the moment of her discovery, and this campaign still creates echoes in French culture many generations later. One recent spring afternoon at the Louvre I listened as a docent brought a group of French schoolgirls, about ten years old, to see the statue. She told them how the Venus was found on Melos and then brought to the Louvre. She pointed out the cracks at the hips and the line in the drapery where the two halves meet and commented on the twists and curves in the body. Then, standing with the girls gathered around her, the docent lowered her voice and said that the Venus had once stood next to a statue of Mars, the god of war. And she assumed the position that both Quatremère and Ravaisson had insisted on for the statue. She extended her left arm as if it were resting on the god's shoulder and brought her right hand across her stomach as if to touch his arm. She held the pose for a moment, looking at the girls. Then she dropped her arms, raised a finger, and said that the most important thing about the statue is that it is an original. "An original!" she repeated with emphasis. How proud Quatrèmere and Ravaisson would have been of her.

But French propaganda is not the reason why the Venus de Milo has fascinated artists for generations or why great masses of tourists arrive at the Louvre each day to see her. They come because the statue is beautiful in a way that even an untrained eye immediately understands. Its classicism is the source of that instant recognition. Ever since Winckelmann brought Greek art back into our culture, we have thought of Greek idealized nude sculpture as both the beginning of Western art and an achievement that has not been surpassed in the two and a half millennia since. There can be only one convenient public symbol of this achievement—two or more would just confuse things. The

Venus de Milo, beautiful and genuinely Greek, not a Roman copy of some earlier masterpiece, has been that symbol from the moment the statue was first displayed at the Louvre.

Classical though her beauty is, it is far easier to see than it is to describe. Although apparently simple and immediately comprehensible, the statue is actually so complex that Sir Kenneth Clark once remarked: "[The] planes of her body are so large and calm that at first we do not realize the number of angles through which they pass. In architectural terms, she is a baroque composition with classic effect." He also said the "Aphrodite of Melos makes us think of an elm tree in a field of corn." I find that last comparison completely baffling, but the large planes and angles are all there to see. We spoke in the last chapter of the conflicting movements to the left in the upper half of the statue and to the right in the lower. These opposing tensions are so strong that they could have made the statue appear to be twisting itself apart. Instead, even more powerful dynamics unify the statue and produce the surprising calm that Clark mentioned.

In the Louvre, it's possible to see the Venus de Milo from every angle. The pose in contrapposto, with her left knee bent slightly inward while her weight rests on her straight right leg, produces a large, elongated S-curve. It begins at her left shoulder, moves to her right armpit, then runs down across her body to her left knee, where it turns again and runs through the lower drapery before ending at the right foot. This long, lazy curve is intersected by two dramatic Xs. The first X is tall and skinny. One line begins just at the right of her neck and goes down to her missing left foot. The second line begins halfway from her neck to her left shoulder and goes down to her right foot. These two lines cross at her navel. The second X, shorter and wider, crisscrosses her torso. One line begins at the edge of her right shoulder and goes to her left hip. The other begins at her left shoulder and goes to her right hip. These lines meet directly above her navel at the fold across her stomach. The languor of the S combined with the rigid simplicity of the two Xs helps give the statue both her baroque complexity and her classic calm.

The line of her shoulders, tilted slightly downward from left to right, is parallel with the line of the fold of drapery around her hips and also parallel with a line from her missing left foot to her right. These parallel lines serve to unite the statue while their slope to the right is neutralized, even dominated, in part by the twist of her torso but even more by her head. It floats on its long neck as the goddess gazes to the left toward the spot where her missing arm once held the apple.

The flesh appears so real that one expects it to be warm to the touch. Some of that is due to the translucence of the marble, but mostly it's the result of the delicate skill Alexandros had with a chisel. One example is the small fold of flesh near the armpit that's been displaced by the right arm. On a grander scale, the back in particular is an expanse of flesh with small undulations of muscle and a long, narrow, bowed furrow for her spine that runs from the bottom of her neck to the line of her buttocks. This bow is echoed in the curve of her right hip and waist. This is the most sensuous back ever carved in stone. The three tendrils of hair on her neck that have come loose from her bun subtly enhance this eroticism.

When her face is seen from the three-quarter right profile, as the artist intended, it appears regular although, as the German anatomists Henke and Hasse were to discover, it is in fact quite irregular. The eyes are not symmetrical. The mouth and chin are slightly to the right of center of the nose. Even the part in her hair is not centered but somewhat to the left. Her eyes are deep in her head and emphasize the roundness of her cheeks. Her eyebrows and upper eyelids are delicate, although a touch severe, and the ends of her mouth turn down slightly, giving to some viewers an impression of disdain.

The face is the most criticized part of the statue. While disdainful to some, it's blank or expressionless to others. In fact, her expression is neither disdainful nor blank but completely absorbed. If her arms were intact, we could see that her apple of victory is what draws her attention. She is pondering her own beauty. That accounts for the pride shown in the slight downward turn of her lips. Her absorption turns out to be self-absorption.

But without the arms we can't see what it is that she contemplates. All we know is that it's something there to her left but invisible to us. That gives the statue a mystery and depth that would be absent if we knew her thoughts were on herself.

It's curious how little the arms are missed. Knowing they *were* there is enough. Their absence doesn't affect the pleasure in seeing the drapery wrapped around her legs, the elegant twist of her torso, the sexuality that even her back exudes, the quizzical irregularity of her face, the unruly strands of hair on her neck, or the subtle displacement of her flesh by the right arm. More than that, the loss of the arms has actually deepened the statue's meaning. Goddesses, after all, and especially Aphrodite, are somewhat frivolous. As immortals, they cannot suffer. As objects of adoration, they cannot lose at love. Their hearts cannot break. The missing arms bring the goddess down to earth among us. Here she is vulnerable just as we are, and her frivolity and her self-absorption vanish. She retains our admiration, but now she has our sympathy, too. That sympathy, which connects the viewer with the statue, secures her enduring popularity.

The Venus de Milo proves that great art transcends its time and place, and even the purpose for which it was intended. Whatever Greek society may have assumed about women, one Greek man, Alexandros, created the Venus de Milo, who is a beauty, a mother, a force of nature, a mortal woman contemplating the unknown, and a goddess absorbed in her own beauty. She was that complex and radiant being more than two thousand years ago. Rediscovered, she immediately resumed her role and has maintained it for almost two centuries. During that time the world has changed many times, but she has not. What is beauty? What is a mother, a force of nature, a mortal woman? What is a goddess? While you look at her, the answers seem within reach. Look away and mystery returns.

NOTES

Works cited here in brief are given in full in the Bibliography.

Preface

xi advertisements and kitsch objects, artists, trip to Japan: Salmon.
xii "immense like the sea": Rodin, 12.

I. From Melos to Paris

3 Alaux, Besnier, and Michon 1900 and 1902 all have detailed accounts of the statue's discovery, acquisition, and arrival at the Louvre. Michon's works publish the many original documents he found in the archives of the Louvre, maritime records, and private family papers and give an extensive commentary on them. Marcellus in his two books (1840, 1851) provides the only account of the negotiations that led to the purchase and, except for maritime records and ships' logs, of the subsequent voyage with the statue in the hold of the *Estafette*. Some later commentators have claimed that he is self-important at best and prevaricating at worst. I see no reason to think so. He was the one person with the authority and responsibility for acquiring the statue, so he could hardly overemphasize his role. Nothing he writes is contradicted by any other reliable source, and his account of the negotiations is quite plausible. It is not overly intricate, and Marcellus shows himself winning more by determination than by brilliant strokes.

3 description and biography of Voutier: Alaux. Voutier's own account of the discovery is in Alaux and de Lorris. Voutier wrote many years after the fact, but there is no reason to doubt his truthfulness. Furthermore, his sketches are strong proof of his veracity. They are undoubtedly genuine, for reasons discussed in the text.

4 April 8: This date for the discovery is established by Duval d'Ailly's letter of April 11 (in Alaux, 175), which speaks of the statue's being discovered three days earlier.

6 erecting the statue: One does wonder how Voutier and Yorgos managed to reassemble the statue, since the top half must weigh half a ton. Perhaps, in addition to the two sailors, Yorgos's son and nephew, both of whom later claimed to have been present at the discovery, lent a hand. Yorgos did manage to transport the top half to his cowshed, so erecting the statue would also have been within the ability of whoever was there.

7 "Those who have seen": de Lorris, 102.

8 "Are you *sure*": per Voutier in de Lorris, 102.

8 sailing for Constantinople: Voutier claims that he persuaded Captain Robert to sail immediately for Constantinople. He repeats this assertion in his letter to Marcellus quoted in Alaux. Alaux has a convoluted argument claiming that, despite all appearances, the *Estafette* must have gone immediately to Constantinople. But naval records quoted in Michon 1900 (318, n. 2) show it arriving in Smyrna on April 26. In his letter of April 25 to Riviere, Pierre David, the French consul in Smyrna, says that he has talked to Robert about the statue. There is a discrepancy between the dates: David couldn't have talked with Robert on the twenty-fifth because the *Estafette* had not yet arrived in port. The simplest explanation is that David made a mistake in dating the letter or began it on the twenty-fifth and finished it the next day after talking with Robert.

8 Robert the Devil: Aicard, 231.

Sulfur and vampires

9 descriptions of Melos: Renfrew, Bradford, Melas, Facaros, Slot, Stanford and Finopoulos, Blount, Sonnini, Slade, Bent, Swan.

11 population in 1820: Slot.

11 customs and superstitions: Sonnini.

11 vampires: Bent.

The hand with an apple

12 neighbors offering money, interest of primates: Voutier's account, quoted in Alaux, de Lorris.

12 description of primates and dragomans: Dakin, 12–15; Slot, 263; Tournefort, 161.

13 life of Brest's grandfather: Sonnini, 145–6.

13 Brest's age: Doussault (7) says Brest was about seventy years old in 1847,

but this is a mistake since Brest was born 20 March 1789, according to his tombstone, making him thirty-one at the time of the discovery and only fifty-eight when Doussault met him.

14 move to cowshed: Yorgos must have moved the pieces on April 9, because on April 10 the other two boats arrived and Brest took their captains to the cowshed to see the statue. On April 11 Captain Dauriac wrote his letter.

14 ships in port, order of arrival: Besnier, 207.

14 Dauriac's letter: Alaux, 175

15 Brest's letter: Besnier, 207.

15 apple myth: Bulfinch.

The ambitious ensign

16 d'Urville's biography: Rosenman, Guillon.

16 d'Urville description: Rosenman, xivii.

17 "I promised myself": ibid., xliii.

18 Matterer quote: ibid., xliv.

18 description of Castro: Swan, 85.

18 provocative women: Sonnini.

18 "The quantity of the insects": ibid., 147.

19 account of visit to the statue: Matterer, as quoted in Aicard, 146.

The kaptan pasha's dragoman

20 primates, dragomans, and the islands under the Ottomans: Dakin, 12; Slot, 263; Tournefort, 161.

21 Prince Morousi: Marcellus, 1840, 201.

22 Oconomos: Aicard, 19.

23 Yorgos and price of statue: Aicard, 203, in Brest's letter to Rivière.

The portrait of a girl

23 *Chevrette*'s voyage to Constantinople: Besnier, 210.

23 description of Marcellus: from Ingres sketch in de Lorris, 55.

23 biographical details about Marcellus: Hoeffer.

23 meeting at ambassador's dinner: Besnier, 212.

23 hike in countryside: Marcellus, 1840, 191.

24 Ender's painting and the girl: Marcellus, 1840.

25 *Chevrette*'s departure: Besnier, 210.

25 arrival of *Estafette* in Constantinople, departure for Melos: Besnier, 215.

Marcellus negotiates a purchase

26 arrival, Voutier quote, other French ships: Alaux, 28.

26 Oconomos raising price: Ravaisson 1892.

26 Russian ship: It is variously reported as Albanian, Russian, Greek, and Austrian. Ravaisson says it was Russian. Discussion of different nationalities in Michon 1900, 313, fn. 1.

27 contrary wind: Marcellus 1840, 192.

27 account of negotiations: All from Marcellus 1840, except the reference to a threat of force, which is in Michon 1900, 317.

29 friendship of Marcellus and dragoman: Marcellus, 1840, 201.

30 750 francs: Per Marcellus 1840. Several different prices have been quoted. Account of different prices in Michon 1900, 312, fn. 3.

30 account of loading the statue: Alaux, 49. For the date as May 24, Alaux cites Robert's log. Marcellus says it was the 23rd, but he must be mistaken.

30 Marcellus quote: Marcellus 1840, 198.

The island girl Maritza

31 Marcellus tells this story himself in *Souvenirs* (1840).

31 prostitution on Melos: Stanford and Finopoulos.

33 anecdote about pilot and Maritza: Marcellus 1851.

Venus by moonlight

33 voyage after purchase: Alaux (Voutier singing, 67, 179).

33 showing Fauvel: ibid., 76.

34 arrival in Smyrna: ibid., 80.

34 Brest in Smyrna, outrage of dragoman, and Morousi's death: Marcellus 1840, 200.

34 "In Smyrna I left": Alaux, 81.

The troublesome inscriptions

35 biography of Rivière: Hoeffer, Michon 1906. The letter quoted is in Michon 1906, 7.

II. Winckelmann

37 "Good taste,": Wohlleben, 172.

37 fifty copies: Winckelmann 1987, xv.

37 "Summoned a submerged continent": Butler, 11.

38 Winckelmann in Enlightenment France: Pommier, 10.

39 superficial descriptions: Winckelmann 1987, xiv.

39 "One learns nothing": Honour 1987, 58.

39 antiquity all of a piece: Honour 1987, 59.

A Greek reincarnated

39 Winckelmann's biography: Butler, 10, 14ff.

40 "I shall bury myself": ibid., 13.

40 "mangy-headed little boys": ibid., 14.

41 "The only way": Winckelmann 1987, 5.

41 "imitation of the Greeks": ibid., 19.

41 Winckelmann on Bernini: ibid., 21.

41 "noble simplicity and quiet grandeur": ibid., 33.

42 September 1755: Butler, 18.

42 Catholic court. ibid., 16.

Signor Giovanni

43 Vernon Lee: quoted in Butler, 18.

43 Casanova: quoted in Potts 1994, 212.

44 "The independence of Greece": Winckelmann 1968, 289.

44 "One can distinguish": Wohlleben, 174.

45 Winckelmann on the Apollo Belvedere: quoted in Honour 1987, 60.

46 "the only precedent": ibid., 60.

47 murder story: Butler, 40ff; Leppmann, 6.

47 Pasolini: Potts 1994, 17.

Perfection by imitation

48 art academies, economic growth: Pevsner, 151, 152.

48 Pompeii: Constantine, 111.

48 insects: Bracken, 87.

48 guards' extortion: Eisner, 75.

48 *Antiquities of Athens:* Bracken, 10.

48 Barthélemy: Augustinos, 137ff.

49 Flaxman prints: Honour 1987, 88.

III. In the Hallways of the Louvre

50 shops, restaurants, etc.: Mansel 2001, 42–3.
51 "No other capital": Willms, 183.
51 boulevards: Mansel 2001, 50; Willms, 164.
51 English guidebook: quoted in Mansel 2001, 47.
51 toast: ibid., 43.
51 descriptions of Paris: Much of this is from Barzun, 519.
52 population 800,000: Willms, 158.
52 sludge in streets: ibid., 179.
52 diseases: Barzun, 536.
52 family economy: Willms, 162.
52 Louis XVIII: Mansel 2001, 191.

The looted masterpieces

54 "These houses . . . lie wrapped": Balzac, 60–61.
55 on the Louvre: Gould, 3ff.
55 official looting of art, books, plants: ibid., 32.
55 "to send secretly after the armies": Chatelain, 163.
56 "These immortal works": ibid.
56 "There is only we": Pommier, 14.
56 new edition of Winckelmann: ibid., 15.
56 Greek influence on revolutionary society: Badolle, 385ff.
57 song lyric: ibid., 386.
57 Napoleon assumes command in Italy: Gould, 44.
57 Convoy of arts from Italy: Chatelain, 165–6.
58 Denon rushing into battles: ibid., 172.
58 De Non: ibid., 21.
58 debauches in remote châteaux: Chatelain, 76.
58 people Denon knew: ibid., 12.
58 Denon-Napoleon meeting: ibid., 78.
59 Denon taking the best: ibid., 168.
59 Musée Napoléon visitor quotes: ibid., 214.
59 soldiers and workers: ibid., 211.

The masterpieces reclaimed

59 Napoleon and art and motivations: Gould, 42–3.
60 "removal of the Apollo": Gould, 41.

60 "this celestial mixture": Haskell and Penny, 148.

60 "Can one find anywhere": ibid., 91.

60 Napoleon and plaque: ibid., 112.

60 quote on plaque: Chatelain, 210–11.

61 Van Dyck, Rembrandt . . . : Chatelain, 302.

61 Respect for museum: Chatelain, 218.

61 numbers of works reclaimed: Chaudonneret, 12; Chatelain, 250.

61 woodcut: reproduced in Chatelain, third group of pictures.

Artist, lover

Unless otherwise noted, the details of Forbin's personal life are from his letters published in Neto 1995.

61 Louis XVIII quote: Chatelain, 223.

62 description of Forbin: from Ingres portrait and various memoirs.

63 Forbin's birth and family: in Hoeffer.

64 Granet meeting: in Hoeffer; Granet's memoirs, 5.

64 "I am a little surprised": Neto 1995, 60.

64 "cemented the affection": Marcellus 1843.

64 David's school and his quote: Delecluze 1883.

65 "Forbin carried": Neto 1995, 301.

The unhappy husband

67 slave market: Carre, 195.

67 Casts of Elgin marble, etc.: casts Angrand, 62; Moses, 63, (Ingres and chapel) 76, (Forbin quote) 63.

69 "It is unfortunate": Neto 1995, 300.

70 "like a rabid dog": Neto 1995, 65.

70 "I believe": Neto 1995, 70.

70 Rumors that Forbin's painting was really by Granet: Neto 1995, 72.

D'Urville returns

The politics inside the Louvre and the letters it produced are from Michon 1900 and 1902 unless otherwise indicated.

72 d'Urville arrives in October: Besnier, 222.

72 d'Urville reads paper: ibid., also 223, (paper he read) 231.

73 "Thus the obscure ensign": ibid., 218.

73 "I owe to a lucky happenstance": ibid., 206.

An embarrassment appears and disappears

73 "Experts are busy": Michon 1900, 307.

75 reasoning of scholars about the slab's inauthenticity: extrapolated from Quatremère de Quincy's footnote in his "Dissertation" and from later rationales as in Michon 1900.

The right scholar

78 Emeric-David and Winckelmann: Potts 1978, 203.

78 Emeric's opinion on the statue: Emeric-David, 234.

79 Quatremère on women: Quatremère 1980, xxxvi.

79 Quatremère dispute with Forbin: Angrand, 199.

80 Forbin knew what was in the paper: Neto, 65.

80 Quotes from "Dissertation": ibid., 240.

Clarac's anger

84 "There are antiquaries": Maury, 756.

85 "I don't really see why you address yourself": Ravaisson 1871b.

86 "pure forgetfulness": Michon 1900, 351.

87 "represent an epoch" and further quotes: Clarac 1821.

The statue comes to the king

88 "I find your ideas": Michon 1900, 353.

89 Fontaine's buildings: Fontaine, liv.

89 Fontaine's personal life: Fouche, 72.

89 anecdote about Fontaine and money: Hoeffer, 323.

90 "The continual buzzing": Fontaine, 537.

92 museum as place of instruction, "a place consecrated": Chaudonneret, 41.

92 "uselessness" and "fantasies": Fontaine, 617.

92 coming to blows: ibid., 617.

92 plaster cast: ibid., 618.

93 jury to decide: ibid., 617–18.

93 "I have the honor": Michon 1900, 358.

93 "I am truly displeased": ibid., 358.
93 "It was only the personal interest": Fontaine, 627.

A cavalier in a corset

94 corset and Spanish fly: Neto 1995, 303.
95 Forbin carried into Récamier salon: Goncourt and Goncourt, 65.

IV. Broken Marble

96 opening anecdote: Delacroix's *Journals.*

The sealed room

97 details of Ravaisson's life: Dulière, Borgson.
98 hiding the statue during the Franco-Prussian War: Gautier.
101 problems exposed by missing sides: Ravaisson 1871b.

The protruding edge

106 "Venus appears": Gautier, 357.

Habitual passivity

107 "Never did a man": Bergson, 278.

The story of the fight on the shore

111 biographical details about Aicard: Guirand, Burnett. Rest of situation: Aicard.
112 "I would have": Aicard, 43.
113 Brest's letter: Runciok 1930, 255.
113 d'Urville's paper: ibid., 253.

The drawings reappear

114 Marcellus, Voutier, and the drawings: Aicard, de Lorris.
115 "a scuffle": Beard, 120.

115 "Years later, Marcellus's account": Augustinos, 233.

116 "Though Marcellus never admits": Arscott and Scott, 3.

The Venus of the Gardens

118 "image expressing divine grace": Ravaisson 1985, 84.

120 Reinach's review of Ravaisson's paper: Reinach 1893.

120 Furtwängler's review: Furtwängler 1893.

V. Two Geniuses

122 Prince Ludwig: Haskell 1981, 116.

122 Heine crying: Galard, 106. He also thought she looked at him with pity as if she wanted to say, "Can't you see I don't have arms and am not able to help you?"

123 Furtwängler's life before work in Athens: Briggs and Calder, 84ff.

123 "all fire": Briggs and Calder, 85.

124 Furtwängler and pottery from Mycenae: Marchand 2000a.

125 Curtius at Olympia: Briggs and Calder.

126 philology and the desirability of finds: Marchand 2000b, 196.

126 Hermes copy: Michaelis, 131.

127 Furtwängler at Olympia, "rubbish of ancient times": Briggs and Calder, Marchand 2000a.

127 "I feel quite satisfied": Marchand, 2000a.

128 Furtwängler after Olympia: Briggs and Calder, Bazant.

128 "I am already": Bazant, 91.

129 "One of my fundamental failings": Briggs and Calder, 88.

129 Furtwängler marriage and family life: Schonzeler, Schuchhardt.

129 appearance and lecturing style: Church.

130 Wilhelm Furtwängler: Schonzeler.

The island

Unless otherwise noted, Reinach's life, bibliography, marriage, beliefs are from introduction to Reinach 1996 or Pottier.

131 Reinach: The final *ch* is hard and is pronounced like *k*.

133 back of a woman's neck: Samuels, 123.

133 Liane de Pougy anecdote and quote: Pougy, 142.

134 "Tell me then": Morra, 269.

134 "Much more romance": Wickes, 158.

136 "She reads nothing": ibid., 8.

136 "Surely the wild girl": Samuels, 207.

136 "physical radiance": ibid.

136 "I was madly in love": Biocca, 150.

137 Liane de Pougy biography: Chalon.

138 "We were passionate": Pougy, 253.

138 Pougy's quotes about Reinach: Pougy, 107, 135, 125, 117, 51.

139 "I blame myself": Reinach, 181.

139 Reinach's letters to Pougy: ibid., 169, 190.

A mystical crisis

140 Joseph Reinach and anti-Semitism: Birnbaum.

142 travels to Athens and the Aegean: Reinach 1996.

A tiara for 200,000 francs

143 walking with Furtwängler: Reinach 1996.

144 story of the tiara: Pasquier 1994.

145 Reinach's refusal to defend himself: Metzger, 39.

A goddess in a limekiln

145 "I repeat today": Reinach 1930, 251. The narrative of the debate between Reinach and Fürtwangler is drawn from Reinach 1930, 250–356.

146 "the style of the Venus" and following quotes: ibid., 259.

Meisterforschung

147 "have preserved . . . the masterpieces": Furtwängler 1964, viii.

148 attacks on Furtwängler's reconstruction of Lemnian Athena: Hartswick, Palagia.

148 "still a center of eager controversy": Furtwängler 1964, 367.

149 "When the statue": ibid., 368.

149 "disappearance of the inscription": ibid., 369.

149 "Not even the most ignorant": ibid., 375.

150 "Therefore he too": ibid., 368.

152 "not altogether happy": ibid., 384.

152 "at least a man": ibid., 401.

152 "lines of the composition": ibid., 386.

An inscription reappears

155 *"if the Venus is contemporary"*: Reinach 1930, 288.
155 "question of the date": ibid., 290.
156 "as if she wanted": ibid., 312.

The patience of a saint

158 "I admit": Reinach 1930, 337.
159 "previously content": ibid., 338.
159 "What a shame": ibid., 340.

Lilacs and tulips

160 Furtwängler's later work: Briggs and Calder.
160 Furtwängler's death: Church.
161 Glozel affair: Renfrew, Pottier.
161 "looked like a dying eagle": Samuels, 397.
161 "saw him lying on a sofa": Pougy, 242.
162 "life itself is a burden": Reinach 1980, 301.
162 "that rather chill giantess": Grigson, 156.

VI. A Goddess with Golden Hair

Much of the discussion of Greek sculpture in this chapter draws on Bruneau.

Foam-born

173 nature of Greek gods: Thornton 1997, 2000.
173 "Nature is primal power": Paglia, 57.
174 sexuality and women in Greece: Blundell; Thornton 1997, 2000.

The nude goddess

178 history of statues of Aphrodite: Brinkerhoff; Havelock 1981 and 1995.
180 "Woman, thus fashioned, is reduced": Salomon, 204.
180 "I question": Havelock 1985, 37.

Roman taste

183 Romans and their conservative taste: Brinkerhoff.

Contrary to the general opinion

185 "Beginning in 1893": Charbonneaux 1951, 8.

A poet and sculptor from Antioch

185 role of the gymnasium: Walbank.
186 Venus in gymnasiums: Corso.
187 Thespiae inscription mentioning Alexandros: ibid.
188 "the alignment": Clarac 1821.

VII. The Last Chapter

193 Facial research: Gunturkun.
195 Magritte quote, other artists, cartoons, ads: Salmon.
198 "matronly": Smith, 81.
198 "mild merits hardly justify": Robertson, 554.
198 "placed beside the original": Smith, 81.
200 "Authors writing on nude classical sculptures": Brown, 18.
202 "planes of her body": Clark, 138.

BIBLIOGRAPHY

Abrantes, Duchesse de. *At the Court of Napoleon*. New York: Doubleday, 1989.

Aicard, Jean. *La Vénus de Milo: Recherches sur l'histoire de la découverte*. Paris: Sandoz et Fischbacher, 1874.

Alaux, Jean-Paul. *La Vénus de Milo et Olivier Voutier*. Paris: Collection du Galion d'Or, 1939.

Angrand, Pierre. *Le comte de Forbin et le Louvre en 1819*. Paris: La Bibliothèque des Arts, 1972.

Antal, Frederick. *Classicism and Romanticism with Other Studies in Art History*. New York: Basic Books, 1966.

Arenas, Amelia. "Broken: The Venus de Milo." *Arion*, Winter 2002: 35.

Aronson, Theo. *The Golden Bees: The Story of the Bonapartes*. Greenwich, Conn.: New York Graphic Society, 1964.

Arscott, Caroline, and Katie Scott, eds. *Manifestations of Venus: Art and Sexuality*. Manchester: Manchester University Press, 2000.

Augustinos, Olga. *French Odysseys: Greece in French Travel Literature from the Renaissance to the Romantic Era*. Baltimore and London: Johns Hopkins University Press, 1994.

Autin, Jean. *La duchesse d'Abrantès*. Paris: Perrin, 1991.

Babelon, E. Review of Furtwängler's *Die antiken Gemmen*. *Journal des Savants*, 1900: 445.

Badolle, Maurice. *L'abbé Jean-Jacques Barthélemy (1716–1795) et l'Hellénisme en France dans la seconde moitié du XVIIIᵉ siècle*. Paris: Presses Universitaires de France, 1926.

Balzac, Honoré de. *Cousin Bette*. Trans. Marion Ayton Crawford. Middlesex: Penguin Books, 1984.

Bann, Stephen. "Romanticism in France." In *Romanticism in National Context*, edited by Roy Porter and Mikuláš Teich. Cambridge: Cambridge University Press, 1988.

Bibliography

Barthélemy-Saint-Hilaire, Jules. *M. Victor Cousin: Sa vie et sa correspondance.* Paris: Hachette et Cie., 1895.

Bazant, Jan. "The Case of the Talkative Connoisseur." *Eirene* 29 (1993): 84.

Barzun, Jacques. *A Jacques Barzun Reader.* New York: HarperCollins, 2002.

Beard, Mary, and John Henderson. *Classical Art from Greece to Rome.* Oxford: Oxford University Press, 2001.

Belting, Hans. "Le musée et la conception du chef-d'oeuvre." Trans. Edouard Pommier. In *Histoire de l'histoire de l'art,* vol. 1. Paris: Klincksieck, 1995.

Benoît, François. *L'art français sous la Révolution et l'Empire.* Geneva: Slatkine-Megariotis Reprints, 1975.

Bent, James Theodore. *Aegean Islands: The Cyclades, or Life among the Insular Greeks.* 1884. Revised edition edited and enlarged by A. N. Oikonomides. Chicago: Argonaut, 1964.

Bergson, Henri. *The Creative Mind.* Trans. Mabelle L. Andison. New York: Philosophical Library, 1946.

Bertier de Sauvigny, G. de. *La Restauration.* Paris: Flammarion, 1955.

Besnier, Maurice. "La Vénus de Milo et Dumont d'Urville." *Revue des Etudes Anciennes,* 1908: 207.

Bieber, Margarete. *The Sculpture of the Hellenistic Age.* New York: Columbia University Press, 1961.

Bikelas, D. "Le philhellénisme en France." *Revue d'Histoire Diplomatique* 5 (1891): 346–65.

Biocca, Dario, ed. *A Matter of Passion.* Berkeley: University of California Press, 1989.

Birnbaum, Pierre. *The Jews of the Republic.* Trans. Jane Marie Todd. Stanford: Stanford University Press, 1996.

Blount, Sir Henry. *A Voyage into the Levant.* Reprint of 1636 edition published by Crooke. London: 1977.

Blundell, Sue. *Women in Ancient Greece.* London: British Museum Press, 1995.

Boardman, John. *Greek Sculpture: The Late Classical Period.* London: Thames and Hudson, 1995.

———. *Greek Art.* London: Thames and Hudson, 1996.

Bois, Joseph. "Une anecdote sur Clarac." *Revue Archéologique,* 1910: 169.

Boutroux, Emile. "La philosophie de Félix Ravaisson." *Revue de Métaphysique et de Morale,* 1900.

Bracken, C. P. *Antiquities Acquired: The Spoliation of Greece.* London: David and Charles, 1975.

Bradford, Ernle. *The Companion Guide to the Greek Islands.* New York: Harper and Row, 1963.

Bremen, Riet van. *The Limits of Participation.* Amsterdam: J. C. Gieben, 1996.

Bresc, Geneviève. *Mémoires du Louvre.* Paris: Découvertes Gallimard, 1989.

Briggs, Ward W., and William M. Calder III, eds. *Classical Scholarship: A Biographical Encyclopedia.* New York: Garland Publishing, 1990.

Brinkerhoff, Dericksen Morgan. *Hellenistic Statues of Aphrodite.* New York: Garland Publishing, 1978.

Broglie, duc de. *Souvenirs 1785–1870.* Paris: Calmann-Lévy, 1886.

Brookner, Anita. *Jacques-Louis David.* New York: Harper and Row, 1980.

Brooks, John I., III. *The Eclectic Legacy: Academic Philosophy and the Human Sciences in Nineteenth-Century France.* Newark: University of Delaware Press, 1998.

Brown, Shelby. " 'Ways of Seeing' Women in Antiquity." In *Naked Truths,* ed. Ann Olga Koloski-Ostrow and Claire L. Lyons. London: Routledge, 1997.

Brown, Wallace Cable. "English Travel Books and Minor Poetry about the Near East, 1775–1825." *Philological Quarterly* 16, no. 3 (July 1937): 249–71.

Bruneau, Philippe. "Greek Art." In *Sculpture from Antiquity to the Present Day,* ed. Georges Duby. Cologne: Taschen, 1996.

Bulfinch, Thomas. *The Age of Fable or Beauties of Mythology.* Ed. J. Loughran Scott. Philadelphia: David McKay, 1898.

Burnett, Andrew Hammond. "The Novels of Jean Aicard (to 1909)." Unpublished Master's thesis, Stanford University, 1935.

Butler, E. M. *The Tyranny of Greece over Germany.* Boston: Beacon Press, 1958.

Canat, René. *La Renaissance de la Grèce Antique (1820–1850).* Paris: Librairie Hachette et Cie., 1911.

Carré, Jean-Marie. *Voyageurs et ecrivains français en Egypte.* Paris: Le Caire, 1932.

Carus, Paul. *Venus: An Archeological Study of Woman.* Chicago: Open Court, 1916.

Ceram, C. W., ed. *The World of Archaeology: The Pioneers Tell Their Own Story.* London: Thames and Hudson, 1966.

Chaffanjon, Arnaud. *Napoléon et l'Univers Impérial.* Paris: SERG, 1969.

Chaffiol-Debillemont, F. *Petite suite excentrique.* Paris: Mercure de France, 1952.

Chalon, Jean. *Liane de Pougy: Courtisane, princesse et sainte.* Paris: Flammarion, 1994.

Charbonneaux, Jean. "La Vénus de Milo et Mithridate le Grand." *La Revue des Arts* 1 (1951): 8.

———. "Le geste de la Vénus de Milo." *La Revue des Arts* 6, no. 2 (1956): 105.

Charbonneaux, Jean, et al. *Hellenistic Art 330–50 B.C.* Trans. Peter Green. London: Thames and Hudson, 1973.

Chateaubriand, vicomte de. *Memoirs.* New York: G. P. Putnam's Sons, 1902.

Chatelain, Jean. *Dominique Vivant Denon et le Louvre de Napoléon.* Paris: Perrin, 1999.

Chaudonneret, Marie-Claude. *L'état et les artistes (1815–1833).* Paris: Flammarion, 1999.

Christiansen, Rupert. *Romantic Affinities: Portraits from an Age 1780–1830*. London: Bodley Head, 1988.

Church, J. E., Jr. "Adolf Furtwängler." *University of Nevada Studies*, 1908–11: 61.

Clarac, Charles-Othon-Frédéric-Jean-Baptiste, comte de. *Sur la statue antique de Vénus Victrix decouverte dans l'ile de Milo, avec un dessin de Debay fils*. Paris, 1821.

———. *Description historique et graphique du Louvre et des Tuileries*. Paris: Imprimerie Impériale, 1853.

Clark, Kenneth. *The Nude*. Garden City, N.Y.: Doubleday Anchor Books, 1959.

Clarke, M. L. *Greek Studies in England 1700–1830*. Cambridge: The University Press, 1945.

Cole, Robert. *A Traveller's History of Paris*. New York: Interlink, 1994.

Constant, Benjamin. *Lettres à Madame Récamier (1807–1830)*. Paris: Librairie C. Klincksieck, 1977.

Constantine, David. *Early Greek Travellers and the Hellenic Ideal*. Cambridge: Cambridge University Press, 1984.

Corso, Antonio. "A Short Note about the Aphrodite of Melos." *Xenia Antiqua* 4 (1995): 27.

Coward, D. A. "Attitudes to Homosexuality in Eighteenth-century France." *Journal of European Studies*, December 1980: 231.

Cuzin, Jean-Pierre, et al. *D'après l'antique*. Catalog for an exhibition at the Louvre, 2000.

Dakin, Douglas. *The Unification of Greece 1770–1923*. New York: St. Martin's Press, 1972.

Delacroix, Eugène. *Journal*. Trans. Walter Pach. New York: Friede Publishers, 1937.

Delecluze, E. J. *Souvenirs de soixante années*. Paris: Michel Levy Frères, 1862.

———. *Louis David: Son école et son temps*. Paris: Macula, 1883.

———. *Journal de Delecluze 1824–1828*. Paris: Editions Bernard Grasset, 1948.

de Lorris, Andrea. *Enlèvement de Vénus*. Paris: La Bibliothèque, 1994.

Demand, Nancy. *Birth, Death, and Motherhood in Classical Greece*. Baltimore: Johns Hopkins University Press, 1994.

Denon, Vivant. *Point de lendemain*. Paris: Gallimard, 1995.

Doussault, C. *La Vénus de Milo: Documents inédits*. Paris: Paul Ollendorff, 1877.

Duchêne, Hervé. "Un Athénien: Salomon Reinach." *Bulletin de Correspondance Hellénique*, 1996: 273.

———, ed. *Notre Ecole Normale*. Paris: Les Belles Lettres, 1994.

Duliere, André. *Visages namurois (1693–1970)*. Namur, Belgium: Les Presses de l'Avenir, 1974.

Durrell, Lawrence. *The Greek Islands*. New York: Viking Press, 1978.

Edwards, Paul, ed. *The Encyclopedia of Philosophy*. New York: Macmillan and Free Press, 1972.

Eisner, Robert. *Travelers to an Antique Land: The History and Literature of Travel to Greece*. Ann Arbor: University of Michigan Press, 1991.

Emeric-David, T. B. *Histoire de la sculpture antique*. Paris: Charpentier, 1853.

Engelhardt, Dietrich Von. "Romanticism in Germany." In *Romanticism in National Context*, edited by Roy Parker and Mikuláš Teich. Cambridge: Cambridge University Press, 1988.

Estève, Edmond. *Byron et le Romantisme français*. Paris: Boivin, 1929.

Etienne, Roland, and Françoise Etienne. *The Search for Ancient Greece*. Trans. Anthony Zielonka. New York: Harry N. Abrams, 1992.

Facaros, Dana. *Greek Island Hopping*. London: Sphere Books, 1979.

Faxon, Alicia. "Cézanne's Sources for 'Les Grandes Baigneuses.'" *Art Bulletin*, June 1983: 320.

Fontaine, Pierre-François-Léonard. *Journal 1799–1853*. Paris: Société de l'Histoire de l'Art Français, 1987.

Forbin, comte de. *Voyage dans le Levant en 1817 et 1818*. Paris: Imprimerie Royal, 1819.

Fouché, Maurice. *Percier et Fontaine*. Paris: Henri Laurens, 1904.

Friedrich, Paul. *The Meaning of Aphrodite*. Chicago: University of Chicago Press, 1978.

Fuller, Peter. *Art and Psychoanalysis*. N.p.: Writers and Readers, 1980.

Furtwängler, Adolf. Review of Ravaisson's *La Vénus de Milo*. *Berliner Philologische Wochenschrift*, August 26, 1893: 1107.

———. *Masterpieces of Greek Sculpture*. Trans. Eugenie Sellers Strong. Chicago: Argonaut, 1964.

Gaehtgens, Thomas W. "Le Musée Napoléon et son influence sur l'histoire de l'art." In *Histoire de l'histoire de l'art*. vol. 2. Paris: Klincksieck, 1995.

Galard, Jean, ed. *Visiteurs du Louvre*. Paris: Réunion des Musées Nationaux, 1993.

Gautier, Théophile. *Paris Besieged*. Trans. F. C. de Sumichrast. N.p.: Jenson Society, 1905.

Goethe, Johann Wolfgang von. *Essays on Art and Literature*. Ed. John Gearey. Trans. Ellen von Nardroff and Ernest H. von Nardroff. New York: Suhrkamp Publishers, 1986.

Gombrich, E. H. *The Story of Art*. London: Phaidon, 1997.

Goncourt, Edmond de, and Jules de Goncourt. *Journal 1862–1865*. Paris: Ernst Flammarion, 1935.

Gould, Cecil. *Trophy of Conquest: The Musée Napoléon and the Creation of the Louvre*. London: Faber and Faber, 1965.

Graves, Robert. *The Greek Myths.* London: Penguin, 1992.

Green, Peter. *Classical Bearings.* London: Thames and Hudson, 1989.

Grigson, Geoffrey. *The Goddess of Love.* London: Constable, 1976.

Grimm, Herman Friedrich. *Essays.* Nuremberg: Glock und Lutz, 1964.

Guillon, Jacques. *Dumont d'Urville 1790–1842.* Paris: Editions France-Empire, 1986.

Guirand, F. "Aicard." *Larousse Mensuel* no. 180 (February 1922): 26.

Gunturkun, Onur. "The Venus of Milo and the Dawn of Facial Asymmetry Research." *Brain and Cognition,* July 1991: 147.

Hadas, Moses. *Hellenistic Culture.* New York: W. W. Norton & Co., 1972.

Haddad, George. *Aspects of Social Life in Antioch in the Hellenistic-Roman Period.* New York: Hafner, 1949.

Hamiaux, Marianne. *Les sculptures grecques,* vol. 2. Paris: Réunion des Musées Nationaux, 1998.

Harmon, A. M. *Lucian with an English Translation.* New York: G. P. Putnam's Sons, 1921.

Hartog, François. "Faire le voyage d'Athènes: Johann Joachim Winckelmann et sa réception française," in *Winckelmann et le retour à l'antique.* Entretiens de la Garenne Lemot, 1994.

Hartswick, Kim J. "The Athena Lemnia Reconsidered." *American Journal of Archaeology,* January 1983: 335.

Haskell, Francis. *History and Its Images: Art and the Interpretation of the Past.* New Haven: Yale University Press, 1993.

———, and Nicholas Penny. *Taste and the Antique: The Lure of Classical Sculpture 1500–1900.* New Haven: Yale University Press, 1981.

Hasse, C. *Antike Bildwerke.* Strasbourg: Heitz und Mundel, 1911.

Hatfield, Henry Caraway. *Winckelmann and His German Critics 1755–1781.* New York: King's Crown Press, 1943.

Hauptman, William. "Juries, Protests, and Counter-Exhibitions before 1850." *Art Bulletin,* March 1985: 95.

Havelock, Christine Mitchell. *Hellenistic Art.* New York: W. W. Norton & Co., 1981.

———. *The Aphrodite of Knidos and Her Successors.* Ann Arbor: University of Michigan Press, 1995.

Hemmerdinger, Bertrand. "La falsification de la Vénus de Milo." *Quaderni di storia* no. 17 (1983): 187.

Hemmings, F. W. J. *Culture and Society in France 1789–1848.* Leicester, England: Leicester University Press, 1987.

Herriot, Edouard. *Madame Récamier.* Trans. Alys Hallard. New York: Boni and Liveright, 1926.

Hitchens, Christopher. *The Elgin Marbles: Should They Be Returned to Greece?* London: Verso, 1997.

Hoeffer, J. C. F., ed. *Nouvelle biographie générale*. Paris: Firmin Didot Frères, 1856.

Honour, Hugh. *Romanticism*. New York: Westview Press, 1979.

———. *Neo-Classicism*. Middlesex, England: Penguin, 1987.

Howard, Seymour. "The Antiquarian Market in Rome and the Rise of Neo-classicism: A Basis for Canova's New Classics." *Studies on Voltaire and the Eighteenth Century*, vol. 153. Oxford: Voltaire Foundation, 1976.

Irwin, David. "The Industrial Revolution and the Dissemination of Neoclassical taste." *Studies on Voltaire and the Eighteenth Century*, vol. 153. Oxford: Voltaire Foundation, 1976.

———, ed. *Winckelmann: Writings on Art*. London: Phaidon, 1972.

Jacob, André, ed. *L'Univers philosophique*. Paris: Presses Universitaires de France, 1997.

Jaincaud, Dominique. *Une généalogie du spiritualisme français*. La Haye, France: Martinus Nijhoff, 1969.

Johns, Christopher M. S. *Antonio Canova and the Politics of Patronage in Revolutionary and Napoleonic Europe*. Berkeley: University of California Press, 1988.

Kangas, Matthew. "Rebirth of Venus." *Sculpture,* November–December 1990: 49.

Kundera, Milan. *Slowness*. Trans. Linda Asher. New York: HarperPerennial, 1997.

Lagrange, Léon. "Dumont d'Urville et la Vénus de Milo." *Archives de l'Art Français* (Paris) 2 (1862): 202.

Lambrichs, Colette, and Corneille Hannoset. *La Vénus de Milo ou Les dangers de la célébrité*. Catalog for an exhibition organized by the Ready Museum. Brussels: 1973.

Larrabee, Stephen A. *English Bards and Grecian Marbles*. New York: Columbia University Press, 1943.

Lavery, Brian. *Nelson's Navy: The Ships, Men, and Organizations 1793–1815*. Annapolis, Md.: Naval Institute Press, 1989.

Lavin, Sylvia. *Quatremere de Quincy and the Invention of a Modern Language of Architecture*. Cambridge: MIT Press, 1992.

Lebensztejn, Jean-Claude. "De l'imitation dans les beaux-arts." *Critique,* January 1982: 3.

Lebovics, Herman. *Mona Lisa's Escort: André Malraux and the Reinvention of French Culture*. Ithaca, N.Y.: Cornell University Press, 1999.

Le Clere, Marcel, ed. *Paris de la préhistoire à nos jours*. Paris; Editions Bordessoules, 1985.

Lenotre, G. "Pourquoi la Vénus de Milo est sans Bras." *Le Jardin des Arts,* November 1954: 46.

Leppmann, Wolfgang. *Winckelmann.* New York: Knopf, 1970.

Lethaby, W. R. "The Venus de Milo and the Apollo of Cyrene." *Journal of Hellenic Studies,* 1919: 206.

Levaillant, Maurice. *Les Amours de Benjamin Constant.* Paris: Hachette, 1958.

Levin, Harry. *The Broken Column: A Study in Romantic Hellenism.* Cambridge: Harvard University Press, 1931.

Lewis, H. D. "The Legal Status of Women in Nineteenth-Century France." *Journal of European Studies,* September 1980: 178.

Livingstone, Marco. *Jim Dine: The Alchemy of Images.* New York: Monacelli Press, 1998.

Lucian. Eng. trans. by A. M. Harmon. London: William Heinemann, 1921.

Luke, Yvonne. "The Politics of Participation: Quatremère de Quincy and the Theory and Practice of 'Concours publiques' in Revolutionary France 1791–1795." *Oxford Art Journal* 10, no. 1 (1987): 15.

Mach, Edmund von. *Greek Sculpture: Its Spirit and Principles.* Boston: Athenaeum Press, 1903.

Malakis, Emile. *French Travelers in Greece (1770–1820): An Early Phase of French Philhellenism.* Philadelphia: University of Pennsylvania, 1925.

Mansel, Philip. *Louis XVIII.* London: Blond and Briggs, 1981.

———. *Paris between Empires 1814–1852.* London: John Murray, 2001.

Marcellus, comte de. *Souvenirs de L'Orient.* Brussels: Société Belge de Librairie, 1840.

———. *Portefeuille de comte de Forbin, ses tableaux, dessius, et equisses les plus remarquable.* Paris: 1843.

———. *Episodes littéraires en Orient.* Paris: Jacques Lecoffre et Cie., 1851.

———. "Un dernier mot sur la Vénus de Milo." *Revue Contemporaine* 13 (1854): 291.

Marchand, Suzanne L. *Down from Olympus: Archaeology and Philhellenism in Germany, 1750–1970.* Princeton: Princeton University Press, 1996.

———. "The Excavations at Olympia, 1868–1881: An Episode in Greco-German Cultural Relations." *Greek Society in the Making, 1863–1913.* Aldershot, England: Ashgate Variorum, 1997.

———. "Adolf Furtwängler at Olympia: On Excavation, the Antiquarian Tradition, and Philhellenism in Nineteenth-Century Germany." Paper delivered at the Olympia symposium, November 2000a.

———. "The Quarrel of the Ancients and Moderns in the German Museums." In *Museums and Memory,* ed. Susan A. Crane. Stanford: Stanford University Press, 2000b.

Marrus, Michael R. *The Politics of Assimilation*. Oxford: Clarendon Press, 1971.

Martin-Fugier. *Les Romantiques: Figures de l'artiste*. Paris: Hachette, 1998.

Marvin, Miranda. "Roman Sculptural Reproductions or Polykleitos: The Sequel." In *Sculpture and Its Reproductions*, eds. Anthony Hughes and Erich Ranfft. London: Reaktion Books, 1997.

Masson, Frédéric. *Napoléon et sa famille*. Paris: Société d'Editions Littéraires et Artistiques, 1900.

Mat-Hasquin, Michèle. *Voltaire et l'antiquité grecque*. Oxford: Voltaire Foundation, 1981.

Mauries, Patrick, ed. *Vies remarquables de Vivant Denon*. Paris: Gallimard, 1988.

Maury, Alfred. "Nécrologie" (Clarac). *Revue Archéologique*, 1846: 754.

McClellan, Andrew. *Inventing the Louvre*. Cambridge: Cambridge University Press, 1994.

Medwid, Linda M. *The Makers of Classical Archaeology*. Amherst, Mass.: Humanity Books, 200.

Melas, Evi, ed. *Greek Islands*. New York: Stewart, Tabori and Chang, 1981.

Ménard, Louis. "Ares (Mars): Prototype des statues impériales." *Gazette des Beaux-Arts*, 1873: 450.

Metzger, Henri, et al. *A la mémoire de Salomon Reinach*. Paris: Mazarine, 1965.

Michaelis, A. *A Century of Archaeological Discoveries*. Trans. Bettina Kahnweiler. London: John Murray, 1908.

Michaud, J. F., and L. G. Michaud, eds. *Biographie universelle ancienne et moderne*. Paris: Delgrave, 1870–73.

Michon, Etienne. "La Vénus de Milo: Son arrivée et son exposition au Louvre." *Revue des Etudes Grecques*, 1900: 302.

———. "La Vénus de Milo." *Revue des Etudes Grecques*, 1902: 11.

———. *Le marquis de Rivière et la donation de la Vénus de Milo*. Paris: Imprimerie Générale Lahure, 1906.

Morra, Umberto. *Conversations with Berenson*. Trans. Florence Hammond. Boston: Houghton Mifflin, 1965.

Mouilleseaux, Jean-Pierre. "David: A Classical Painter against the Academy and a Teacher of the French School." In *The French Academy: Classicism and Its Antagonists*, ed. June Ellen Hargrove. Newark: University of Delaware Press, 1990.

Munhall, Edgar. *François-Marius Granet: Watercolors from the Musée Granet at Aix-en-Provence*. Trans. Joseph Focarino. New York: Frick Collection, 1988.

Nead, Lynda. *The Female Nude: Art, Obscenity, and Sexuality*. London: Routledge, 1992.

Neto, Isabelle. *Granet et son entourage*. Paris: Editions Jacques Laget, 1995.

———. "Auguste de Forbin et les salons de la Restauration: Les tribulations d'un directeur de musées." *Collections Parisiennes,* December 1997.

Nicolson, Harold. *Benjamin Constant.* Garden City, N.Y.: Doubleday and Company, 1949.

Niemeier, Jorg-Peter. *Kopien und Nachahmungen im Hellenismus.* Bonn: Dr. Rudolf Habelt, 1985.

Nur, Amos. "Poseidon's Horses: Plate Tectonics and Earthquake Storms in the Late Bronze Age Aegean and Eastern Mediterranean." *Journal of Archaeological Science* 27 (2000): 43–63.

———, and Eric H. Cline. "Earthquake Storms." *Archaeology Odyssey,* September–October 2001: 31–6.

Orenstein, Gloria Feman. "The Salon of Natalie Clifford Barney: An Interview with Berthe Cleyrergue." *Signs,* spring 1979: 484.

Overbeck, J. *Geschichte der Griechischen Plastik.* Leipzig: J. C. Hinrichs'sche Buchhandlung, 1882.

Ozgan, Ramazan. *Die griechischen und romischen Skulpturen aus Trailleis.* Bonn: Dr. Rudolf Habelt, 1995.

Paglia, Camille. *Sexual Personae.* New Haven: Yale University Press, 1990.

———. *Sex, Art, and American Culture.* New York: Vintage Books, 1992.

Palagia, Olga. "In Defense of Furtwängler's Athena Lemnia." *American Journal of Archaeology,* 1987: 81.

Pasquier, Alain. "La tiare de Saitapharnes: Histoire d'un achat malheureux." In catalog for "La jeunesse des musées." Paris: Musée d'Orsay, 1994.

———. *La Vénus de Milo et les Aphrodites du Louvre.* Paris: Editions de la Réunion des Musées Nationaux, 1985.

———. "Les salles de sculpture grecque au Louvre." *La Revue du Louvre et des Musées de France,* 1987: 91.

———. "Les voyages de la Vénus de Milo." *Revue des Deux Mondes,* September 1999: 35.

Pater, Walter. *The Renaissance.* London: Senate, 1998.

Perrot, Georges. Review of Furtwängler's *Die antiken Gemmen. Revue Archéologique,* July–December 1900: 474.

Peters, F. E. *The Harvest of Hellenism.* New York: Simon and Schuster, 1970.

Pevsner, Nikolaus. *Academies of Art Past and Present.* New York: Da Capo Press, 1973.

Plato. *The Collected Dialogs.* Ed. Edith Hamilton and Hunnington Cairns. Princeton: Princeton University Press, 1985.

Pollitt, J. J. *The Art of Ancient Greece: Sources and Documents.* Cambridge: Cambridge University Press, 1990.

Pommier, Edouard. "Winckelmann et la vision de l'antiquité classique dans la

France des Lumières et de la Révolution." *Gazette des Beaux-Arts,* April 1968: 9.

Pottier, Edmund. "Salomon Reinach." *Revue Archéologique,* 1937: 137.

Potts, Alex. "Political Attitudes and the Rise of Historicism in Art Theory." *Art History,* June 1978: 191.

———. *Flesh and the Ideal: Winckelmann and the Origins of Art History.* New Haven: Yale University Press, 1994.

Pougy, Liane de. *My Blue Notebooks.* Trans. Diana Athill. New York: Harper and Row, 1977.

Preuner, A. *Über die Restauration der Venus von Milo.* Greifswald: 1873.

Prévost, Michel, and Roman d'Amat, eds. *Dictionnaire de biographie française.* Paris: Librairie Letouzey et Ané, 1956.

Quatremère de Quincy, M. *Recueil de dissertations archéologiques.* Paris: Adrien Le Clere et Cie., 1836.

———. *De l'imitation.* Archives d'Architecture Moderne (Brussels), 1980.

———. *Considérations morales sur la destination des ouvrages de l'art.* Paris: Fayard, 1989.

Ramljak, Suzanne, et al. *A Disarming Beauty.* Catalog for an exhibition at the Salvador Dalí Museum. St. Petersburg, Fla.: 2001.

Raoul-Rochette. Review of Quatremère de Quincy's *Recueil de Dissertations archéologiques. Journal des Savants* (Paris), March and April 1837.

———. "Percier: Sa vie et ses ouvrages." *Revue des Deux Mondes* (Paris), October 15, 1840: 246.

Ravaisson, Félix. *Essai sur la Métaphysique d'Aristote.* Paris: Librairie Philosophique J. Vrin, 1837.

———. "La Vénus de Milo." *Revue des Deux Mondes* (Paris), September 1871a.

———. *La Vénus de Milo.* Paris: Librairie Hachette et Cie., 1871b.

———. "La Vénus de Milo." *Revue Archéologique* (Paris) 16 (1890).

———. "La Vénus de Milo." *Des Mémoires de l'Académie des Inscriptions et Belles Lettres* (Paris), 1892.

———. *La philosophie en France au XIXe siècle.* Paris: Librairie Philosophique J. Vrin, 1983.

———. *L'art et les mystères grecs.* Paris: L'Herne, 1985.

———. *De l'habitude.* Paris: Rivages Poche, 1997.

Reinach, Salomon. Review of Ravaisson on Venus de Milo. *Revue Critique d'Histoire et de Littérature* 35 (1893): 445.

———. Review of Furtwängler's *Die antiken Gemmen. Revue Critique,* 1900: 102.

———. "La tiare de Saitapharnes." *L'Anthropologie,* 1903: 238, 361.

———. "Documents nouveaux sur Frédéric de Clarac." *Revue Archéologique,* 1907: 304.

———. "Adolf Furtwängler." *Revue Archéologique,* 1907: 326.

———. "Pauline Tarn." *Notes and Queries,* 1914: 488.

———. *Répertoire de la statuaire grecque et romaine.* Paris: Editions Ernest Leroux, 1920.

———. *Monuments nouveaux de l'art antique.* Paris: Simon Kra, 1924.

———. *Apollo.* Trans. Florence Simms. New York: Charles Scribner's Sons, 1924.

———. "Souvenirs sur Furtwängler." *Revue Archéologique,* 1928: 204.

———. "Pour le 'sottisier' de la Vénus de Milo." *Revue Archéologique,* 1929: 181.

———. *Amalthée.* Paris: Librairie Ernst Leroux, 1930.

———. *Lettres à Liane de Pougy.* Paris: Plon, 1980.

———. *Cultes, mythes, et religions.* Paris: Robert Laffont, 1996.

Renfrew, Colin. "Glozel and the Two Cultures." *Antiquity* 49: 219.

———, and Malcolm Wagstaff. *An Island Polity: The Archaeology of Exploitation in Melos.* Cambridge: Cambridge University Press, 1982.

Robertson, Martin. *A History of Greek Art.* Cambridge: Cambridge University Press, 1975.

Rodin, Auguste. *Venus: To the Venus of Melos.* Trans. Dorothy Dudley. New York: B. W. Huebsch, 1912.

Rosenman, Helen, ed. and trans. *Two Voyages to the South Seas by Jules S-C Dumont D'Urville.* Melbourne: Melbourne University Press, 1987.

Saint-Victor, Paul de. *Hommes et dieux.* Paris: Michel Lévy Frères, 1867.

Salmon, Dimitri. *La Vénus de Milo: Un mythe.* Paris: Découvertes Gallimard, 2000.

Salomon, Nanette. "Making a World of Difference: Gender, Asymmetry, and the Greek Nude." In *Naked Truths,* ed. Ann Olga Koloski-Ostrow and Claire L. Lyons. London: Routledge, 1997.

Samuels, Ernest. *Bernard Berenson: The Making of a Legend.* Cambridge: Belknap Press, 1987.

Sandys, John Edwin. *A History of Classical Scholarship.* Cambridge: Cambridge University Press, 1908.

Sargeaunt, G. M. *Classical Studies.* London: Chatto and Windus, 1929.

Scarborough, John. *Facets of Hellenic Life.* Boston: Houghton Mifflin, 1976.

Schneider, R. "Un ennemi du Musée des Monuments Français." *Gazette des Beaux-Arts* (Paris), 1909: 353.

Schonzeler, Hans-Hubert. *Furtwängler.* London: Duckworth, 1990.

Schuchhardt, Walter-Herwig. *Adolf Furtwängler.* Freiburg: Rombach and Co., 1956.

Seward, Desmond. *Napoleon's Family.* London: Weidenfeld and Nicolson, 1986.

Shreve, William Price. *The Venus of Milo: Its Discovery, the Theories Concerning It, Its Subsequent History.* Boston: Shreve, Crump and Low, 1878.

Sichtermann, Helmut. *Kulturgeschichte der klassischen Archäologie.* Munich: Beck, 1996.

Slade, Adolphus. *Records of Travels in Turkey, Greece, &c.* London: Saunders and Otley, 1833.

Slot, B. J. *Archipelagus Turbatus.* Istanbul: Nederlands Historisch-Archaeologisch Instituut, 1982.

Smith, R. R. R. *Hellenistic Sculpture.* London: Thames and Hudson, 1991.

Sonnini, Charles-Sigisbert. *Voyage en Grèce et en Turque (1801).* Paris: Editions L'Harmattan, 1997.

Spencer, Terence. *Fair Greece, Sad Relic.* London: Weidenfeld and Nicolson, 1954.

Spivey, Nigel. *Understanding Greek Sculpture.* London: Thames and Hudson, 1996.

Stanford, W. B., and E. J. Finopoulos, eds. *The Travels of Lord Charlemont in Greece & Turkey 1749.* London: Trigraph, 1984.

Stern, Bernard Herbert. *The Rise of Romantic Hellenism in English Literature 1732–1786.* Menasha, Wis.: George Banta Publishing Company, 1940.

Steward, John Hall. *The Restoration Era in France: 1814–1830.* Princeton: D. Van Nostrand Company, 1968.

Stillman, W. J. *On the Track of Ulysses Together with an Excursion in Quest of the So-Called Venus of Melos.* Boston: Houghton Mifflin, 1888.

Suhr, Elmer G. *Venus de Milo, the Spinner.* New York: Exposition Press, 1958.

———. "The Spinning Aphrodite in Sculpture." *American Journal of Archaeology* no. 64 (1960): 253.

Swan, Rev. Charles. *Journal of a Voyage Up the Mediterranean.* London: C. and J. Rivington, 1826.

Tarn, W. W. *Hellenistic Civilization.* New York: New American Library, 1961.

Taylor, Joshua C. *Nineteenth Century Theories of Art.* Berkeley: University of California Press, 1987.

Thornton, Bruce S. *Eros: The Myth of Ancient Greek Sexuality.* New York: Westview Press, 1997.

———. *Greek Ways.* San Francisco: Encounter, 2000.

Tournefort, Joseph Pitton de. *A Voyage into the Levant.* Trans. John Ozell. London: D. Midwinter, 1741.

Turquan, Joseph. *A Great Coquette: Madame Récamier and Her Salon.* New York: Brentano's, 1913.

Vermeule, Cornelius. *European Art and the Classical Past.* Cambridge: Harvard University Press, 1964.

Vitry, Paul. *The Museum of the Louvre: A Concise Guide to the Various Collections.* Trans. Charles H. Hauff. Paris: Gaston Braun, 1913.

Vrettos, Theodore. *The Elgin Affair.* New York: Arcade, 1997.

Wagener, Françoise. *Madame Récamier 1777–1849.* Paris: J. C. Lattes, 1986.

Walbank, F. W. *The Hellenistic World.* Cambridge: Harvard University Press, 1992.

Wickes, George. *The Amazon of Letters.* New York: G. P. Putnam's Sons, 1976.

Willms, Johannes. *Paris, Capital of Europe.* Trans. Eveline L. Kanes. New York: Holmes and Meier, 1997.

Winckelmann, Johann Joachim. *History of Ancient Art.* Trans. Alexander Gode. New York: Frederick Ungar Publishing, 1968.

———. *Reflections on the Imitation of Greek Works in Painting and Sculpture.* Trans. Elfriede Heyer and Roger C. Norton. La Salle, Ill.: Open Court, 1987.

Wohlleben, Joachim. "Germany 1750–1830." Trans. Andrew Knight. In *Perceptions of the Ancient Greeks,* ed. K. J. Dover. Oxford: Blackwell, 1992.

Wolf, John B. *France 1814–1919.* New York: Harper Torchbooks, 1963.

Woodhouse, C. M. *The Philhellenes.* Rutherford, N.J.: Fairleigh Dickinson University Press, 1969.

———. *Modern Greece: A Short History.* London: Faber and Faber, 1991.

ACKNOWLEDGMENTS

THE IDEA for *Disarmed* took shape when my friend Daniel Okrent told me that the book I was describing to him—a book with chapters on various masterpieces of art—"sounded more like a series of magazine articles than a book. Why don't you pick just one?" I owe the existence of this book to Dan's sensible advice. He also kindly read the manuscript and gave helpful suggestions.

Stephen Harrigan, my neighbor and longtime friend, was always generous with his advice and enthusiasm during the time it took me to research and write. He read the manuscript at every stage and made incisive comments that greatly improved the final result.

My agent, David McCormick, believed in the project and in me even though I had never written a book before. During many conversations and much correspondence, he helped set me on the right path with his strong editorial voice and also handled the business affairs faultlessly.

William Broyles, Jr., was a friend and colleague in this as he has been in everything for more years than either of us want to count.

Lawrence Wright saved me from much wasted time and confusion with his suggestions about research and organization.

I'm very grateful to my editor, Ann Close, not only for her careful reading and notes, but also for believing in this book and its author from the beginning.

Norman Pearlstine has been a friend for many years. Recently he has shown great kindness toward me, without which this book could not have been written.

Alain Pasquier, general conservator of the Department of Greek, Etruscan, and Roman Antiquities at the Louvre, was generous on several occasions with his time and expertise.

Candy Gianetti's copyediting improved the manuscript in many ways. Chester Rosson's careful translation of many German sources helped immea-

Acknowledgments

surably. Claire Davenport spent many tedious hours poring through journals and databases for sources. Holly Brady of the Stanford Publishing Courses helped me navigate the perils of the Stanford library and bureaucracy. Suzanne Marchand of Louisiana State University provided very helpful information about German archeology and saved me from many errors and misinterpretations. Denise Schulze has spent long hours listening to me puzzle through French grammar. Thomas Palaima of the University of Texas was kind enough to read and comment incisively on my chapter on Greek society and art. Kevin Kwan in New York and Maria Vincenza Aloisi in Paris tracked down photographs and illustrations for me that were difficult to find. Caroline Wright did several searches for sources. I must also mention William Wiegand, now retired but formerly of San Francisco State College, from whom I learned most of what I know about writing and literature. The staff of the University of Texas at Austin libraries was unfailingly helpful.

Finally, I dedicate this book to my wife, Tracy. What she has given me is beyond measure. Also, many thanks to my son, Ben; my daughter, Vivian; and the other Venuses in my life, the members of T.L.L.W.C. You know who you are.

INDEX

ILLUSTRATION CREDITS

Big Ben

Peter Mac Donald

Big Ben is perhaps the most famous clock in the world. This book tells its story, from its conception in the 1830s, after fire destroyed the ancient Palace of Westminster, to its establishment as the national timepiece and the symbol of Britain.

Peter Mac Donald is the author of *Eclipse* and has also contributed articles to *Heritage* magazine and other publications, and written articles for the British Astronomical Society.

November 2004 • (HB) • 224pp • 216 x 135mm
16 b&w illustrations • ISBN 0 7509 3827 7

Strapless: John Singer Sargent and the Fall of Madame X

Deborah Davis

Sargent's painting Madame X is one of the world's best-known portraits. Few people, though, know the fascinating story behind it. 'Madame X' was 23-year-old, Amelie Gautreau, who moved to Paris and quickly became the 'it girl'. Sargent painted her with one strap of her dress dangling from her shoulder, suggesting to outraged Parisian viewers, either the prelude or the aftermath of sex. Her reputation ruined, Sargent's reputation grew and he became both rich and renowned. Today, his work is admired, and Madame X has become an iconic image of an age.

Deborah Davis is a writer and veteran film executive who has worked as a story editor and story analyst. She is co-organising an exhibition of Sargent's Women for exhibition in New York with Richard Ormond and writing the exhibition catalogue.

April 2004 • (HB) • 256pp • 216 x 135mm
28 b&w 12 colour illustrations • ISBN 0 7509 3706 8